Theory and Practice of Public International Law

Series Editor

Vincent Chetail

VOLUME 3

The titles published in this series are listed at *brill.com/tppi*

International Law and Transition to Peace in Colombia

International Law and Transition to Peace in Colombia

Assessing Jus Post Bellum *in Practice*

By

César Rojas-Orozco

BRILL

NIJHOFF

LEIDEN | BOSTON

This is an open access title distributed under the terms of the CC BY-NC 4.0 license, which permits any non-commercial use, distribution, and reproduction in any medium, provided the original author(s) and source are credited. Further information and the complete license text can be found at https://creativecommons.org/licenses/by-nc/4.0/

The terms of the CC license apply only to the original material. The use of material from other sources (indicated by a reference) such as diagrams, illustrations, photos and text samples may require further permission from the respective copyright holder.

Published with the support of the Swiss National Science Foundation.

Library of Congress Cataloging-in-Publication Data

Names: Rojas-Orozco, César, author.
Title: International law and transition to peace in Colombia : assessing jus post bellum in practice / by César Rojas-Orozco.
Identifiers: LCCN 2021014017 (print) | LCCN 2021014018 (ebook) | ISBN 9789004440524 (hardback) | ISBN 9789004440531 (ebook)
Subjects: LCSH: Transitional justice. | Peace-building–Law and legislation. | Peace-building–Law and legislation–Colombia. | Postwar reconstruction–Law and legislation–Colombia. | Peacekeeping forces, Colombian.
Classification: LCC KZ6787 .R65 2021 (print) | LCC KZ6787 (ebook) | DDC 341.6/8009861–dc23
LC record available at https://lccn.loc.gov/2021014017
LC ebook record available at https://lccn.loc.gov/2021014018

Typeface for the Latin, Greek, and Cyrillic scripts: "Brill". See and download: brill.com/brill-typeface.

ISSN 2405-6847
ISBN 978-90-04-44052-4 (hardback)
ISBN 978-90-04-44053-1 (e-book)

Copyright 2021 by Cesar Rojas-Orozco. Published by Koninklijke Brill NV, Leiden, The Netherlands.
Koninklijke Brill NV incorporates the imprints Brill, Brill Nijhoff, Brill mentis, Vandenhoeck & Ruprecht, Böhlau Verlag and V&R Unipress.
Koninklijke Brill NV reserves the right to protect this publication against unauthorized use.

This book is printed on acid-free paper and produced in a sustainable manner.

Contents

Acknowledgments IX
List of Abbreviations X

Introduction 1
1 Transition to Peace as a Matter of International Law 4
2 A Framework on the Legal Dimension of Transition: *Jus Post Bellum* 7
3 The Relevance of the Colombian Transition 12
4 Empirical Analysis from the Perspective of NIACS 16
5 Purpose of the Study 19
6 Methodological Considerations 20
7 Structure of the Book 21

1 *Jus Post Bellum*
A Normative Framework for the Transition from Armed Conflict to Peace 23
1 Approaches to a Definition 24
  1.1 *A New Legal Regime* 24
  1.2 *Ordering System of Norms, Practices, and Discourses* 27
  1.3 *Interpretative Framework* 29
2 Principles of *Jus Post Bellum* 31
3 Temporal and Functional Approach to *Jus Post Bellum* 35
4 The Object of *Jus Post Bellum* 39
5 *Jus Post Bellum* and Related Concepts 42
  5.1 *Transitional Justice* 43
  5.2 *Lex Pacificatoria* 47
6 *Jus Post Bellum* in Non-international Armed Conflicts 49
7 Conclusions 51

2 International Law in the Colombian Transition 53
0 A General Overview of the Colombian Armed Conflict and Its Transition to Peace 54
  0.1 *Origin and Evolution of the Armed Conflict* 54
  0.2 *Transitional Legal Mechanisms in the Ongoing Conflict* 56
  0.3 *Peace Process and Final Agreement (2012–2016)* 57
1 The Legal Status of the Peace Agreement 57
  1.1 *The Discussion on the Domestic or International Legal Status of Internal Peace Agreements* 59

1.2 *Formulas of Normative Internationalization of the Colombian Peace Agreement* 62
    1.2.1 The Peace Agreement as a Special Agreement under IHL 62
    1.2.2 The Peace Agreement as a Document of the UN Security Council 67
1.3 *Consequences of the Peace Agreement's International Legal Status* 71

2 Socioeconomic and Political Reforms 74
  2.1 *Legal and Policy Framework on Socioeconomic and Political Reforms for Transition to Peace* 75
  2.2 *Socioeconomic and Political Reforms in the Colombian Peace Agreement* 79

3 Criminal Justice 83
  3.1 *Legal Framework on Amnesties and Criminal Responsibility* 84
    3.1.1 Amnesties at the End of NIACS 84
    3.1.2 The Duty to Prosecute International Crimes 87
  3.2 *Conciliating Peace and Justice in Peace Negotiations* 91
  3.3 *The Colombian Approach: A Negotiated System of Criminal Justice* 95
    3.3.1 The Precedent of the Justice and Peace Law 96
    3.3.2 The Special Jurisdiction for Peace 98

4 Reparations for Victims 101
  4.1 *Legal Framework on Reparations for Victims of Armed Conflict* 101
    4.1.1 The Right to Reparation in International Law 102
    4.1.2 Reparations for Armed Conflict-related Violations of Human Rights and IHL 105
  4.2 *Colombian Approach to Reparations* 107
    4.2.1 Judicial Reparation: Justice and Peace Law 107
    4.2.2 Comprehensive Administrative Reparations: Law on Victims and Land Restitution 108
    4.2.3 Reparations in the 2016 Peace Agreement 109

5 Inclusive Transitions 110
  5.1 *Legal Framework on Inclusiveness* 112
    5.1.1 On Women and Gender Issues 112
    5.1.2 On Ethnic Minorities Issues 115
    5.1.3 On the Participation of Victims and Civil Society in General 116

CONTENTS VII

    5.2   *The Colombian Approach* 117
        5.2.1   Differential Approach for the Attention and Reparation of Victims of Armed Conflict 117
        5.2.2   Participation of Victims and Civil Society in the Peace Negotiations 118
        5.2.3   Differential Gender and Ethnic Approaches in the Peace Agreement 119
6   Conclusions 121

3 *Jus Post Bellum* Viewed from the Colombian Transition 124
1   A Definition of *Jus Post Bellum* from the Colombian Experience 125
2   The Formation and Operation of *Jus Post Bellum* 129
3   Principles of *Jus Post Bellum* identified in the Colombian Case 132
    3.1   *Reconstruction and Transformation* 133
    3.2   *Criminal Accountability* 136
    3.3   *Reparation* 138
    3.4   *Reconciliation* 140
    3.5   *Proportionality* 142
    3.6   *Inclusiveness* 144
    3.7   *Environmental Protection* 146
4   The Actors of *Jus Post Bellum* in Colombia 149
    4.1   *The Parties in Negotiation* 150
    4.2   *External Guarantors* 150
    4.3   *The Colombian Constitutional Court* 152
    4.4   *The Prosecutor of the International Criminal Court* 154
    4.5   *The Inter-American System of Human Rights* 156
    4.6   *Victims and Civil Society Organizations* 157
    4.7   *Insights on the Type and Role of Actors of Jus Post Bellum* 158
5   The Functions Played by International Law in the Colombian Transition: Possible Functions of *Jus Post Bellum*? 160
    5.1   *Increasing International Legitimacy of Transitional Mechanisms* 160
    5.2   *Offering Legal Certainty to the Peace Agreement* 161
    5.3   *Delimitating a Bargaining Zone for Negotiations* 162
    5.4   *Creating Confidence among the Parties* 162
    5.5   *Empowering Traditional Marginalized Actors* 163
    5.6   *Promoting Comprehensiveness in the Guarantee of Rights* 164
    5.7   *Encouraging the Transformative Role of Transition* 165
    5.8   *Insights for the General Functions of Jus Post Bellum* 166
6   Conclusions 167

General Conclusions 169
1 A Summary of the Study 169
2 The Main Contributions of the Colombian Transition to International Law and to *Jus Post Bellum* 170
3 *Jus Post Bellum* from Theory to Practice: Challenges and Opportunities 174
4 The Future of *Jus Post Bellum* 176

Bibliography 179
Index 193

Acknowledgments

This book is the result of my PhD thesis in International Law at the Graduate Institute of International and Development Studies in Geneva. I am deeply grateful to Professor Vincent Chetail, my mentor and supervisor, both for his guidance and support during my doctoral studies and for encouraging me to pursue this publication.

I also thank Professors Paola Gaeta and Carsten Stahn for their insightful comments in the examination of my thesis. Professor Gaeta has also been an inspiring guide during my studies. And I had the privilege to have my work reviewed by Professor Stahn, a great leading scholar on *jus post bellum*.

This research would not have been possible without the generous support of the Graduate Institute. I thank the Institute both for the doctoral scholarship I was awarded and for offering me an extraordinarily rich and diverse space of personal and academic growth. I also thank the Fundación para el Futuro de Colombia—Colfuturo for its support for my doctoral program.

I wish to express my gratitude to Brill for considering my work and making this publication real, and to the team that has supported me through the process. Along this line, I am very grateful to the Swiss National Science Foundation for its generous funding to publish this book in Open Access.

Geneva has meant much more than an academic process. I have met wonderful people and lived extraordinary experiences both during my LLM at the Geneva Academy of International Humanitarian Law and Human Rights and during my PhD at the Graduate Institute. I am extremely grateful for that and I want to thank all my friends that in many different ways offered me their support to complete this project.

Finally, I thank my family, for whose love and courage I am who I am. Achieving this project is fully devoted to them. The same, I thank Alejandro, for his patience, for his care, and for his love.

Abbreviations

AmCHR	American Convention on Human Rights
ELN	National Liberation Army (*Ejército de Liberación Nacional*)
FARC	Revolutionary Armed Forces of Colombia (*Fuerzas Armadas Revolucionarias de Colombia*)
IAC	International Armed Conflict
ICC	International Criminal Court
ICCPR	International Covenant on Civil and Political Rights
ICERD	International Convention on the Elimination of All Forms of Racial Discrimination
ICESCR	International Covenant on Economics, Social, and Cultural Rights
ICL	International Criminal Law
ICRC	International Committee of the Red Cross
IHL	International Humanitarian Law
IHRL	International Human Rights Law
ILC	International Law Commission
ILO	International Labor Organization
NGOS	Non-Governmental Organizations
NIAC	Non-International Armed Conflict
UN	United Nations
UNSC	United Nations Security Council
VCLT	Vienna Convention on the Law of Treaties

Introduction

Under current international law, the transition to peace after a non-international armed conflict (NIAC) is no longer a matter of the exclusive discretion of the conflicting parties within a state. Several international legal standards are progressively shaping the ways in which internal peace negotiations are conducted as well as the content of peace agreements.[1] These standards are represented in legal obligations, principles, and practices mainly derived from International Human Rights Law (IHRL), International Humanitarian Law (IHL), International Criminal Law (ICL), and the United Nations (UN) and states practice in peacemaking and peacebuilding.

Colombia provides the most recent and notorious example of a peace process and a peace agreement ending a NIAC conducted under an international legal frame.[2] The 2012–2016 peace negotiations between the Colombian government and the guerilla movement *Fuerzas Armadas Revolucionarias de Colombia* (FARC) and their final agreement are internationally considered a model for resolving other conflicts around the world.[3] The Colombian Peace Agreement[4] has been recognized both for its

---

1   Carsten Stahn, '*Jus Post Bellum*: Mapping the Discipline(s),' in *Jus Post Bellum. Towards a Law of Transition from Conflict to Peace*, ed. Carsten Stahn and Jann Kleffner (The Hague: T.M.C. Asser Press, 2008), 104. For Sthan: "The substantive components of peace-making are no longer exclusively determined by the discretion and contractual liberty of the warring factions, but are governed by certain norms and standards of international law derived from different fields of law and legal practice."

2   Even though other peace agreements have been signed around the world after the 2016 Colombian deal was adopted, they do not have the comprehensive dimension of the Colombian one. They are mostly partial or ceasefire agreements, in which an international legal dimension is not as large and comprehensive as in the Colombian case. On this point, see Escola de Cultura de Pau, *Peace Talks in Focus 2019. Report on Trends and Scenarios* (Barcelona: Icaria, 2019), 27.

3   See, among others: UN Peacebuilding Commission, Informal Meeting on Colombia, Chairperson's Summary of the Discussion, 13 November 2017, available at: http://www.un.org/es/peacebuilding/pdf/oc/PBCmeetingonColombia13November2017-Chair's%20summary FINAL.pdf, accessed on 10 June 2018; Jean-Arnault, Chief of the UN Mission in Colombia, "Este proceso de paz es un ejemplo para el mundo": Jean Arnault, available at: caracol.com.co/radio/2017/06/27/nacional/1498581031_512926.html, accessed on 20 November 2017; Report of the Secretary-General on the UN Verification Mission in Colombia, Security Council, S/2018/1159, 26 December 2018, para. 91.

4   The expressions Colombian Peace Agreement, Peace Agreement, Final Agreement, and Agreement (with capitalization) will be used interchangeably to refer to the peace agreement signed by the Government of Colombia and the *Fuerzas Armadas Revolucionarias de Colombia* (FARC) on 24 November 2016 and called *Final Agreement to End the Armed*

© CÉSAR ROJAS-OROZCO, 2021 | DOI:10.1163/9789004440531_002
This is an open access chapter distributed under the terms of the CC BY-NC 4.0 license.

comprehensive approach to ending armed violence and addressing structural causes of the conflict and for its compliance with international law. As noted by Huneeus and Urueña:

> That agreement, and, indeed, the entire negotiation process, has been exceptional in the central role that international law plays. Colombia is an intensely legalistic society, with a legal system that has been traditionally open to international law. Moreover, the peace talks are conducted in a global legal context that imposes strict legal limits—in particular, international criminal law and Inter-American human rights law are of constant concern to the negotiators. [...] [M]any of the deal's particular choices seemed specifically designed to comply with Colombia's international legal obligations.[5]

The central role of international law in the Colombian transition is due and is expressed in at least two ways. First, several external actors participated in the negotiations or they sent messages that influenced the discussions. These actors included the UN, the Inter-American System of Human Rights, the Prosecutor of the International Criminal Court (ICC), and the guarantor countries. Second, the negotiation and the Agreement not only incorporated international legal standards of justice, truth, reparations, and inclusiveness, but also used international law and international enforcement mechanisms to ensure its compliance.

However, this case also evinces the complexity of the legal regulation of transitioning from armed conflict to peace. There is no specific legal regime governing such transitions, but a disparate set of applicable provisions enshrined by different branches of international law that are not specifically designated for that purpose. Thus, these provisions must be interpreted and adapted in their application to the specific transitional context. This process implies a dual role for the parties involved in the transition as both the subjects and creators of law: the apply general existing norms and define, through this practice, new ways to interpret and adapt them to the context. As Kreß and

---

Conflict and Build a Stable and Lasting Peace. See Government of Colombia and FARC, 'Final Agreement to End the Armed Conflict and Build a Stable and Lasting Peace,' 2016, especiales.presidencia.gov.co/Documents/20170620-dejacion-armas/acuerdos/acuerdo-final-ingles.pdf.

5 Alexandra Huneeus and Rene Urueña, 'Introduction to Symposium on the Colombian Peace Talks and International Law,' *American Journal of International Law* 110 AJIL Unbound Symposium on the Colombian Peace Talks and International Law (2016): 161–62.

Grover wrote, "States in transition apply existing law and, in so doing, contribute to its refinement."[6]

The academic debate on this role of international law in transition has been framed under the concept of *jus post bellum*. This concept has been proposed as a normative framework to gather—under a common frame of reference—the myriad of international legal considerations applicable to the transition from armed conflict to sustainable peace.[7] However, the relative novelty of the concept, which only entered the international legal scholarship in 2005,[8] is marked by divergent conceptions around its content and scope, and few empirical studies have been conducted on it.

Considering the above-presented elements, this study analyzes the role of international law in transition from internal armed conflict to peace by using the Colombian transition as a case study. Based on this analysis, it discusses to what extent this case fits within the scholarly debate on *jus post bellum* by identifying what elements are applicable from theory to practice and what lessons can be drawn from the Colombian case toward further developing the concept.

This introduction first discusses how transition to peace became a matter of international law and how the concept of *jus post bellum* offers a framework for such a debate, examining the state of research on this topic. Then, the introduction discusses the relevance of the Colombian case in assessing the role of international law in the transition to peace and why this case is useful to attaining a better understanding of the concept of *jus post bellum*. According to these discussions, the introduction reflects on the empirical analysis from the perspective of NIACs and the use of a case study. Lastly, this introduction will delimitate the purpose, some methodological considerations, and the structure of the study.

---

6   Claus Kreß and Leena Grover, 'International Criminal Law Restraints in Peace Talks to End Armed Conflicts of a Non-International Character,' in *Law in Peace Negotiations*, ed. Morton Bergsmo and Pablo Kalmanovitz (Oslo: Torkel Opsahl Academic EPublisher, 2010), 46.

7   Vincent Chetail, 'Introduction: Post-Conflict Peacebuilding: Ambiguity and Identity,' in *Post-Conflict Peacebuilding: A Lexicon*, ed. Vincent Chetail (Oxford: Oxford University Press, 2009), 1–33; Vincent Chetail and Oliver Jütersonke, 'Peacebuilding: A Review of the Academic Literature' (White Paper Series No. 23, Geneva Peacebuilding Platform, 2015), 5, https://papers.ssrn.com/sol3/papers.cfm?abstract_id=2684002.

8   As it will be analyzed in Section 2 of this Introduction, the first academic work addressing *jus post bellum* from a legal point of view appeared in 2005, analyzing how the concept could frame the application of IHL in the post-occupation context in Iraq: Daniel Thürer and Malcom MacLaren, ' "Ius Post Bellum" in Iraq: A Challenge to the Applicability and Relevance of International Humanitarian Law?,' in *Weltinnenrecht: Liber Amicorum Jost Delbrück*, ed. Klaus Dicke, and et al. (Berlin: Duncker & Humblot, 2005), 753–82.

1   Transition to Peace as a Matter of International Law

Law plays a fundamental role in the transition from armed conflict to peace. Although peace is a politically-oriented goal, legal considerations frame the process of negotiating and building peace.[9] In particular, international law is gaining increasing relevance in domestic transitions to peace. The international obligations of states according to IHRL, IHL, and ICL are unavoidable considerations for negotiating parties when defining their conditions to end conflict and achieve peace.[10] These obligations serve as a framework outlining limits, possibilities, and duties that ought to be followed when negotiating, defining, and implementing measures of transition from armed conflict to peace.

The increasing involvement of international law in domestic transitions is mainly due to the development of IHRL as a reliable means of protecting individuals, including from their own state.[11] To Cecile Fabre, this phenomenon represents a new paradigm in international relations with at least two rules: "a) individuals are the fundamental unit of moral concern [...], b) whatever rights and privileges states have, they have them only in so far as they thereby serve individual's fundamental interests."[12] This argument is reinforced by the fact that IHRL has increased its protection of individuals not only by the substantial development of rights but also through the creation of effective mechanisms to enforce them internationally.

Regarding this paradigm, Stahn affirms that "The rise of human rights obligations and growing limitations on sovereignty [...] have not only changed the attitude toward the ending of conflicts, but have also set certain benchmarks for behavior. The process of peace-making itself has become a domain of international attention and regulatory action."[13] Here, one should add also the processes of peacekeeping and peacebuilding as matters of international concern. These concepts came to the international policy and legal arena since the 1992 UN Secretary-General's Agenda for Peace.[14] Chetail defines

---

9   Stahn, 'Jus Post Bellum: Mapping the Discipline(s),' 2008, 101.
10 Philipp Kastner, *Legal Normativity in the Resolution of Internal Armed Conflict* (Cambridge: Cambridge University Press, 2015), 1.
11 Michael Walzer, *Just and Unjust Wars. A Moral Argument with Historical Illustrations* (New York: Basic Books, 2006), XI.
12 Cecile Fabre, 'Cosmopolitanism, Just War Theory and Legitimate Authority,' *International Affairs* 84, no. 5 (2008): 964.
13 Stahn, 'Jus Post Bellum: Mapping the Discipline(s),' 2008, 100–101.
14 UN Secretary-General, 'An Agenda for Peace' (New York: United Nations, 1992); UN Secretary-General, 'Supplement to An Agenda for Peace' (New York: United Nations, 1995).

them as: *peacekeeping*, meaning the actions aimed to end the immediate violence and hostilities; *peacemaking*, involving the peaceful resolution of the conflict through negotiation, mediation, or arbitration; and *peacebuilding*, as the process of addressing the root causes of the conflict with a view to establishing a sustainable peace.[15] From the three concepts, peacemaking and peacebuilding are more closely related to the idea of transitioning to sustainable peace.

Peacemaking and peacebuilding processes have received increasing legal regulation through UN documents, IHRL, and international jurisprudence,[16] mainly since the early 2000s after the adoption of the ICC Statute and different UN guidelines on transitional justice.[17] This phenomenon is described by Christine Bell in the following terms:

> Indeed, legal analysis suggests a more pivotal role for international law in assisting, and perhaps even acting as catalyst to, the trend towards negotiated settlements in intrastate conflicts.
>
> Throughout the 1980s, a number of legal developments relevant to the peace agreement landscape took place and can be argued to have played a little-acknowledged role in creating the peace agreement phenomenon. These legal developments all worked to undo the concept of international law as the law of states, by opening up the black box of 'the state' to scrutiny of its internal configurations—traditionally the preserve of state sovereignty. In so doing, they increased the scope for international law to address intrastate conflict.[18]

Then, she adds:

> The contemporary peace agreement is negotiated in a context where an expanding international machinery has a clear mandate in the areas that many peace agreements deal with, such as human rights, refugees and displaced persons, independence of the judiciary, policing, and economics.

---

15 Chetail, 'Introduction,' 1.
16 Guglielmo Verdirame, 'What to Make of *Jus Post Bellum*: A Response to Antonia Chayes,' *European Journal of International Law* 24, no. 1 (2013): 307–8.
17 Astri Suhrke, 'Post-War States: Differentiating Patterns of Peace,' in *Jus Post Bellum: Mapping the Normative Foundations*, ed. Carsten Stahn, Jennifer Easterday, and Jens Iverson (Oxford: Oxford University Press, 2014), 270–72.
18 Christine Bell, *On the Law of Peace: Peace Agreements and the Lex Pacificatoria* (Oxford: Oxford University Press, 2008), 31.

Never before have international law and international institutions had such an array of tools capable of application to intrastate conflict.[19]

The expansion of the influence of international law in peacemaking and peacebuilding is reflected in a growing number of UN guidelines, reports, and resolutions addressing this matter and recommending the observance and incorporation of international legal standards in reparations, transitional justice, inclusiveness, and the rule of law.[20] The General Assembly and the Security Council created the UN Peacebuilding Commission[21] aimed at providing international support to countries in transition, and the Council has intervened in many transitional settings—most of them related to NIACs—pursuing its fundamental mandate to safeguard international peace and security.[22]

However, as Bell argues, "peace agreement practice is increasingly posing a fundamental challenge to the existing international legal order."[23] Despite the rising influence of international law in peace processes and peace agreements, there is no specific legal regime regulating transition from armed conflict to peace, and different branches of law can apply. As such, states and other parties in conflict must interpret and apply relevant international norms according to the specific needs and conditions of their own transitional context, but with no legal framework given to provide coherence to the matter. Offering such a framework is the purpose of *jus post bellum*.[24]

---

19 Bell, 104.
20 See, among others: UNSC, 'Resolution 1325 (2000),' Pub. L. No. S/RES/1325 (2000); UN Secretary-General, 'Report of the Secretary-General on the Rule of Law and Transitional Justice in Conflict and Post-Conflict Societies' (New York: UN Security Council, 23 August 2004); UN Secretary-General, 'Women, Peace and Security,' 13 October 2004; UN General Assembly, 'Basic Principles and Guidelines on the Right to a Remedy and Reparation for Victims of Gross Violations of International Human Rights Law and Serious Violations of International Humanitarian Law,' Pub. L. No. A /RES/60/147 (2005); UN Secretary-General, 'The Rule of Law and Transitional Justice in Conflict and Post-Conflict Societies' (New York: UN Security Council, 12 October 2011); UN Secretary-General, 'Strengthening the Role of Mediation in the Peaceful Settlement of Disputes, Conflict Prevention and Resolution' (UN General Assembly, 25 June 2012).
21 UNSC Resolution 1645, S/RES/1645(2005), 20 December 2005, and General Assembly Resolution 180, A/RES/60/180, 30 December 2005.
22 See, for example: UNSC Resolution 1127 (1997), UN. Doc. S/RES/1127 (1997), Resolution 1383 (2001), UN. Doc. S/RES/1383 (2001), Resolution 1740 (2007), UN. Doc. S/RES/1740 (2007), Resolution 1464 (2013), UN. Doc. S/RES/1464, Resolution 1590 (2005), UN. Doc. S/RES/1590 (2005), Resolution 2259 (2015), UN. Doc. S/RES/2259 (2015).
23 Christine Bell, 'Peace Agreements: Their Nature and Legal Status,' *American Journal of International Law* 100, no. 2 (2006): 384.
24 Chetail and Jütersonke, 'Peacebuilding: A Review of the Academic Literature,' 5.

2 A Framework on the Legal Dimension of Transition: *Jus Post Bellum*

In the same way that the conditions for engaging in war are regulated under a legal framework known as *jus ad bellum*, and the legal regime for conducting armed conflict is defined as *jus in bello*, moral and legal scholarship has proposed the concept of *jus post bellum* to designate the legal framework applicable to transition from armed conflict to peace. However, while *jus ad bellum* and *jus in bello* are unified legal regimes, the law applicable to the transition from armed conflict to peace is not gathered into a specific legal framework but involves a complex interaction between different branches of law and between international and national law.

Therefore, the concept of *jus post bellum* appeared as a space to hold the debate around the interaction between law and transition to peace,[25] and to offer a normative framework for peacemaking and peacebuilding practice. Following this logic, Vincent Chetail suggests that:

> *Jus post bellum* can be generally defined as the set of norms applicable at the end of an armed conflict—whether internal or international—with a view to establishing a sustainable peace. [...] [T]he grouping disparate standards within the same frame of reference underscores the need for a comprehensive and coordinated approach to the numerous rules governing post-conflict situations. From a systemic perspective, it paves the way for a contextualized interpretation—and, by extension, a contextualized application—of existing norms in order to better take into account the specificities which characterize the difficult transition from war to peace.[26]

This definition addresses different components of the concept: the substance of *jus post bellum* as a set of norms; a temporal scope placed to the end of armed conflict; its applicability to both international armed conflicts (IACs) and NIACs; and its systemic function to group different standards governing transition from armed conflict to peace under a common framework, allowing their contextualized interpretation and application. However, notwithstanding the comprehensiveness of this definition, the concept is far from reaching consensus, and Easterday, Iverson and Stahn even sustain that "there are

---

25 Inger Österdahl and Esther van Zadel, 'What Will *Jus Post Bellum* Mean? Of New Wine and Old Bottles,' *Journal of Conflict and Security Law* 14, no. 2 (2009): 176.
26 Chetail, 'Introduction,' 18.

almost as many conceptions of *jus post bellum* as scholars" working in this field.[27]

Looking at the origin of the concept, Stahn sustains that this tripartite conception of the law of war can be found since St. Agustine (City of God, 410), Vitoria, Suarez, Grotius (Laws of War and Peace, 1625) and Kant (Science of Right, 1790).[28] However, the first systematization of the idea of *jus post bellum* is generally attributed to Kant, who referred to a right to war (*jus ad bellum*), a right in war (*jus in bello*), and a right after war (*jus post bellum*).[29]

Nevertheless, these three elements have not been developed at the same level. Both *jus ad bellum* and *jus in bello* were largely theorized since the 19th century. Then, *jus in bello* was codified since the 1899 and 1907 The Hague Conventions, and *jus ad bellum* in the 1945 UN Charter provisions on the use of force. However, *jus post bellum* did not receive the same attention neither in theory nor in legal codification. For Stahn, this situation is due to at least three reasons. First, until the 20th century there was a split conception of war or peace without intermediate states of transition from one to other.[30] Second, peace has been traditionally considered as a matter of the discretion of states.[31] And, third, peace-making has been regarded as a case-by-case issue and some legal scholars "even continued to conceive peace-making as an 'art' rather than a legal paradigm until the 1980s."[32]

Having this background, the concept of *jus post bellum* had only entered into the academic debate at the beginning of the 21st century, after the US-led interventions in Iraq and Afghanistan.[33] This contemporary discussion on *jus post bellum* has been held within the framework of two disciplines: moral

---

27 Jennifer Easterday, Jens Iverson, and Carsten Stahn, 'Exploring the Normative Foundations of *Jus Post Bellum*: An Introduction,' in *Jus Post Bellum: Mapping the Normative Foundations*, ed. Carsten Stahn, Jennifer Easterday, and Jens Iverson (Oxford: Oxford University Press, 2014), 3.

28 Stahn, '*Jus Post Bellum*: Mapping the Discipline(s),' 2008, 94. The same view is shared by Larry May, '*Jus Post Bellum*, Grotius, and Meionexia,' in *Jus Post Bellum: Mapping the Normative Foundations*, ed. Carsten Stahn, Jennifer Easterday, and Jens Iverson (Oxford: Oxford University Press, 2014), 16.

29 Brian Orend, '*Jus Post Bellum*: The Perspective of a Just-War Theorist,' *Leiden Journal of International Law* 20, no. 3 (2007): 574.; Brian Orend, *War and International Justice: A Kantian Perspective* (Wilfrid Laurier University Press, 2000). Chetail, 'Introduction,' 18.

30 Stahn, '*Jus Post Bellum*: Mapping the Discipline(s),' 2008, 96. On this idea, see also Philip Jessup, 'Should International Law Recognize an Intermediate Status between Peace and War?,' *American Journal of International Law* 48, no. 1 (1954): 98–103.

31 Stahn, '*Jus Post Bellum*: Mapping the Discipline(s),' 2008, 96.

32 Stahn, 98.

33 Stahn, 98.

philosophy and international law.[34] The first has been focused on the moral obligation of reparation and reconstruction in the aftermath of a military intervention, under the just war theory. On the other hand, international legal scholars have tried to identify and articulate the international legal regulation applicable to the transition from armed conflict to peace under this concept.[35]

From the perspective of the just war theory, Orend proposed the first contemporary approach to *jus post bellum*. For him, the "just war theory, as currently conceived, is incomplete", and now it is necessary to look at "the justice [...] of the move back from war to peace."[36] Then, since 2004, some philosophers used the concept to discuss the moral obligation of reparation and reconstruction after a military intervention.

Walzer presented an analysis on different wars around the world under a just war perspective; and, when referring to the Iraqi case, he has suggested the development of a *jus post bellum* component within the just war theory.[37] Bass used the concept to analyze "the justice of a belligerent power's postwar conduct,"[38] which Iasiello supported mapping the moral responsibilities of victors in war.[39] In another perspective, Rigby[40] discussed the concept and its implications in terms of forgiveness and reconciliation. Later, in 2006, DiMeglio[41] continued working on the definition of *jus post bellum* as part of the just war tradition, and Williams and Caldwell insisted on connecting the justness of "how we *intend* to fight and what we *intend* to do after we have fought."[42]

In 2012, Larry May published one of the most influential works on *jus post bellum*, entitled *After War Ends: A Philosophical Perspective*.[43] Written under the umbrella of the just war theory, this book proposes six normative principles of

---

34 Stahn, 112.
35 Christine Bell, 'Of *Jus Post Bellum* and Lex Pacificatoria: What's in a Name?,' in *Jus Post Bellum: Mapping the Normative Foundations*, ed. Carsten Stahn, Jennifer Easterday, and Jens Iverson (Oxford: Oxford University Press, 2014), 181.
36 Brian Orend, '*Jus Post Bellum*,' *Journal of Social Philosophy* 31, no. 1 (2000): 117–18.
37 Michael Walzer, *Arguing About War* (New Haven: Yale University Press, 2004), 162.
38 Gary Bass, '*Jus Post Bellum*,' *Philosophy & Public Affairs*, 2004, 385.
39 Louis Iasiello, '*Jus Post Bellum*: The Moral Responsibilities of Victors in War,' *Naval War College Review* 57, no. 3-4 (2004): 33–52.
40 Andrew Rigby, 'Forgiveness and Reconciliation in *Jus Post Bellum*,' in *Just War Theory: A Reappraisal*, ed. Mark Evans (Edinburgh: Edinburgh University Press, 2005), 177–200.
41 Richard DiMeglio, 'The Evolution of the Just War Tradition: Defining *Jus Post Bellum*,' *Military Law Review* 186 (2006): 116–63.
42 Robert Williams and Dan Caldwell, '*Jus Post Bellum*: Just War Theory and the Principles of Just Peace,' *International Studies Perspectives* 7, no. 4 (2006): 309–20.
43 Larry May, *After War Ends: A Philosophical Perspective* (Cambridge: Cambridge University Press, 2012).

jus post bellum: rebuilding, retribution, restitution, reparation, reconciliation and proportionality. Subsequent works have considered this proposal of principles as a solid basis to develop the content of *jus post bellum*.[44]

From the perspective of international law, Thürer and MacLaren were the first authors to address the issue in 2005. In an article, entitled *'Ius Post Bellum' in Iraq*, they analyzed the role of the concept to improve the application of IHL in the occupation and post-occupation period in Iraq.[45] Similarly, Boon used the concept to assess the limits of occupant's law-making powers,[46] which Cohen further addressed in 2006 examining the role of international law in post-conflict constitution-making.[47] The same year, Stahn presented the first article exploring *jus post bellum* in a comprehensive way as a legal category.[48]

Later, in 2007, under the direction of Stahn, the University of Leiden's Grotius Center for International Legal Studies undertook the *Jus Post Bellum* Project.[49] This project was conceived to "investigate whether and how a contemporary *jus post bellum* may facilitate greater fairness and sustainability in conflict termination and peacemaking."[50] In ten years, the Project published three volumes presenting the most comprehensive contributions to the legal understanding of contemporary *jus post bellum*. The first one, published in 2008, *Jus Post Bellum. Towards a Law of Transition from Conflict to*

44　Easterday, Iverson, and Stahn, 'Exploring the Normative Foundations of *Jus Post Bellum*: An Introduction'; Aurel Sari, 'The Status of Foreign Armed Forces Deployed in Post-Conflict Environments: A Search for Basic Principles,' in *Jus Post Bellum: Mapping the Normative Foundations*, ed. Carsten Stahn, Jennifer Easterday, and Jens Iverson (Oxford: Oxford University Press, 2014), 467–501; Carsten Stahn, '*Jus Post Bellum* and the Justice of Peace: Some Preliminary Reflections' (Final Conference: *Jus Post Bellum* and the Justice of Peace, The Hague, 2016), http://postconflictjustice.com/jus-post-bellum-and-the-justice-of-peace-some-preliminary-reflections-part-1-2/.

45　Thürer and MacLaren, ' "Ius Post Bellum" in Iraq: A Challenge to the Applicability and Relevance of International Humanitarian Law?'

46　Kristen Boon, 'Legislative Reform in Post-Conflict Zones: *Jus Post Bellum* and the Contemporary Occupant's Law-Making Powers,' *McGill Law Journal* 50, no. 2 (2005): 285–326.

47　Jean Cohen, 'The Role of International Law in Post-Conflict Constitution-Making: Toward a *Jus Post Bellum* for "Interim Occupations",' *New York Law School Law Review* 51 (2007 2006): 497–532.

48　Carsten Stahn, ' "Jus Ad Bellum", "jus in Bello" ... "*Jus Post Bellum*"?—Rethinking the Conception of the Law of Armed Force,' *European Journal of International Law* 17, no. 5 (2006): 921–43.

49　This is the website of the *Jus Post Bellum* Project, where information about its activities, its team, and its publications can be found: http://juspostbellum.com/default.aspx (accessed on 21 September 2016).

50　Ibid.

INTRODUCTION   11

Peace,[51] has focused on the foundations, contemporary challenges, and the future of the concept. Later, in 2014, they published *Jus Post Bellum. Mapping the Normative Foundations*,[52] with a broader analysis on the different dimensions of the concept, its functions, and dilemmas. Finally, in 2017 the Project released the work *Environmental Protection and Transitions from Conflict to Peace: Clarifying Norms, Principles, and Practices*,[53] in which several scholars have addressed the connection between *jus post bellum* and environmental protection. At present, these works represent the most advanced analysis of contemporary *jus post bellum*.[54]

However, despite the existing contributions, the concept is still fragmented and contested. Lewkowicz considers that *jus post bellum* creates semantic confusions on the law of the use of force,[55] and it is just an abstract doctrine without any substantial contribution to peace practice.[56] De Brabandere criticizes the usefulness of the concept,[57] and he even affirms "that certain conceptions of *jus post bellum* pose a danger to some very foundational principles of international law."[58] In turn, even if Bell admits some usefulness in the concept, she has considered it as an aspirational regime for the future, being the current normativity applicable to transitions more a question of *lex pacificatoria*, understood as the law of peacemakers.[59]

---

51   Carsten Stahn and Jan Kleffner, eds., *Jus Post Bellum: Towards a Law of Transition from Conflict to Peace* (The Hague: T.M.C. Asser Press, 2008).
52   Carsten Stahn, Easterday, Jennifer, and Iverson, Jens, eds., *Jus Post Bellum: Mapping the Normative Foundations* (Oxford: Oxford University Press, 2014).
53   Carsten Stahn, Jens Iverson, and Jennifer Easterday, eds., *Environmental Protection and Transitions from Conflict to Peace: Clarifying Norms, Principles, and Practices* (Oxford: Oxford University Press, 2017).
54   For Bell, Carsten Stahn and the Leiden School have led the contemporary discussion on *jus post bellum* under the perspective of international law. Bell, 'Of *Jus Post Bellum* and Lex Pacificatoria: What's in a Name?,' 181.
55   Gregory Lewkowicz, 'Présentation. Le *Jus Post Bellum*: Nouveau Cheval de Troie Pour Le Droit Des Conflit Armés?,' *Revue Belge de Droit International* 44, no. 1–2 (2011): 5.
56   Lewkowicz, 'Présentation. Le *Jus Post Bellum*: Nouveau Cheval de Troie Pour Le Droit Des Conflit Armés?'
57   Eric De Brabandere, 'International Territorial Administrations and Post-Conflict: Reflections on the Need of a *Jus Post Bellum* as Legal Framework,' *Revue Belgue de Droit International* 44, no. 1–2 (2011): 69.
58   Eric De Brabandere, 'The Concept of *Jus Post Bellum* in International Law: A Normative Critique,' in *Jus Post Bellum: Mapping the Normative Foundations*, ed. Carsten Stahn, Jennifer Easterday, and Jens Iverson (Oxford: Oxford University Press, 2014), 123–41.
59   The concept of *lex pacificatoria*, as related to *jus post bellum*, will be analyzed in Chapter 1, Section 5.2. Bell, *On the Law of Peace*; Bell, 'Of *Jus Post Bellum* and Lex Pacificatoria: What's in a Name?'

Those discussions have evidenced the need for further research to clarify the concept and its concrete scope. In 2009 Chetail pointed out the importance "to recognize post-war law as a concept in its own right."[60] In 2012 May and Forcehimes considered *jus post bellum* scholarship as an "emerging field [...] still in its formative years".[61] In 2014, Easterday, Iverson, and Stahn argued that despite "the expansion of references to *jus post bellum* in a variety of journals [...], there has been an increase of ambiguity, [instead of] a consolidation around a consensus definition."[62] And, in 2017 Iverson sustained that the concept "remains comparatively under-theorized, and frequently referenced without realizing that many authors be talking past each other, meaning different things while using the same term."[63]

Having this background on the scholarly debate of *jus post bellum*, this study is aimed at offering an empirical analysis of the concept by testing its theoretical development in practice throughout a relevant case study.

3   The Relevance of the Colombian Transition

The Colombian transitional process from armed conflict to peace offers a proper test case to assess both the role of international law in transition to peace and the viability of *jus post bellum* as the concept to frame such a role. Several reasons explain the relevance of the Colombian transition for this purpose.

First, the 2016 Peace Agreement in Colombia is the most recent comprehensive[64] peace deal ending a NIAC in the world.[65] The comprehensiveness of the

---

60   Chetail, 'Introduction,' 18.
61   Larry May and Andrew Forcehimes, eds., *Morality, Jus Post Bellum, and International Law* (Cambridge: Cambridge University Press, 2012), 1.
62   Jens Iverson, Jennifer Easterday, and Carsten Stahn, 'Epilogue: *Jus Post Bellum*—Strategic Analysis and Future Directions,' in *Jus Post Bellum: Mapping the Normative Foundations*, ed. Carsten Stahn, Jennifer Easterday, and Jens Iverson (Oxford: Oxford University Press, 2014), 547.
63   Jens Iverson, 'The Function of *Jus Post Bellum* in International Law' (Leiden, Leiden University, 2017), 8, https://openaccess.leidenuniv.nl/handle/1887/55949.
64   According to the Peace Accords Matrix, of the University of Notre Dame's Kroc Institute for International Peace Studies, which offers extensive data on the implementation of several peace agreements ending armed conflicts around the work, a peace agreement is considered comprehensive when: "(1) the major parties to the conflict were involved in the negotiations that led to the written agreement; and (2) the substantive issues underlying the conflict were included in the negotiations." Peace Accords Matrix (Date of retrieval: (1/16/2019), https://peaceaccords.nd.edu/about, Kroc Institute for International Peace Studies, University of Notre Dame.
65   Up to the end of 2018, peace agreements concluded in other countries after the 2016 Colombian Peace Agreement were mostly partial or ceasefire agreements, which did not

INTRODUCTION 13

agreement implies both ending the armed conflict between the main opposing actors and addressing its root causes with a view to establishing lasting peace.[66] In this sense, the Agreement addresses matters of justice, truth, reparation, socio-economic and political issues related to the causes of the conflict, the participation and inclusion of different groups in society, and other relevant questions.[67]

Second, the 2012–2016 peace process has been designed to integrate and apply international legal standards. In the preamble of the Agreement, the parties expressly stated their strict respect for the Colombian Constitution and for the general principles of international law, IHRL, IHL, and the ICC Statute.[68] Further, the Agreement contains several references to international law, incorporating international legal standards applicable to different matters of the deal and using international enforcement mechanisms to ensure its compliance. The Agreement's international legal status was affirmed through its configuration as a special agreement under IHL and a unilateral declaration by the Colombian State before the UN.[69] The process has incorporated an inclusive perspective that follows UN Security Council (UNSC) Resolution 1325 (2000) and other legal instruments and guidelines on the participation of women, ethnic groups, minorities, victims, and civil society.[70] Crucial matters such as criminal justice for international crimes and reparations to victims were defined according to IHRL and ICL standards.[71] Moreover, a monitoring role was assigned to the UNSC, which created a special mission for verifying the implementation phase.[72]

---

address comprehensively the root causes of armed conflict. This is the reason why the Colombian agreement can be considered the most recent comprehensive peace deal. On this point, see Escola de Cultura de Pau, *Peace Talks in Focus 2019. Report on Trends and Scenarios*, 27.

66 This purpose of the Agreement is seen from its very title: Government of Colombia and FARC, 'Final Agreement to End the Armed Conflict and Build a Stable and Lasting Peace.'
67 The main components of the Agreement will be developed in detail in Chapter 2 of the book.
68 Government of Colombia and FARC, 'Final Agreement to End the Armed Conflict and Build a Stable and Lasting Peace,' 1.
69 Gobierno de Colombia and FARC, 'Comunicado Conjunto No. 69,' 12 May 2016, http://es.presidencia.gov.co/noticia/160512-Comunicado-Conjunto-numero-69. A detailed analysis on the international legal status of the Peace Agreement is offered in Chapter 2.1.
70 See Chapter 2, Section 5.
71 See Chapter 2, Sections 3 and 4.
72 Government of Colombia and FARC, 'Final Agreement to End the Armed Conflict and Build a Stable and Lasting Peace,' 216. The UN mission for verification of disarmament and reincorporation was created by UNSC Resolutions 2307 (2016) and 2366 (2017). The mandate of the Mission has been renewed by Resolutions 2381 (2017) and 2435 (2018).

Third, there was significant international involvement in the peace process through foreign support,[73] observatory statements by the ICC Prosecutor,[74] a UN Secretary-General Representative, and welcoming messages by the UNSC,[75] which monitors the implementation of the Agreement. These actors have played a crucial role influencing the peace agreement discussions. Norway, as a guarantor of the process, sponsored a group of international legal experts to advise the parties on the conformity of the Agreement with international law.[76] During the negotiations, the ICC Prosecutor's Office sent letters and statements to Colombian institutions reminding them of their obligations in the prosecution of international crimes.[77] In addition, various non-governmental organizations (NGOs) openly invoked the international legal obligations of the State when negotiating victim's rights to justice, truth, and reparation.[78]

---

73 Cuba and Norway serve as permanent guarantors. The process has been supported by the UN, the EU, the OAS, the US, the Vatican, and different foreign and international actors. In addition, it should be mentioned the Nobel Peace Prize awarded to Colombian President Juan Manuel Santos, acknowledging his leaderships and commitment to the peace process.

74 Office of the ICC Prosecutor, 'Statement of ICC Prosecutor, Fatou Bensouda, on the Conclusion of the Peace Negotiations between the Government of Colombia and the Revolutionary Armed Forces of Colombia,' 1 September 2016, https://www.icc-cpi.int//Pages/item.aspx?name=160901-otp-stat-colombia (accessed on 1 April 2018). On the conclusion of a Final Agreement in Colombia, the ICC Prosecutor stated: "As a State Party to the Rome Statute of the International Criminal Court, Colombia has recognised that grave crimes threaten the peace, security and well-being of the world and stated its determination to put an end to impunity for the perpetrators and thus contribute to the prevention of such crimes. I note, with satisfaction, that the final text of the peace agreement excludes amnesties and pardons for crimes against humanity and war crimes under the Rome Statute [...]. I have supported Colombia's efforts to bring an end to the decades-long armed conflict in line with its obligations under the Rome Statute since the beginning of the negotiations. I will continue to do so during the implementation phase in the same spirit."

75 UN Security Council, 'Resolution 2307 (2016),' Pub. L. No. S/RES/2307 (2016); UN Security Council, 'Resolution 2366 (2017),' Pub. L. No. S/RES/2366 (2017) (2017).

76 Hugo García and Juan David Laverde. Los arquitectos del acuerdo. *El Espectador*, 26 September 2015, https://www.elespectador.com/noticias/politica/los-arquitectos-del-acuerdo-articulo-588936 (accessed on 7 July 2018).

77 Letter of 26 July 2013, sent by the Prosecutor of the ICC to the Colombian Constitutional Court. Corte Constitucional de Colombia, Sentencia C-579/13 (26 August 2013). paragraph 3.16.1. Letter of 7 August 2013, sent by the Prosecutor of the ICC to the Colombian Constitutional Court. Corte Constitucional de Colombia, paragraph 3.16.2.

78 Prominent international human rights NGOs claimed the consideration of human rights standards during the discussion and adoption of transitional justice mechanisms. Among them, the Commission of Jurists, the International Center for Transitional Justice, Human Rights Watch and Amnesty International. An analysis on this question takes place in Chapter 3 of the book.

INTRODUCTION   15

Fourth, transition in Colombia has been a complex and prolonged process, during which international legal considerations related to peace have been present at different moments within the armed conflict. Before the recent peace process, the country had developed other domestic mechanisms of transitional justice (2005)[79] and reparation for victims (2011)[80] closely inspired by international standards. Some authors have even defined the Colombian experience as a case of transitional justice without transition.[81] Because of these aspects, the Colombian case is particularly useful for assessing the application of *jus post bellum* during an ongoing armed conflict.

Fifth, Colombia has a legal system particularly receptive to international law, in which IHRL and IHL treaties are considered to have the same legal level of the Constitution.[82] Additionally, as Céspedes points out, the country has relied "so much on international norms to understand its own conflict."[83] Regarding transitional instruments, this feature has been ensured by an outstanding Constitutional Court controlling the domestic legal and constitutional framework under both the Colombian Constitution and international law.[84] This condition offers advantageous insights on the relationship between international and domestic law, which is a crucial discussion regarding *jus post bellum*.[85]

Finally, while international involvement has marked different stages of transition in Colombia, the peace efforts have maintained a solid local ownership. It can be attributed to, among other reasons, a strong institutional system and a vigorous civil society. This situation is almost paradoxical in a country living an armed conflict for more than five decades.[86] For that reason,

---

79 Congreso de la República de Colombia, 'Ley 975 (Ley de Justicia y Paz)' (2005).
80 Congreso de la República de Colombia, 'Ley 1448 (Ley de Víctimas y Restitución de Tierras)' (2011).
81 Rodrigo Uprimny et al., eds., *¿Justicia Transicional Sin Transición? Verdad, Justicia y Reparación Para Colombia* (Bogota: DeJusticia, 2006).
82 Constitución Política de Colombia, 1991, Art. 93.
83 Lina Céspedes-Báez, 'Gender Panic and the Failure of a Peace Agreement,' *American Journal of International Law* 110 AJIL Unbound Symposium on the Colombian Peace Talks and International Law (2016): 183–87.
84 The Constitutional Court is playing a fundamental role in the process, since all the legal and constitutional instruments developed to implement the agreement have constitutional control. For a view to the main decisions of the Court on the matter, see Corte Constitucional de Colombia, Sentencia C-579/13; Corte Constitucional de Colombia, Sentencia C-379/16 (18 July 2016).
85 Iverson, Easterday, and Stahn, 'Epilogue: *Jus Post Bellum*—Strategic Analysis and Future Directions,' 553.
86 As noted by Saffon and Uprimny, there is certain ambiguity in the Colombian case, because there is a protracted armed conflict aside to a functional institutional system.

the case offers specific insights on the role of domestic actors voluntarily relying on international norms and institutions to resolve their own internal armed conflict.[87]

The above discussion highlights the substantial role of international law in Colombia's domestic transition from armed conflict to peace, in which the parties in negotiation and other domestic and international actors have been involved in reaching peace under a normative framework seeking not only to end the conflict but also to achieve sustainable peace. Said features of the Colombian case offer a broad picture of the relevance of this transition in legal and policy terms, making this experience an especially insightful case study for an empirical analysis of the concept of *jus post bellum*.

4 Empirical Analysis from the Perspective of NIACS

The Colombian transition provides an opportunity to identify how international law shapes peacemaking and peacebuilding by analyzing the actors and discourses involved in that process, as well as the interaction between legal and political considerations and between international and domestic law. Moreover, framing such analysis under the concept of *jus post bellum* offers an opportunity to assess how theory works in practice and how practice provides new insights for theoretical development.

The 2014 publication of the University of Leiden's *Jus Post Bellum* Project raised some questions that should guide future research on the topic, acknowledging that today there are "more questions than answers."[88] Some of those questions relevant for this study include the following: "Who is the addressee of *jus post bellum*? How does it impact the societies in which it is applied or practiced?" "How, exactly, does *jus post bellum* incorporate, blend, or otherwise draw on its various legal sources? To what extent is it feasible to contemplate further regulation and stocktaking, and what form should it take?" "What

---

For them, "In spite of the persistence of the armed conflict and the seriousness of the human rights abuses therein produced, Colombian institutions have managed to maintain important democratic features." Maria Saffon and Rodrigo Uprimny, 'Uses and Abuses of Transitional Justice in Colombia,' in *Law in Peace Negotiations*, ed. Morgen Bergsmo and Pablo Kalmanovitz (Oslo: Torkel Opsahl Academic EPublisher, 2010), 363.

87   Chapter 3 will analyze the actors of *jus post bellum* in Colombia.
88   Iverson, Easterday, and Stahn, 'Epilogue: *Jus Post Bellum*—Strategic Analysis and Future Directions,' 553.

would guiding principles include?" And, "How can, or should, *jus post bellum* be adopted and applied by practitioners?"[89]

Most of these questions will be addressed by this work. Additionally, the empirical approach from a case study within a NIAC context provides new ideas to advance elements from theory and practice looking to give concrete substance to *jus post bellum*.

Thus far, few studies have examined concrete cases of transition from a *jus post bellum* perspective. In 2005, Thürer and MacLaren[90] used Iraq as a test case to examine practical concerns in the application of the law of occupation. Their conclusions addressed the concrete responsibilities of post-occupant powers, suggesting that rather than reforming occupation law, *jus post bellum* provides a framework for better application of IHL in those contexts. In 2009, Labonte[91] wrote a comprehensive case study on *jus post bellum*, examining the Afghan context. However, her analysis is conducted exclusively from the perspective of the just war theory rather than from the perspective of international law. She examined to what extent different peacemaking and peacebuilding measures adopted in Afghanistan respected *jus post bellum* principles as proportionality, discrimination, reconciliation and restoration, focusing on the challenges of non-state actors involved in these processes. In 2011, Ryngaert[92] assessed the role of ICL and *jus post bellum* in Uganda following the country's peace efforts after its situation was referred to the ICC in 2004. This study is concentrated on the role of the ICC when a country is conducting internal peace efforts, but it does not offer a systematic analysis in terms of *jus post bellum*. Finally, in 2012, Benson suggested how the development of emerging norms for economic reform in post conflict countries, discussing the Iraqui case, could be an expression of a rule of *jus post bellum*,[93] though she does not assess the very application of the concept. As such, the Colombian

---

89 Iverson, Easterday, and Stahn, 553.
90 Thürer and MacLaren, '"Ius Post Bellum" in Iraq: A Challenge to the Applicability and Relevance of International Humanitarian Law?'
91 Melissa Labonte, '*Jus Post Bellum*, Peacebuilding and Non-State Actors: Lessons from Afghanistan,' in *Ethics, Authority, and War: Non-State Actors and the Just War Tradition*, ed. Eric Heinze and Brent Steele (New York: Palgrave Macmillan, 2009), 205–57.
92 Cédric Ryngaert and Lauren Gould, 'International Criminal Justice and *Jus Post Bellum*: The Challenge of ICC Complementarity: A Case-Study of the Situation in Uganda,' *Revue Belge de Droit International* 44, no. 1–2 (2011): 91–124.
93 Christina Benson, '*Jus Post Bellum* in Iraq: The Development of Emerging Norms for Economic Reform in Post Conflict Countries,' *Richmond Journal of Global Law & Business* 11, no. 4 (2012): 315–55.

peace process represents a useful example with which to examine the concept under a legal empirical perspective, given the relevance of this case as discussed previously.

Moreover, using a NIAC as a case study challenges the current theorization on *jus post bellum*, which has been focused on IACs. Since the end of World War II, NIACs have been more common than IACs, and the termination of NIACs through peace processes has become more popular following the end of the Cold War.[94] Between 1989 and 2008, only 7 of 124 active armed conflicts were interstate,[95] and between 1990 and 2007, 646 documents of peace agreements were produced addressing 102 conflicts, of which 91% were NIACs.[96] In 2017, 43 peace negotiations were in place around the world, of which 34 referred to NIACs and only 9 to IACs.[97] Therefore, while the concept continues to be more frequently associated with IACs, today we have more cases of transitions from NIACs to peace from which to extract elements of *jus post bellum*.[98]

In addition to the above quantitative argument, substantive considerations increase the relevance of an analysis of *jus post bellum* with respect to NIACs. Negotiating peace in IACs is relatively easier than in NIACs. As highlighted by Kastner, "Whereas the main goal of state-to-state negotiations aiming to end traditional wars is to negotiate a truce and resolve an underlying easily identifiable problem, intrastate negotiations must address numerous issues and involve a wider range of actors, whose relationships are characterized by a higher degree of interdependence."[99] In NIACs, the parties ought to address matters as complex and diverse as criminal accountability, reparations to victims, gender and minority issues, the building of civil trust and reconciliation, the reestablishment of the rule of law, and the guarantee of civil, political, economic, social, and cultural rights. Therefore, a comprehensive analysis of *jus post bellum* in those contexts can provide further clarity on the contours and functions of the concept.

---

94 Jonathan Tonge, *Comparative Peace Processes* (Cambridge: Polity Press, 2014), 5–6.
95 Charles Kegley and Shannon Blanton, *World Politics: Trend and Transformation* (Boston: Wadsworth, 2010), 377–78.
96 Bell, *On the Law of Peace*, 5.
97 Escola de Cultura de Pau, *Peace Talks in Focus 2018. Report on Trends and Scenarios* (Barcelona: Icaria, 2018), 11–12.
98 Kristen Boon, 'The Application of *Jus Post Bellum* in Non-International Armed Conflicts,' in *Jus Post Bellum: Mapping the Normative Foundations*, ed. Carsten Stahn, Jennifer Easterday, and Jens Iverson (Oxford: Oxford University Press, 2014), 259–60.
99 Kastner, *Legal Normativity in the Resolution of Internal Armed Conflict*, 3.

5   Purpose of the Study

Summarizing the above-discussed elements, the study is conceived under three premises. First, international law has an increasingly greater role in transition from armed conflict to peace. Second, the Colombian transition is the most recent and comprehensive example of such a role. And third, extensive legal scholarship has proposed the concept of *jus post bellum* to designate the normative framework for transition from armed conflict to peace.

In this way, the study aims to answer what role international law plays in the transition from armed conflict to peace by using the Colombian transition as a case study, and to what extend this experience can be framed under the concept of *jus post bellum*. By addressing this question, the study explores new ways to understand the role of international law in transition to peace as well as the concrete content and functioning of *jus post bellum* as the concept framing such a role.

As examined in the previous sections, it is necessary to understand the role of international law in transition under an analytical framework,[100] in order to seek some coherence around the disparate set of legal considerations applicable to peacemaking and peacebuilding. Additionally, since *jus post bellum* is the framework proposed for said analysis, the current state of research on the concept reveals the need for further research, especially from an empirical perspective and from the point of view of NIACs. For both reasons, as previously discussed, the Colombian case offers advantageous elements for the analysis.

The main argument of this book is that the Colombian transition has been shaped by different international legal norms, discourses, and practices and that the concept of *jus post bellum* frames such a normative framework. In that way, the study will sustain a definition of the concept as a normative framework of principles guiding the contextualized interpretation and application of international law—understood in a broad sense as including positive and customary norms, legal discourses, and legal practices—to transition to peace, showing how it works in practice, what principles and functions can be identified, and who are its actors. In that sense, the study will show how the theoretical development of the concept mostly matches with practice in Colombia, and that practice also challenges some of its components, providing new insights to keep developing the theory.

---

100   As argued by Kastner, most analysis on the role of legal norms in the resolution of armed conflicts have been conducted "in a superficial manner and without grounding such an examination in a theoretical framework." Kastner, 15.

6 Methodological Considerations

Four considerations should be offered to delineate the methodology of this study. First, even if transitions from armed conflict to peace have more political features than legal ones, this book is focused on the legal elements shaping the political decisions. However, this does not mean that the policy aspects of peacemaking and peacebuilding will be neglected. They will be incorporated into the analysis of the context and implications of the legal formulas adopted in the case study and used to understand the rationale of the principles and functions of *jus post bellum*. Additionally, some aspects of the analysis, such as the socioeconomic and political components of transition, should be considered more so in terms of policy than from a legal perspective.

Second, the concept of *jus post bellum* is considered from the perspective of international law. Though the concept emerged within the just war theory and has been inspired by moral considerations on the justness of peace,[101] this study will consider *jus post bellum* as referring to the legal norms, discourses, and practices governing the transition from armed conflict to peace. This does not mean that moral considerations will be excluded from the analysis; rather, the study will assume that those moral elements are already incorporated into or reflected by international law.

The third consideration concerns what this book understands by international law. The study will follow a broad understanding of law encompassing not only positive norms but also principles, discourses, and practices with a legal dimension. This understanding includes, in addition to conventional and customary law, soft law documents such as guidelines and declarations, as well as jurisprudential rules and legal principles and discourses built through peacemaking and peacebuilding practice.

Fourthly, it is important to mention that while the main emphasis of the analysis of the case study is given to the 2016 Peace Agreement and its negotiation process, other mechanisms of transition in Colombia since 2005 will also be considered.

With the above considerations in mind, the object of the study will be addressed using an inductive and a deductive methodological approach, as well as both primary and secondary sources. An inductive approach is necessary

---

101 Following the just war perspective, Larry May affirms that the normative character of *jus post bellum* derives from its moral nature. May, *After War Ends*. On this line, see also, among other authors, Orend, '*Jus Post Bellum*: The Perspective of a Just-War Theorist'; Williams and Caldwell, '*Jus Post Bellum*: Just War Theory and the Principles of Just Peace'; DiMeglio, 'The Evolution of the Just War Tradition: Defining *Jus Post Bellum*.'

for the examination of the Colombian case in order to determine lessons that could bring new insights to the academic debate on the role of international law in the transition from armed conflict to peace. At the same time, a deductive approach will allow the assessment of existing theory on the relationship between international law and transition to peace through the framework of *jus post bellum*.

For the empirical analysis of the case study, the official documents related to the Colombian transitional process from armed conflict to peace will be considered, including the agenda of negotiations, rules of procedure, joint communiqués, and the 2016 Peace Agreement. Also included are the constitutional and legal domestic framework to implement the Agreement, the legal instruments on transitional justice and reparations existing before the recent peace process, and the jurisprudence of the Constitutional Court, which has played a fundamental role in interpreting those norms under the Constitution and international law. In addition to these primary sources, other relevant international instruments such as treaties, jurisprudence, soft law and UN documents will be used to identify the legal frameworks.

Finally, secondary sources will be used such as bibliography on the different topics of the book, in particular those regarding the concept of *jus post bellum*, as well as the literature on subjects such as socioeconomic and political transitional reforms, criminal justice, reparations, inclusiveness, and the legal nature of peace agreements.

7 Structure of the Book

The book is divided into three chapters. The first chapter will explore the conceptual ground of *jus post bellum*. It will analyze different approaches to a definition of the concept, highlighting the challenges to achieving a unified understanding of *jus post bellum*. The chapter will then explore the object of *jus post bellum*, which is generally described as helping to achieve a sustainable peace. Here, the study will discuss what a sustainable peace would mean under a legal approach to *jus post bellum*. In relation to this subject, the chapter will explore the question of the principles of *jus post bellum*, as the substantive content of the concept. Finally, the chapter will examine similar categories related to the legal framework of transition, discussing how the concepts of transitional justice and *lex pacificatoria* could compete with *jus post bellum*, to then argue that the third term is the most appropriate for designating a comprehensive normative framework for the transition from armed conflict to peace.

The second chapter will assess how international law is reflected in the Colombian transition to peace. The chapter will first offer a general overview of the Colombian armed conflict and its transitional process to peace. It will then examine different components of transition in Colombia, identifying the applicable international legal framework and the way in which it shaped the formulas adopted in the country. The chapter will discuss how aspects such as the legal status of the peace agreement, socioeconomic and institutional reforms, criminal justice for serious crimes committed during armed conflict, reparations, and the inclusive dimension of the peace process were significantly influenced by international legal standards. As such, the chapter will offer the empirical elements that will then be contrasted, in the third chapter, against the conceptual elements of *jus post bellum* discussed in the first chapter.

The third chapter is aimed at connecting the previous two, analyzing what elements can be drawn from the Colombian case toward developing a better understanding of the concept of *jus post bellum*. It will address the conceptual elements of *jus post bellum* presented in Chapter 1 and assess them from the perspective of the Colombian case examined in Chapter 2. The purpose of Chapter 3 is to assess how the Colombian transitional process exemplifies elements of *jus post bellum* in practice and to draw conclusions on the potential definition, content, operation, actors, and functions of the concept based on this case study. As such, this chapter gathers the core of analysis of the study and offers new practical insights for the theory of *jus post bellum*.

Finally, a general conclusion will be presented. It will summarize the three chapters of the study. Then, the conclusion will reflect on the main contributions of the Colombian case to understanding the role of international law in transition to peace and the concept of *jus post bellum*. Lastly, from the perspective of the empirical analysis conducted by the study, the conclusion will discuss the challenges and opportunities of bringing *jus post bellum* from theory to practice, and what could be the future of the concept.

CHAPTER 1

Jus Post Bellum

A Normative Framework for the Transition from Armed Conflict to Peace

This chapter offers the conceptual basis for understanding *jus post bellum* as the normative framework for transition from armed conflict to peace. As presented in the Introduction, the origin and development of *jus post bellum* have taken place under a moral and a legal perspective.[1] While within the just war theory the concept is built from the moral perspective of the justness of the cause and the termination of the conflict, under international law its purpose is to address legal obligations aimed at protecting people's rights in transition to peace.[2]

This chapter—and the study in general—focuses its analysis on the legal dimension of *jus post bellum*. Though the concept is being discussed in legal scholarship for around 15 years,[3] there is no agreement on its content and scope as a legal concept.[4] The discussion has moved from maximalist to minimalist approaches,[5] including authors for whom it seems still premature to consider *jus post bellum* into law.[6] In this context, Easterday, Iverson, and Stahn highlight that "there are almost as many conceptions of *jus post bellum* as scholars, within and across disciplines."[7]

---

1   See Introduction, Section 2.
2   Stahn, '*Jus Post Bellum*: Mapping the Discipline(s),' 2008, 112.
3   The first works on *jus post bellum* from a legal perspective were conducted by Thürer and MacLaren, '"Ius Post Bellum" in Iraq: A Challenge to the Applicability and Relevance of International Humanitarian Law?'; Boon, 'Legislative Reform in Post-Conflict Zones: *Jus Post Bellum* and the Contemporary Occupant's Law-Making Powers'; Cohen, 'The Role of International Law in Post-Conflict Constitution-Making: Toward a *Jus Post Bellum* for "Interim Occupations"'; Stahn, '"Jus Ad Bellum", "jus in Bello" ... "*Jus Post Bellum*"?—Rethinking the Conception of the Law of Armed Force'.
4   Iverson, 'The Function of *Jus Post Bellum* in International Law,' 8.
5   Lonneke Peperkamp, '*Jus Post Bellum*: A Case of Minimalism versus Maximalism?,' *Ethical Perspectives* 21, no. 2 (2014): 255–88.
6   Gregory Fox, 'Navigating the Unilateral/Multilateral Divide,' in *Jus Post Bellum: Mapping the Normative Foundations*, ed. Carsten Stahn, Jennifer Easterday, and Jens Iverson (Oxford: Oxford University Press, 2014), 229–58.
7   Easterday, Iverson, and Stahn, 'Exploring the Normative Foundations of *Jus Post Bellum*: An Introduction,' 3.

© CÉSAR ROJAS-OROZCO, 2021 | DOI:10.1163/9789004440531_003
This is an open access chapter distributed under the terms of the CC BY-NC 4.0 license.

This uncertainty undermines the development of the concept, which can also be attributed to the lack of empirical assessment. The only way to move forward from the theoretical discussion is to assess the concept in practice. As such, this chapter presents the main conceptions of *jus post bellum* as a legal concept across existing literature, addressing the approaches to a definition of the concept, its principles, its objective, its relationship with similar concepts, and its application in the context of transition from NIACs to peace—given the character of the case study. Then, the conceptual mapping provided by this chapter will be the reference for the empirical assessment of *jus post bellum* in the other two chapters of the study.

1 Approaches to a Definition

Jus post bellum is a polysemous concept.[8] The definitions and characterizations around the concept are diverse. Easterday defines *jus post bellum* as a broad and holistic category that covers four spectrums: "as a body of law, as an interpretive framework, as a site of coordination, and as a site of discourse or dialogue."[9] For her, *jus post bellum* should be understood as referring to the rules, norms, and principles governing those spectrums in post-conflict with the goal of reaching sustainable peace.

In 2016, Stahn classified the existing definitions of *jus post bellum* under three approaches: 1) as a system of norms; 2) as an ordering system; and 3) as an interpretative framework.[10] This classification is similar to the four spectrums identified by Easterday if one considers the second approach as including both the spectrums of a site of coordination and a site of discourse or dialogue proposed by her. This section explores each of these approaches as follows.

1.1 *A New Legal Regime*

This approach is based on the alleged existence of a normative gap in the regulation of transition from armed conflict to peace.[11] Its proponents sustain that

---

8 Emmanuel Vianès, 'Le *Jus Post Bellum*: Rupture Ou Continuité?,' *Études Internationales*, 2013, 622. Iverson, 'The Function of *Jus Post Bellum* in International Law,' 8.
9 Jennifer Easterday, 'Peace Agreements as a Framework for *Jus Post Bellum*,' in *Jus Post Bellum: Mapping the Normative Foundations*, ed. Carsten Stahn, Jennifer Easterday, and Jens Iverson (Oxford: Oxford University Press, 2014), 379.
10 Stahn, '*Jus Post Bellum* and the Justice of Peace: Some Preliminary Reflections.'
11 Orend, '*Jus Post Bellum*,' 222; Stahn, '*Jus Post Bellum*: Mapping the Discipline(s),' 2008, 101; Österdahl and van Zadel, 'What Will *Jus Post Bellum* Mean? Of New Wine and Old Bottles,' 182.

such a gap ought to be fulfilled through new legal instruments. There is no discussion on accepting that *jus post bellum* does not exist as a defined branch of international law, as *jus ad bellum* and *jus in bello* do. However, the exponents of this approach sustain that *jus post bellum* should get such a status in international law. While most of them accept that this regime is based on existing norms of international law, all suggest that new norms should be created.

Orend is the main advocate of this approach. In 2000, at the very beginning of the contemporary discussion on *jus post bellum*, he argued the existence of a legal gap in the law of armed force.[12] For him, this "situation requires rectification, ideally through the establishment of international laws of war termination which are codified and effectively observed."[13] His idea was supported by DiMeglio, who considers that such a legal gap represents a risk that the "winner's justice can prevail," which may be addressed through a new legal regulation on the matter.[14] Later, in 2007, Orend proposed that this regulation should be done through a new Geneva Convention on *jus post bellum*.[15]

In the same line, Österdahl and van Zandel affirm that "new international laws, codified and effectively observed, are necessary in order to tackle the problems created by this legal gap in the regulation of post-conflict conduct,"[16] and they suggest that it should be done "through the incorporation of all *jus post bellum* rules in a new Geneva Convention."[17] At this regard, Österdahl noted that "the current post-conflict practice would necessarily provide a lot of experience and normative ideas that would fuel the negotiations on any such comprehensive legal instrument."[18]

This conception of *jus post bellum* is the most ambitious and contested one.[19] Most authors disagree, or doubt that such a codification could be possible.[20]

---

12   Orend, *War and International Justice: A Kantian Perspective*.
13   Orend, 222.
14   DiMeglio, 'The Evolution of the Just War Tradition: Defining *Jus Post Bellum*,' 131–32.
15   Orend, '*Jus Post Bellum*: The Perspective of a Just-War Theorist,' 591.
16   Österdahl and van Zadel, 'What Will *Jus Post Bellum* Mean? Of New Wine and Old Bottles,' 182.
17   Österdahl and van Zadel, 207.
18   Inger Österdahl, 'Just War, Just Peace and the "*Jus Post Bellum*"', *Nordic Journal of International Law* 81, no. 3 (2012): 273.
19   Easterday, Iverson, and Stahn, 'Exploring the Normative Foundations of *Jus Post Bellum*: An Introduction,' 5–6.
20   Among other authors, see Frederik Naert, 'International Humanitarian Law and Human Rights Law in Peace Operations as Parts of a Variable Ius Post Bellum,' *Revue Belge de Droit International* 44, no. 1–2 (2011): 26–37; De Brabandere, 'The Concept of *Jus Post Bellum* in International Law: A Normative Critique'; Bell, 'Of *Jus Post Bellum* and Lex Pacificatoria: What's in a Name?'

And, indeed, codifying *jus post bellum* into a new convention seems an unlikely task, for at least three reasons.

First, a codification of *jus post bellum* will involve the ordinary political and practical challenges of a treaty-making process or the formation of customary law.[21] It does not seem a likely task in a matter that by its very nature requires flexibility and the permanent balance of political and legal considerations, where states want to keep their autonomy. Additionally, peacemaking and peacebuilding are processes full of ambiguities and contradictions, that by no means could be addressed through a "conclusive body of law, i.e., as a (vertical) *lex specialis*."[22] Peace is a political matter, and "the more law specifies peace settlement terms, the less the parties are able to negotiate."[23]

Second, even if some authors argue the existence of a legal gap, such a gap should not be understood as a lack of legal regulation, but of a framework to coordinate and to apply existing rules in a contextualized way in transitional settings. Transition from armed conflict to peace involves a diversity of matters that are already governed by rules belonging to different branches of international law.[24] The application of any specific rule depends on each context, and it is not possible to regulate all of them by a singular branch of law.[25] Different international norms play a role, even if they were not specifically designed to regulate transitions. Thus, the problem is not about lack of law, but how to coordinate and interpret those norms properly in transitional processes.

And third, even if *jus post bellum* appeared as a systemic adaptation of the current divide of the law of armed force,[26] it is not possible to conceive the concept in the same way as *jus ad bellum* and *jus in bello*. These last two regimes operate in a top-down logic, where external norms are applied with no substantial margin of decision by the parties. On the contrary, in *jus post bellum* the parties take and adapt external norms according to the circumstances of their context. If we think, for instance, about *jus in bello* in NIACs,

---

21 De Brabandere, 'The Concept of *Jus Post Bellum* in International Law: A Normative Critique,' 136.
22 Carsten Stahn, 'The Future of *Jus Post Bellum*,' in *Jus Post Bellum. Towards a Law of Transition from Conflict to Peace*, ed. Carsten Stahn and Jann Kleffner (The Hague: T.M.C. Asser Press, 2008), 234. See also Hilary Charlesworth, 'Law After War,' *Melbourne Journal of International Law* 8, no. 2 (2007): 241.
23 Bell, 'Of *Jus Post Bellum* and Lex Pacificatoria: What's in a Name?,' 200.
24 Chetail, 'Introduction'; Österdahl and van Zadel, 'What Will *Jus Post Bellum* Mean? Of New Wine and Old Bottles.'
25 Vianès, 'Le *Jus Post Bellum*: Rupture Ou Continuité?,' 632.
26 De Brabandere, 'The Concept of *Jus Post Bellum* in International Law: A Normative Critique,' 126.

external imperative rules are required, since some parties in conflict—non-state actors—usually do not recognize internal rules and institutions. Thus, to ensure the protection of minimum humanitarian standards, an external top-down regulation should be imposed without internal margin of appreciation or derogation by the parties. For that reason, there is a single *jus in bello* for all kind of NIACS, regardless of the causes or dynamics of the conflict. However, this is not the nature of *jus post bellum*. Even if some limits and standards are imposed by international law, they must be interpreted and applied in a way that allows the search of peace according to the conditions of the specific transitional context. In that way, *jus post bellum* involves a permanent bottom-up normative process, given by the way in which parties involved in transition apply and develop applicable international norms.

1.2 *Ordering System of Norms, Practices, and Discourses*

The second approach to a definition of *jus post bellum* recognizes that rather than new substantive law, an overarching framework for normative coordination and dialogue in transition is required. This framework should include norms to manage the interplay of applicable rules of international law from different legal branches and help to resolve eventual conflicts among them.[27]

Stahn points out that transition from conflict to peace "requires a multilayered structure, which addresses the sequencing and simultaneous application of different bodies of law (including peacetime law or domestic law, if needed)."[28] This interaction of different branches and levels of law in the post-conflict scenario demands an overarching framework providing rules of coordination.[29] Along this line, Easterday argues that *jus post bellum* "can provide the needed coherence and determinacy in the post-conflict legal landscape,"[30] serving two functions. First, *jus post bellum* offers a site of coordination, which "provides a space for a common legal language for the process of transition from conflict to peace, and a unified mode of interpretation for its different underlying legal frameworks when they are applied in post-conflict situations."[31] Second, *jus post bellum* creates a site of discourse and dialogue, which "provides a way to connect different discourses dealing with issues of peace and conflict, and can create synergies between

---

27 Chetail, 'Introduction,' 18.
28 Stahn, 'The Future of *Jus Post Bellum*,' 234.
29 Chetail, 'Introduction,' 18.
30 Easterday, 'Peace Agreements as a Framework for *Jus Post Bellum*,' 385.
31 Easterday, 383.

disciplines such as international relations, legal anthropology, political science, and peace and conflict studies."[32]

Sari goes even further and describes *jus post bellum* "as a normative process which envisages the progressive evolution of the legal framework applicable to post-conflict situations over a period of time."[33] In this sense, the concept should offer elements to identify relevant rules and principles and help to balance them in a concrete context of transition. Similarly, Vatanparast considers *jus post bellum* as "a concept of mixed utility", which offers a "conceptual space" to hold the debate on the "complexities of warfare and the evolving relationships between law, war, and peace."[34]

In a critic to this approach—and to *jus post bellum* in general—, De Brabandere sustains that this view has been justified arguing that *jus post bellum* helps "bringing the existing rules and obligations to the forefront of legal discussion and political decision making."[35] However, for him, such a conception would mean that *jus post bellum* "simply brings together already existing obligations under a new name,"[36] without any "added value from a purely legal perspective."[37]

Based on the discussed elements, this approach offers important insights to understand *jus post bellum* in systemic terms. The disparate set of rules applying in transitional contexts requires some integration. Thus, if *jus post bellum* operates as an overarching system to group those norms and regulate their interplay, the concept would provide such an integration and coordination of norms. However, gathering the norms applicable to the transition from armed conflict to peace is a useful step, but it does not offer a legal function by itself. The next approach offers complementary elements in that direction.

---

32 Easterday, 383–84.
33 Sari, 'The Status of Foreign Armed Forces Deployed in Post-Conflict Environments: A Search for Basic Principles,' 482–83.
34 Roxana Vatanparast, 'Waging Peace: Ambiguities, Contradictions, and Problems of a *Jus Post Bellum* Legal Framework,' in *Jus Post Bellum: Mapping the Normative Foundations*, ed. Carsten Stahn, Jennifer Easterday, and Jens Iverson (Oxford: Oxford University Press, 2014), 153.
35 De Brabandere, 'The Concept of *Jus Post Bellum* in International Law: A Normative Critique,' 137.
36 Eric De Brabandere, 'The Responsibility for Post-Conflict Reforms: A Critical Assessment of *Jus Post Bellum* as a Legal Concept,' *Vanderbilt Journal of Transnational Law* 43, no. 1 (2010): 122.
37 De Brabandere, 'The Concept of *Jus Post Bellum* in International Law: A Normative Critique,' 137.

1.3 Interpretative Framework

In 2009, Chetail pointed out how *jus post bellum* serves as a framework for the "contextualized interpretation" of existing norms applicable to the transition from armed conflict to peace.[38] This interpretative approach to the concept was then developed by James Gallen,[39] defining *jus post bellum* "as an interpretive framework for international law through the various dimensions of complexity that arise in transitions."[40] For him, "the distinctive value of *jus post bellum* should be in recognizing that the various norms, regulations, and practices relevant to transitions are inter-dependent and mutually re-enforcing and as a result can be evaluated and interpreted in a unified fashion."[41] As such, he argues that this framework integrates three dimensions of complexity that must be addressed in transition: 1) the variety of legal obligations that apply in transitions; 2) the international legal status of actors involved in the process; and 3) the particularities of each transitional context.[42]

Although Gallen considers a suitable end the development of a codification on *jus post bellum*, he agrees that it would be difficult to achieve.[43] Nevertheless, he points out that "the absence of a conventional *jus post bellum* does not preclude the interpretation of existing international law and policy" under a unified framework.[44]

On this point, even if De Brabandere is skeptical about *jus post bellum*, he admits that this minimalistic approach to the concept as an interpretative framework is "theoretically is the most viable."[45] For him, under this perspective *jus post bellum* responds to the "need to interpret uniformly the various norms, rules, and practices applicable in post-conflict reconstruction," and

---

38 Chetail, 'Introduction,' 18.
39 James Gallen, '*Jus Post Bellum*: An Interpretive Framework,' in *Jus Post Bellum: Mapping the Normative Foundations*, ed. Carsten Stahn, Jennifer Easterday, and Jens Iverson (Oxford: Oxford University Press, 2014), 58–79.
40 Gallen, 59.
41 Gallen, 59.
42 Gallen, 61–65.
43 In a later article, he admits that in the future *jus post bellum* could lead to a codification into a Geneva Convention or in policy documents. In his words, "*jus post bellum* may eventually lead to concrete changes in existing public international law and find expression in a future Geneva Convention or in the policy documents of international organisations. At present it may effectively operate as an interpretation of the laws, actors, issues and fields relevant to the achievement of a just and sustainable peace after conflict." James Gallen, 'Odious Debt and *Jus Post Bellum*,' *Journal of World Investment & Trade* 16, no. 4 (2015): 670.
44 Gallen, '*Jus Post Bellum*: An Interpretive Framework,' 69.
45 De Brabandere, 'The Concept of *Jus Post Bellum* in International Law: A Normative Critique,' 127.

thus it should be seen "as a normative set of principles rather than substantive rules."[46] As such, he suggests the identification of existing principles of international law relevant to transition for interpreting applicable "rules in function of the identified overarching principles."[47]

Similarly, although Bell has proposed the concept of *lex pacificatoria* as an alternative to *jus post bellum*,[48] her approach is close to the notion of an interpretative framework. She says that the emerging *lex* is the result of the evolution of legal understandings on how international law should be applied to peace processes and agreements. As such, rather than "regulate negotiations outcomes," this *lex* sets out normative parameters that offer the elements to reach agreements combining the specific needs of justice and peace.[49] In her words, "this new *lex* does not operate as a clear new legal regime establishing a set of legal obligations but rather as a set of programmatic standards that provides guidance and, at times, goes further in creating a normative expectation as to how the dilemmas of peace settlements can be resolved concomitantly with the requirements of international law."[50]

This approach is the most accurate in terms of identifying the legal function of *jus post bellum*. It does not call for new norms but for a framework to interpret the existing norms of international law in a consistent and contextualized way in transitional settings.[51] This interpretative function is required to resolve conflicts between a general legal norm, on the one hand, and the specific conditions of post-conflict contexts in which such a norm should be applied, on the other. However, this approach takes elements from the previous one, since the interpretative function played by *jus post bellum* implies an ordering system or a space of dialogue to combine legal and practical considerations to achieve the adequate formula for a particular context of transition.

As such, combining elements from the last two approaches, an integrative definition becomes possible. *Jus post bellum* can be seen, then, as a normative framework ordering norms, discourses, and practices to allow the contextualized interpretation and application of relevant international law to the transition from armed conflict to sustainable peace. With this idea on mind, the study will continue exploring elements from theory and practice in the first

---

46   De Brabandere, 124.
47   De Brabandere, 137.
48   Bell, 'Of *Jus Post Bellum* and Lex Pacificatoria: What's in a Name?,' 192.
49   Bell, 205.
50   Bell, 192.
51   Chetail, 'Introduction,' 18.

two chapters, and then it will develop its own approach to the definition and content of *jus post bellum* in Chapter 3 from the perspective of the case study.

2   Principles of *Jus Post Bellum*

Regardless of their approach to a definition, most authors have proposed different series of principles of *jus post bellum*. While just war theorists have suggested moral principles informing the conditions to reach a just peace, in legal scholarship principles have been proposed with various purposes. Authors claiming for the codification of *jus post bellum* through a new conventional instrument suggest principles to develop such a body of law. Authors understanding *jus post bellum* as an ordering framework propose overarching principles to organize the disparate set of norms applicable to transitional contexts. And authors approaching *jus post bellum* as an interpretative framework argue that principles are the tool for interpreting international law in a contextualized way in transitional settings.

For Stahn, the configuration of a *jus post bellum* framework would allow to identify "specific legal principles which serve as guidance in making legal policy choices in situations of transitions."[52] To this effect, in one of his first works on the topic, he proposed six principles of *jus post bellum*: 1) Fairness and inclusiveness of peace settlements; 2) Demise of the concept of punishment for aggression; 3) Humanization of reparations and sanctions; 4) Moving from collective to individual responsibility for wrongs committed during conflict; 5) Combining justice and reconciliation models; and 6) Fostering people-centered governance.[53] Similarly, Orend suggests as *jus post bellum* principles: 1) Rights vindication; 2) Proportionality and publicity, 3) Discrimination between leader, soldiers and civilians, 4) Punishment, 5) Compensation, and 6) Rehabilitation.[54]

In the context of post-occupation situations, where the concept of *jus post bellum* started its contemporary development, principles related to occupiers'

---

52   Stahn, '*Jus Post Bellum*: Mapping the Discipline(s),' 2008, 101–2.
53   Stahn, ' "Jus Ad Bellum", "jus in Bello" … "*Jus Post Bellum*"?—Rethinking the Conception of the Law of Armed Force,' 938–41.
54   Brian Orend, '*Jus Post Bellum*: A Just War Theory Perspective,' in *Jus Post Bellum. Towards a Law of Transition from Conflict to Peace*, ed. Carsten Stahn and Jann Kleffner (The Hague: T.M.C. Asser Press, 2008), 37–42. In a previous work, Orend suggested five principles of *jus post bellum*: 1) Just cause for termination; 2) Right intention; 3) Public declaration and legitimate authority; 4) Discrimination; and, 6) Proportionality. Orend, '*Jus Post Bellum*,' 128–29.

duties have been proposed. Boon suggests three principles: trusteeship, accountability, and proportionality.[55] And later, Coady proposed other three: rebuilding and reconstruction, punishment and reparations, and the role of occupiers, peacemakers and peacekeepers.[56]

Gallen and De Brabandere, who define *jus post bellum* as an interpretative framework, also suggest their principles. For Gallen, *jus post bellum* should be based on three principles: accountability (individual criminal responsibility and state responsibility), stewardship (respect of local ownership), and proportionality.[57] In a similar formulation, De Brabandere coincides with those principles, that he describes as proportionality, accountability of foreign actors (he is focused on post-occupation), and the principle that post-conflict reconstruction should be for the benefit of the population.[58]

Just as there is no agreed definition, there is no agreement in terms of *jus post bellum* principles. The above-mentioned principles have been formulated in general ways, in works aimed at discussing conceptual aspects of *jus post bellum*. There is no a systematic analysis on these principles, and each author suggests new ones without discussing principles formulated previously. Additionally—as common with other aspects of the existing legal scholarship on *jus post bellum*—the principles which have been proposed are mainly addressed to IACs. This situation does not correspond to the fact that NIACs are currently more common than IACs nor to the need to provide greater consistency to the concept of *jus post bellum*.

In his 2012 book *After War Ends: A Philosophical Perspective*, May developed a systematic scheme of six principles of *jus post bellum*: rebuilding, retribution, restitution, reparation, reconciliation, and proportionality.[59] These principles integrate some of the principles proposed by other authors, and his proposal has received significant endorsement by other scholars.[60]

---

55   Boon, 'Legislative Reform in Post-Conflict Zones: *Jus Post Bellum* and the Contemporary Occupant's Law-Making Powers'.
56   Cecil Anthony Coady, 'The *Jus Post Bellum*,' in *New Wars and New Soldiers: Military Ethics in the Contemporary World*, ed. Jessica Wolfendale and Paolo Tripodi (London: Ashgate Press, 2011), 49–66.
57   Gallen, '*Jus Post Bellum*: An Interpretive Framework'.
58   De Brabandere, 'The Concept of *Jus Post Bellum* in International Law: A Normative Critique,' 137–38.
59   May, *After War Ends*.
60   Among the authors referring May's principles as a base to develop *jus post bellum*, see: Easterday, Iverson, and Stahn, 'Exploring the Normative Foundations of *Jus Post Bellum*: An Introduction'; Matthew Saul, 'Creating Popular Governments in Post-Conflicts Situations: The Role of International Law,' in *Jus Post Bellum: Mapping the Normative Foundations*, ed. Carsten Stahn, Jennifer Easterday, and Jens Iverson (Oxford: Oxford

For May, these normative principles are the constituent substance of *jus post bellum*. However, since his proposal was conceived under the perspective of the just war theory, he considers that the normative character of these principles derives not from law but from moral. In his words,

> *Jus post bellum* principles are primarily moral principles that are meant to inform decisions about how international law is best to be established down the road. Here it is important to note that on this construal, *jus post bellum* principles are not legal principles themselves. *Jus post bellum* principles are normative in that they are moral norms and they tell us what should become law. But until there is some lawmaking act, such as an international convention (a multilateral treaty), what I will identify as *jus post bellum* principles are primarily moral norms that have strong force in our thinking about what norms should be enacted into international law. [...] In setting out a group of *jus post bellum* principles I am making a plea for them to become instituted, but my arguments in favor of having them become legal norms should not be confused with thinking that they already have legal status, which they do not.[61]

Sustaining this idea, in a later article May argues that the proposed set of *jus post bellum* principles is comparable to the content and scope of the Martens Clause to The Hague Convention (II).[62] As such, he states that even if *jus post bellum* principles are not yet enshrined in legal instruments, they are the embodiment of moral obligations written in the human conscience that dictates the way to proceed in post-conflict settings. In consequence, for him, *jus*

University Press, 2014), 447–66; Fionnuala Ní Aoláin and Dina Haynes, 'The Compatibility of Justice for Women with *Jus Post Bellum* Analysis,' in *Jus Post Bellum: Mapping the Normative Foundations*, ed. Carsten Stahn, Jennifer Easterday, and Jens Iverson (Oxford: Oxford University Press, 2014), 161–77; Stahn, '*Jus Post Bellum* and the Justice of Peace: Some Preliminary Reflections'. Iverson, 'The Function of *Jus Post Bellum* in International Law,' 8.

61   May, *After War Ends*, 5.

62   May, '*Jus Post Bellum*, Grotius, and Meionexia,' 24. On this point, the Martens Clause is formulated in the following terms: "Until a more complete code of the laws of war is issued, the High Contracting Parties think it right to declare that in cases not included in the Regulations adopted by them, population and belligerents remain under the protection and empire of the principles of international law, as they result from the usages established between civilized nations, from the laws of humanity and the requirements of the public conscience". Preamble, Hague Convention (II) Respecting the Laws and Customs of War on Land (adopted 29 July 1899, entered into force 4 September 1900).

post bellum is "a regime of international law that is not strictly speaking *lex lata* but is also more than mere *lex ferenda*."[63]

In the 2014 publication of the *Jus Post Bellum* Project, its editors acknowledge that May's principles constitute a solid basis for *jus post bellum*. Nonetheless, they point out that "the question remains: (how) are those moral norms reflected in international law?"[64]

Regarding this matter, May's principles are certainly useful and they offer a strong basis to reach a unified approach to the content and scope of *jus post bellum*.[65] However, contrary to May's view on the exclusive moral nature of these principles, they already have a basis in international law.[66] To this effect, through Chapters 2 and 3 the study will explore the legal foundation of the principles of *jus post bellum* in contexts of NIACs, and their role in coordinating, interpreting, and applying international legal obligations in the Colombian transition from armed conflict to peace.[67] Along this line, Saul argues that we need to explore in practice the legal components of *jus post bellum* following May's principles, to give them "a more concrete form without completely loosing" their inherent flexibility.[68]

---

63 May, 23. Supporting the idea of *jus post bellum* as being moral, but not having a legal basis, see also: Antonia Chayes, 'Chapter VII½: Is *Jus Post Bellum* Possible?,' *European Journal of International Law* 24, no. 1 (2013): 293.

64 Easterday, Iverson, and Stahn, 'Exploring the Normative Foundations of *Jus Post Bellum*: An Introduction,' 1.

65 At this point, it is important to clarify that even if this study addresses *jus post bellum* form a legal perspective, as stated before, it does not exclude the reference to elements proposed under the just war theory, as they are expressed in international law. In this line, Stahn evokes that is "wrong to construe a 'moral' and a 'legal' *jus post bellum* in isolation from each other. There are important and justified differences between the two. But none of them is completely detached from the other". Stahn, 'The Future of *Jus Post Bellum*,' 232.

66 In the case of *jus ad bellum* and *jus in bello*, their legal principles and rules were originally conceived as moral duties, which were later translated into positive and customary legal obligations. So, even if the nature of *jus post bellum* is different, its development was also initially grounded in a moral perspective. But, as sustained by Evans, moral principles look to "animate the body of law that constitutes 'legal' *jus post bellum*", Mark Evans, 'At War's End: Time to Turn to *Jus Post Bellum*?,' in *Jus Post Bellum: Mapping the Normative Foundations*, ed. Carsten Stahn, Jennifer Easterday, and Jens Iverson (Oxford: Oxford University Press, 2014), 26.

67 Chapter 2 will offer the legal framework on the main components of the Colombian peace agreement. Then, Chapter 3, Section 3, will address the principles of *jus post bellum* as they are viewed in the Colombian transition. However, the legal foundation of those principles is referred mainly in Chapter 2.

68 Saul, 'Creating Popular Governments in Post-Conflicts Situations: The Role of International Law,' 466.

Different views support this argument on the legal foundation of *jus post bellum* principles. *Jus post bellum* is based on existing principles and rules of international law, which are inspired on a liberal view of law centered in the protection of the individual and his fundamental rights.[69] On this point, Österdahl affirms that *jus post bellum* "could gradually lead to new organizing principles" around democracy, the rule of law, and human rights.[70] Similarly, authors as Walzer[71] and Williams and Caldwell[72] coincide sustaining that human rights are the foundation of *jus post bellum* principles. Even May affirms that these principles are aimed at building a just peace, which for him means that "human rights are protected."[73]

Considering this background, this study sustains that principles express the substantive content of *jus post bellum*. As such, Chapter 3 will analyze each of the principles proposed by May, along with some other principles proposed by other authors, assessing how they are reflected in the Colombian case, according to the practice analyzed in Chapter 2.[74]

3 Temporal and Functional Approach to *Jus Post Bellum*

The very use of the concept of *jus post bellum* is problematic to refer a matter that is transitional by nature. Scholars agree that notwithstanding *jus post bellum* is intended to apply to the post-conflict phase, it is not clear how to determine when does it occur.[75] At this regard, Kennedy considers the term

---

69 For a literature review on the liberal dimension of peacebuilding, see Chetail and Jütersonke, 'Peacebuilding: A Review of the Academic Literature,' 5–7. Chetail specifically relates this liberal view to the legal foundation of *jus post bellum*, since he defines *jus post bellum* as the normative framework of peacebuilding: Chetail, 'Introduction.'
70 Inger Österdahl, 'The Gentle Modernizer of the Law of Armed Conflict,' in *Jus Post Bellum: Mapping the Normative Foundations*, ed. Carsten Stahn, Jennifer Easterday, and Jens Iverson (Oxford: Oxford University Press, 2014), 209.
71 Michael Walzer, 'The Aftermath of War. Reflections on *Jus Post Bellum*,' in *Ethics Beyond War's End*, ed. Eric Patterson (Washington: Georgetown University Press, 2012), 43.
72 Williams and Caldwell, '*Jus Post Bellum*: Just War Theory and the Principles of Just Peace,' 309.
73 May, *After War Ends*, 86. On this line, he asserts that *jus post bellum* principles look to guarantee the human rights of the people affected by the conflict, "as well as the human rights of the people of the world." May, 22.
74 As previously mentioned, in Chapter 2 the study will offer the legal framework on the main components of the Colombian Peace Agreement, which will then be addressed in Chapter 3, Section 3, identifying principles of *jus post bellum* in the Colombian transition.
75 Vatanparast, 'Waging Peace: Ambiguities, Contradictions, and Problems of a *Jus Post Bellum* Legal Framework,' 146; Carsten Stahn, '*Jus Post Bellum*: Mapping the Discipline(s),' *American University International Law Review* 23, no. 2 (2007): 322; Doug McCready,

post-conflict inadequate, since the process of transition is a series of continuities where is not possible to determine the end of war or the beginning of peace.[76]

The transition from conflict to peace is a process with no clear starting and ending points.[77] This problem is common in all *jus ad bellum*, *jus in bello*, and *jus post bellum*,[78] since the *before*, the *during*, and the *after* of armed confrontation are usually complex and no linear periods. But, the very name of *jus post bellum* implies a temporary dimension. On this point, Stahn admits that "the '*post*' in this equation is a fragile concept."[79]

The application of *jus post bellum* does not depend on the end of the conflict or the cessation of the application of *jus in bello*. Determining the end of armed conflicts is a complicated matter under IHL. Article Common 3 and Protocol Additional II do not say anything on this matter, and the main criteria to determine the end of the conflict are: 1) the decreasing intensity of the confrontation,[80] or, 2) a peace settlement establishing the end of hostilities.[81] However, the end of a NIAC does not imply the automatic cessation of the application of humanitarian provisions. Some matters keep being regulated by humanitarian norms when their effects last longer than the end of the conflict—such as questions of landmines, displaced persons, or missing

---

'Ending the War Right: *Jus Post Bellum* and the Just War Tradition,' *Journal of Military Ethics* 8, no. 1 (2009): 75; Österdahl and van Zadel, 'What Will *Jus Post Bellum* Mean? Of New Wine and Old Bottles,' 175–76; Stahn, ' "Jus Ad Bellum", "jus in Bello" … "*Jus Post Bellum*"?—Rethinking the Conception of the Law of Armed Force,' 923.

76 David Kennedy, *Of War and Law* (Princeton: Princeton University Press, 2006), 113–14.

77 Jan Kleffner, 'Towards a Functional Conceptualization of Temporal Scope of *Jus Post Bellum*,' in *Jus Post Bellum: Mapping the Normative Foundations*, ed. Carsten Stahn, Jennifer Easterday, and Jens Iverson (Oxford: Oxford University Press, 2014), 288–89.

78 Martin Wählisch, 'Conflict Termination from a Human Rights Perspective: State Transitions, Power-Sharing, and the Definition of the "Post",' in *Jus Post Bellum: Mapping the Normative Foundations*, ed. Carsten Stahn, Jennifer Easterday, and Jens Iverson (Oxford: Oxford University Press, 2014), 317.

79 Stahn, 'The Future of *Jus Post Bellum*,' 233.

80 For Bartels, "if a NIAC only starts when organized armed groups are engaged in fighting of a certain degree of intensity, then, logically, the armed conflict ends when these two criteria are no longer present." Rogier Bartels, 'From Jus in Bello to *Jus Post Bellum*: When Do Non-International Armed Conflicts End?,' in *Jus Post Bellum: Mapping the Normative Foundations*, ed. Carsten Stahn, Jennifer Easterday, and Jens Iverson (Oxford: Oxford University Press, 2014), 303.

81 Gabriella Venturini, 'The Temporal Scope of Application of the Conventions,' in *The 1949 Geneva Conventions*, ed. Andrew Clapham, Paola Gaeta, and Marco Sassoli (Oxford: Oxford University Press, 2015), 61–62.

people.[82] As such, Bartels sustains that it is not necessary to wait until *jus in bello* ceases to apply to start applying *jus post bellum*, and thus both regimes could apply simultaneously.[83]

A more complicated question concerns to the determination of the end of applicability. If *jus post bellum* is a law of transition from armed conflict to peace, it could be said that it ceases to apply when there is peace.[84] Regarding this matter, Kleffner considers that if the purpose of *jus post bellum* is to establish sustainable peace, *jus post bellum* would cease to apply when conflict has been addressed to a point in which there is no risk to come back to violence.[85] He says that there are some components of *jus post bellum* for which it would be possible to identify an end, such as criminal proceedings, reparations to victims, and disarmament and demobilization. Nevertheless, all those processes do not happen at the same time.[86] The question would be even more difficult regarding matters of positive peace.

As such, Kleffner proposes a functional approach to determine the temporal scope of *jus post bellum*, which he sees as a body of law. Since this regime applies to transitional environments, "its applicability *ratione temporis* is equally transitional."[87] Thus, the temporal scope should be regarded in a flexible way, because even if some components have a clear end, others last over the time.

Indeed, transitional periods are fluids, and therefore it is difficult—if not impossible—to establish a temporal scope.[88] On this point, Wählisch argues that the "continuum of practical and legal dynamics [...] set the 'post' into a relative state."[89] However, he suggests some criteria to determine the end of *jus post bellum* application through the reestablishment of human rights guarantees: completed elections, constitutional amendments, compliance with human rights conventional obligations, return of internally displaced persons, etc.[90]

---

82   Venturini, 61; ICRC, *Commentary on the First Geneva Convention*, 2nd edition, 2016, para. 850.
83   Bartels, 'From Jus in Bello to *Jus Post Bellum*: When Do Non-International Armed Conflicts End?,' 314.
84   Kleffner, 'Towards a Functional Conceptualization of Temporal Scope of *Jus Post Bellum*,' 293.
85   Kleffner, 293–94.
86   Kleffner, 294–95.
87   Kleffner, 295.
88   Wählisch, 'Conflict Termination from a Human Rights Perspective: State Transitions, Power-Sharing, and the Definition of the "Post",' 316.
89   Wählisch, 318.
90   Wählisch, 321.

Similarly, other authors consider the question of the temporal scope of *jus post bellum* from a functional angle. Iverson emphasizes that what matters "from a *jus post bellum* perspective is not whether a status of *post bellum* has technically been achieved but rather whether legal norms are being applied with *post bellum* as the goal."[91] Along these lines, May sustains:

> We should be flexible on how we regard the 'post', mainly in contexts where there is not a formal ending of war. [...] *Jus post bellum* refers to any principles that govern the mopping up efforts, namely the efforts at the end and after the end of war that lead into a position of peace. In this way, we don't have to decide precisely when war ends but only when the practices of mopping up begin. It is conceivable that mopping up efforts occur even while it is pretty clear that war is still waging, although often this will be a very dangerous thing to do.[92]

The overall discussion on a temporal or a functional approach in the application of *jus post bellum* is closely connected to the meaning given to the concept. The question of the temporal scope is particularly relevant under the approach to *jus post bellum* as an independent legal regime. However, if one sees *jus post bellum* under other approaches, the focus shifts to a functional rather than a temporal application. In *jus post bellum* as an ordering system or as an interpretative framework, there is no need to discuss a temporal applicability. Under these approaches, *jus post bellum* plays a role guiding the application of norms in the process of transition from armed conflict to peace, but it does not constitute a *corpus* of norms applicable by itself.

In this way, rather than a legal order with specific *ratione temporis* application, *jus post bellum* is a framework offering a space to coordinate and apply relevant norms to the process of transition from armed conflict to peace. This vision conveys a functional and teleological perspective. It means that, instead of a temporal frame of application, *jus post bellum* involves the function and the goal of applying law to end armed conflict and build sustainable peace.

On this point, it is relevant the above-quoted May's idea, arguing that "*jus post bellum* refers to any principles that govern the mopping up efforts [...] that lead into a position of peace."[93] Therefore, there is no need to determine

---

91 Iverson, Jens, 'Transitional Justice, *Jus Post Bellum* and International Criminal Law: Differentiating the Usages, History and Dynamics,' *The International Journal of Transitional Justice* 7 (2013): 426.
92 May, *After War Ends*, 3.
93 May, 3.

"when war ends but only when the practices of mopping up begin."[94] As such, the principles of *jus post bellum* embody a set of legal standards, practices, and discourses guiding the application of law in transitional processes, which could occur during the ongoing conflict, through a peace process, or during the implementation of a peace agreement. This question is particularly visible in the Colombian case, where several elements of *jus post bellum* can be identified in the legal regulation of matters like reparation and criminal justice during the conflict.[95] Similarly, the framework of *jus post bellum* guided the recent peace process in Colombia and its 2016 Peace Agreement even if armed conflict continues in the country, since, at least, one rebel group remains in hostilities.[96]

In consequence, there is no need to establish a beginning or an end in the application of *jus post bellum*. This question is rooted in the function played by *jus post bellum* rather than in a temporal sequence.[97] As such, the concept covers the normative framework guiding the transition from armed conflict towards sustainable peace, regardless of the existence of a peace process or the effective end of the conflict.

4 The Object of *Jus Post Bellum*

Determining the goal pursued by *jus post bellum* is an essential task to develop its functional approach. As delineated in the previous sections, regardless of the approach to a definition, the concept has been conceived as a normative framework to guide societies emerging from armed conflict to reach a solid peace.

Under the just war theory, the concept is linked to the justness of peace and, thus, interconnected and interdependent to *jus ad bellum* and *jus in bello*.[98]

---

[94] May, 3.
[95] Different legal transitional instruments in Colombia can be seen as having a *jus post bellum* approach, even if they were adopted during the ongoing armed conflict, and with no peace agreement in mind. See: Congreso de la República de Colombia, Ley 975 (Ley de Justicia y Paz), 2005; Congreso de la República de Colombia, Ley 1448 (Ley de Víctimas y Restitución de Tierras); Congreso de la República de Colombia, 'Acto Legislativo 01 de 2012 (Marco Jurídico Para La Paz)' (2012).
[96] Despite the broad scope of the 2016 Peace Agreement, another guerrilla goup (the ELN) remains in hostilities in the country. Chapter 2, Section 0, will offer an overview of the Colombian armed conflict.
[97] Iverson, 'The Function of *Jus Post Bellum* in International Law,' 13.
[98] Walzer, *Just and Unjust Wars. A Moral Argument with Historical Illustrations*; May, *After War Ends*, 220.

For Orend, one must consider the justice of the resort to war, the justice in the conduct of war, and the justice after war.[99] In the same way, May suggests that "nearly everyone to have written on the subject of war would agree that the object of a just war is the achievement of a just and lasting peace."[100] Similarly, Walzer sustains that *jus post bellum* implies to have a look at the justice of war's goals,[101] and Lucas even affirms that *jus post bellum* "includes the demand for a right intention to both fight and conclude wars with justice."[102] Lastly, Labonte states that for a just war theorist *jus post bellum* matters because "how war ends—including the substantive terms of a negotiated peace agreement—can be a key factor in determining its justness."[103]

However, such an approach to the objective of *jus post bellum* is problematic from a legal point of view. The notion of the justness of peace is rooted in the moral tradition of the just war theory, and it would be difficult to apply it in a legal perspective. Additionally, international law has understood *jus ad bellum*, *jus in bello*, and *jus post bellum* as independent legal frameworks.[104] Contrary to the just war theory's conception on the linear justness of the three regimes, international law sustains that each regime is independent, and must be observed regardless of the others. It means that the breach of one of them does not imply that the others are consequently broken too.

On this perspective, Vatanparast affirms that "*jus post bellum* is thought to provide a legal framework that can address the underlying causes of conflict to prevent relapse into hostilities."[105] Thus, the object of *jus post bellum* goes beyond the end of hostilities and looks at creating long-term peace. As such, she sustains that the concept's goal is "to eliminating the root causes of conflict and creating a lasting peace."[106] Stahn shares a similar view, arguing that a "modern *jus post bellum* would be focused on the sustainability of peace, rather than on simply brokering an end to violence."[107] This

---

99 Orend, 'Jus Post Bellum,' 118.
100 May, *After War Ends*, 10.
101 Walzer, *Just and Unjust Wars. A Moral Argument with Historical Illustrations.*
102 George Lucas, 'Jus Ante and Post Bellum. Completing the Circle, Breaking the Circle,' in *Ethics Beyond War's End*, ed. Eric Patterson (Washington: Georgetown University Press, 2012), 60.
103 Labonte, '*Jus Post Bellum*, Peacebuilding and Non-State Actors : Lessons from Afghanistan,' 208.
104 Stahn, '"Jus Ad Bellum", "jus in Bello" ... "*Jus Post Bellum*"?—Rethinking the Conception of the Law of Armed Force,' 925.
105 Vatanparast, 'Waging Peace: Ambiguities, Contradictions, and Problems of a *Jus Post Bellum* Legal Framework,' 144.
106 Vatanparast, 145.
107 Stahn, '*Jus Post Bellum*: Mapping the Discipline(s),' 2008, 107.

perspective is reaffirmed in the 2017 *Jus Post Bellum* Project's volume, where its editors state that "the concept is inherently liked to the idea of sustainable peace."[108]

Österdahl affirms that "the purpose of *jus post bellum* is to achieve a just and stable peace based on democracy, human rights and the rule of law."[109] Even though she uses the notion of just peace, she grounds her view on legal elements. In another article authored by her and by van Zadel, they expose this viewpoint in further detail. For them,

> The aim of the rules of *jus post bellum* is to achieve a durable peace by helping the state return to its sovereign pre-conflict situation, if such was a desirable one measured by standards of international law, or by helping the state achieve an improved version of its pre-conflict situation. Ideally, the state should achieve a higher level of human rights protection, accountability and good governance in the post-conflict phase than in the period before the conflict.[110]

According to the above-discussed elements, one can conclude that the final goal of *jus post bellum* is not simply about ending conflict but about establishing a qualified and sustainable peace.[111] On this matter, the UN General Assembly has noted that:

'Peace' is understood as meaning sustainable peace.

> While the cessation of hostilities, restoration of public security and meeting basic needs are urgent and legitimate expectations of people who have been traumatized by armed conflict, sustainable peace requires a long-term approach that addresses the structural causes of conflict, and promotes sustainable development, rule of law and governance, and

---

108 Carsten Stahn, Jens Iverson, and Jennifer Easterday, 'Introduction: Protection of the Environment and *Jus Post Bellum*: Some Preliminary Reflections,' in *Environmental Protection and Transitions from Conflict to Peace: Clarifying Norms, Principles, and Practices*, ed. Carsten Stahn, Jens Iverson, and Jennifer Easterday (Oxford: Oxford University Press, 2017), 7.
109 Österdahl, 'The Gentle Modernizer of the Law of Armed Conflict,' 208.
110 Österdahl and van Zadel, 'What Will *Jus Post Bellum* Mean? Of New Wine and Old Bottles,' 179.
111 Chetail, 'Introduction,' 18; Iverson, Easterday, and Stahn, 'Epilogue: *Jus Post Bellum*— Strategic Analysis and Future Directions,' 548; Boon, 'The Application of *Jus Post Bellum* in Non-International Armed Conflicts,' 265.

respect for human rights, making the recurrence of violent conflict less likely.[112]

In the same view, referring to his guidelines to UN peace envoys, the UN Secretary-General noted that his envoys "can assist in brokering agreements in conformity with law and in a manner which may provide the basis for lasting peace."[113] It involves Galtung's idea of reaching not only negative but also positive peace.[114] In other words, in this context peace "means long-term peace."[115]

In conclusion, the object of *jus post bellum* must be understood in terms of offering a normative framework for societies in transition to establishing a sustainable peace, which requires, at least, two conditions. First, addressing the root causes of the conflict, which is the only way to promote reconciliation and prevent recurrence to violence. Second, observing relevant standards of international law, which are essential to ensure the rule of law, human rights, governance, and international legitimacy.[116]

Both conditions can be appreciated in the Colombian transition. A comprehensive peace process was conceived for both addressing the root causes of the armed conflict and dealing with its consequences in terms of justice, truth, and reparation under an international legal framework. Chapter 2 will analyze how the root causes and the consequences of armed conflict were addressed in Colombia, integrating legal, political, and practical considerations. Then, Chapter 3 will discuss how the Colombian experience offers empirical elements to delineate the object of *jus post bellum* as presented in this section.

5   *Jus Post Bellum* and Related Concepts

In addition to the critics around its definition and scope, *jus post bellum* is challenged by the existence of other concepts related to the transition from armed conflict to peace. There are several notions associated to transitional

---

112   UN General Assembly, 'Nuremberg Declaration on Peace and Justice,' Pub. L. No. A/62/885 (2008), II.1.
113   United Nations, "press Release: Secretary-General Comments on Guidelines Issued to Envoys," UN Doc. SG/SM/7257 (10 December 1999).
114   Johan Galtung, 'Violence, Peace, and Peace Research,' *Journal of Peace Research* 6, no. 3 (1969): 167–91.
115   Chetail and Jütersonke, 'Peacebuilding: A Review of the Academic Literature,' 1.
116   On this question, Kastner sustains that "respecting legal obligations confers legitimacy and increases the effectiveness of peace negotiations and eventually of a peace agreement" Kastner, *Legal Normativity in the Resolution of Internal Armed Conflict*, 14.

processes, though not all of them address the legal dimension of transition. For example, peacemaking and peacebuilding define the process of resolving armed conflicts and building sustainable peace, and even if such processes have received increasing legal regulation they are not legal notions as such.[117] Therefore, this section will only analyze two concepts that, like *jus post bellum*, have been understood as defining the legal framework of transition to peace. One is the concept of transitional justice, which has been extensively developed in theory and practice. The other one is *lex pacificatoria*, proposed by Bell[118] as an alternative concept to *jus post bellum*. This section will explore both concepts and their similarities and differences with *jus post bellum*, arguing why this last concept is preferable to the others for the purpose of naming the normative framework for the transition from armed conflict to peace.

5.1 Transitional Justice

The concept of transitional justice is rooted in political transitions from authoritarian regimes to democracy in Southern Europe in the 1970s, Latin America in the 1980s, and South Africa and Eastern Europe in the late 1980s and early 1990s.[119] For Teitel, one of the most authoritative authors on transitional justice, it "can be defined as the conception of justice associated with periods of political change, characterized by legal responses to confront the wrongdoings of repressive predecessor regimes."[120] Developing this concept, the 2004 Report of the UN Secretary-General on the Rule of Law and Transitional Justice in Conflict and Post-Conflict Societies defines transitional justice as:

> [...] the full range of processes and mechanisms associated with a society's attempts to come to terms with a legacy of large-scale past abuses, in order to ensure accountability, serve justice and achieve reconciliation. These may include both judicial and non-judicial mechanisms, with differing levels of international involvement (or none at all) and individual

---

117 Chetail, for example, defines *jus post bellum* as the law of peacebuilding, which implies that peacebuilding embodies the practice of building peace, and *jus post bellum* designates the norms applicable to such a process. See Chetail, 'Introduction,' 17.
118 Bell, *On the Law of Peace*.
119 Mark Freeman and Drazan Djukic, '*Jus Post Bellum* and Transitional Justice,' in *Jus Post Bellum. Towards a Law of Transition from Conflict to Peace*, ed. Carsten Stahn and Jann Kleffner (The Hague: T.M.C. Asser Press, 2008), 213–14; Iverson, Jens, 'Transitional Justice, *Jus Post Bellum* and International Criminal Law: Differentiating the Usages, History and Dynamics,' 415.
120 Ruti Teitel, 'Transitional Justice Genealogy,' *Harvard Human Rights Journal* 16 (2003): 69.

prosecutions, reparations, truth-seeking, institutional reform, vetting and dismissals, or a combination thereof.[121]

Both definitions are related to the measures adopted by a society for dealing with past abuses, which can occur both in contexts of armed conflict or repressive political regimes. As such, transitional justice is a special form of justice for contexts of transition, ensuring individual criminal responsibility, reparations, truth, and institutional reforms, with a view to prosecute those responsible for abuses, offer a redress to victims, and prevent new abuses to occur. This view is shared with *jus post bellum*. However, even though both concepts relate to transitional contexts and have some common purposes, they are substantially different for at least three reasons.

First, the simplest difference between both concepts is that while transitional justice refers to both contexts of transition from dictatorship to democracy and from armed conflict to peace,[122] *jus post bellum* only applies to the last scenario. Here, we have that transitional justice emerges as a concept during the transitions from dictatorship to democracy from the 1970s,[123] whereas "the post-Cold War questions of transformative occupation, peacebuilding, and international territorial administration set the frame for *jus post bellum*."[124]

Second, as showed in the definition above, transitional justice is focused on how a society deals with past human rights violations. In turn, *jus post bellum* is a broader concept and refers to the general transition from conflict to peace, going beyond human rights abuses. As Iverson states,

---

121 UN Secretary-General, 'Report of the Secretary-General on the Rule of Law and Transitional Justice in Conflict and Post-Conflict Societies,' para. 8.
122 On this point, Porter highlights that the academic study of transitional justice began with the transitions from dictatorship to democracy in Argentina, Brazil, Chile, East Germany, Greece, Hungary, Poland, Spain, Uruguay, and South Africa. Its reference to contexts of armed conflict takes place in DRC, Liberia, Sierra Leone, Sudan, Timor-Leste, and Uganda. Elisabeth Porter, *Connecting Peace, Justice and Reconciliation* (Boulder: Lynne Rienner Publishers, 2015), 10.
123 Teitel points out that the origins of transitional justice can be traced to WWI, but it becomes an international issue since the Allied-run Nuremberg trials in 1945. Then, it was in the last decades of the 20th century that transitional justice took its contemporary form. See Ruti G. Teitel, *Globalizing Transitional Justice: Contemporary Essays* (Oxford: Oxford University Press, 2014), 49–56.
124 Jens Iverson, 'Contrasting the Normative and Historical Foundations of Transitional Justice and *Jus Post Bellum*: Outlining the Matrix of Definitions in Comparative Perspective,' in *Jus Post Bellum: Mapping the Normative Foundations*, ed. Carsten Stahn, Jennifer Easterday, and Jens Iverson (Oxford: Oxford University Press, 2014), 81.

The substantive emphasis of *jus post bellum* is broader than human rights violations. It also clearly includes, *inter alia*, violation of the laws of armed conflict, the rights and privileges that spring from the laws of armed conflict, environmental law (including legal access to natural resources and regulating the toxic remnants of war), state responsibility outside the realm of human rights, recognition of states and governments, laws and norms applicable to peace treaties and peace agreements, peacekeeping, occupation, and post-conflict peacebuilding—laws that directly or through interpretation regulate and enable the transition to a just and sustainable peace.[125]

The third difference is referred to the content of both concepts. Transitional justice designates "the ways countries emerging from periods of conflict and repression address large-scale or systematic human rights violations so numerous and so serious that the normal justice system will not be able to provide an adequate response."[126] In other words, transitional justice does not pretend to be a substantive framework, but the term to designate the specific model of justice adopted by a given society to deal with its past abuses.[127] Conversely, *jus post bellum* is conceived as a set of norms or principles guiding the interpretation and application of law in contexts of transition from armed conflict to peace.[128] It means, *jus post bellum* looks at offering a substantial framework for guiding transitions.

Notwithstanding their different scope of application, authors like Teitel consider the concept of *jus post bellum* vague and unnecessary, arguing that transitional justice already cover the matters that *jus post bellum* is intended to frame.[129] Additionally, she affirms that *jus post bellum* is basically concerned with the restoration of the *status quo ante*, whereas transitional justice is more comprehensive to deal with the expectations and needs emerging in periods of transition.[130] On this point, it is worth to mention that, as Walzer[131] and

---

125   Iverson, 86.
126   International Center for Transitional Justice, *What is Transitional Justice?* Available at: https://www.ictj.org/about/transitional-justice (accessed on 1 April 2018).
127   Kai Ambos, 'The Legal Framework of Transitional Justice,' in *Building a Future on Peace and Justice: Studies on Transitional Justice, Conflict Resolution and Development: The Nuremberg Declaration on Peace and Justice*, ed. Kai Ambos, Judith Large, and Marieke Wierda (Berlin: Springer, 2009), 21.
128   May, '*Jus Post Bellum*, Grotius, and Meionexia,' 25.
129   Teitel, *Globalizing Transitional Justice*, 143.
130   Ruti Teitel, 'Rethinking *Jus Post Bellum* in an Age of Global Transitional Justice: Engaging with Michael Walzer and Larry May,' *European Journal of International Law* 24, no. 1 (2013): 336.
131   Walzer, *Just and Unjust Wars. A Moral Argument with Historical Illustrations*.

Orend[132] point out, even though a certain *status ante* should be restored at the end of armed conflict, *jus post bellum* goes beyond, recognizing that sometimes the *ante* situation was precisely the very cause of conflict, and then it must be changed.

Contrary to Teitel's critics, *jus post bellum* is a broader concept, in which transitional justice can be integrated. Transitional justice has a concrete and limited scope, regarding the treatment of human rights past abuses,[133] whereas *jus post bellum* is addressed to the overall restoration and construction of peace. Regarding this question, Turgis warns about the risk of broadening the concept of transitional justice. For her,

> [...] it can be dangerous to broaden the scope of the objectives of transitional justice to extremely ambitious and varied aspirations, going from peace building to economic development. It is obviously a good thing if transitional justice can facilitate and promote other ambitions of a particular society. But transitional justice should not be used and thought of as a kind of magic wand [...] The risk of broadening the meaning of the concept is to dilute it and turning it into something meaningless [...] The core element of transitional justice is here: offering a "toolbox" filled with elements designed to deal with the violation of human rights from a predecessor regime to form the basis of an order to prevent their reoccurrence.[134]

In this way, having the elements discussed above, one can conclude that transitional justice and *jus post bellum* are two different and related concepts, which do not exclude each other. Transitional justice is a more developed field in theory and practice, but its aim does not comprise all the aspects of transition to peace. In this way, having *jus post bellum* the intention to cover transition to peace in a comprehensive way, transitional justice can be one of

---

132   Orend, 'Jus Post Bellum,' 122.
133   At this point, Kastner affirms that "Transitional justice is thus part of a bigger normative picture." In that sense, even if he does not use the concept of *jus post bellum*, he considers transitional justice only as a part of the normative framework on transition to peace, which he refers as much broader. Kastner, *Legal Normativity in the Resolution of Internal Armed Conflict*, 21.
134   Noémi Turgis, 'What Is Transitional Justice?,' *International Journal of Rule of Law, Transitional Justice and Human Rights* 1 (2010): 14. In this line, Iverson even sustains that the concept of *jus post bellum* should help transitional justice scholars to "refocus their field." Iverson, 'Contrasting the Normative and Historical Foundations of Transitional Justice and *Jus Post Bellum*: Outlining the Matrix of Definitions in Comparative Perspective,' 101.

its components.[135] Among the different matters involved in transition from armed conflict to peace, the treatment of human rights violations occurred during the conflict is an essential aspect for establishing a sustainable peace. That is the role for transitional justice. However, other aspects must be considered as well, as those related to the root causes of the conflict, the legal status of peace deals, the participation of different actors in peace talks, and environmental issues, for example. To frame all these aspects of transition to peace *jus post bellum* is a more capacious concept.

5.2 *Lex Pacificatoria*

The concept of *lex pacificatoria* was proposed in 2008 by Bell[136] as an alternative to *jus post bellum*.[137] She takes the parallel of the *lex mercatoria*, to refer to an emerging law of peacemakers as a set of legal practices, rather than a legal regime. For her, legal practices around peacemaking suggest a developing law that would be better captured by the term *lex pacificatoria*. In her words, *lex pacificatoria* is the outcome of the "interaction of both state and nonstate actors involved in the transition process, who respond to legal norms and try to craft solutions that comply with them in creative ways so as to respond to the distinctive dilemmas of peace-making."[138]

Contrasting *lex pacificatoria* to *jus post bellum*, Bell sustains that currently this *lex* is a matter of *lege ferenda*, "whose natural trajectory would seem to be toward a more established *lex lata* in the form of a fully worked out body of law capable of regulating transitions from conflict." In that sense, she suggests that "we might, from this perspective, view the *lex pacificatoria* as *lex ferenda* and *jus post bellum* as its possible future as imagined new *lex lata*."[139] Then, she sees *jus post bellum* rather as a "discursive project or a way of understanding the practical pressures which push for a distinctive normative revision."[140]

---

135 On this idea, see Freeman and Djukic, '*Jus Post Bellum* and Transitional Justice,' 226; Österdahl and van Zadel, 'What Will *Jus Post Bellum* Mean? Of New Wine and Old Bottles,' 193.
136 Bell, *On the Law of Peace*.
137 Christine Bell explicitly presents *lex pacificatoria* "as an alternative to *jus post bellum*." Bell, 'Of *Jus Post Bellum* and Lex Pacificatoria: What's in a Name?,' 192.
138 Christine Bell, 'Lex Pacificatoria Colombiana: Colombia's Peace Accord in Comparative Perspective,' *American Journal of International Law* 110 AJIL Unbound Symposium on the Colombian Peace Talks and International Law (2016): 165.
139 Bell, 'Of *Jus Post Bellum* and Lex Pacificatoria: What's in a Name?,' 193.
140 Christine Bell, 'Post-Conflict Accountability and the Reshaping of Human Rights and Humanitarian Law,' in *International Humanitarian Law and International Human Rights Law*, ed. Orna Ben-Naftali (Oxford: Oxford University Press, 2011), 369.

Unlike *jus post bellum*, the concept of *lex pacificatoria* has had a very limited treatment in academic scholarship. Bell has devoted several works to its conceptualization,[141] and even to its application to the Colombian case.[142] However, few authors have discussed the notion of *lex pacificatoria*.[143]

Additionally, the main difference between the two concepts appears when *jus post bellum* is viewed by Bell as "a new coherent distinctive legal regime,"[144] which, as argued above, is neither possible nor desirable. But if one looks at the other approaches to a definition of *jus post bellum* discussed in this chapter, there is no substantial difference with the concept of *lex pacificatoria*. Indeed, the understanding of *jus post bellum* as an ordering system, or a space of dialogue, or as an interpretative framework is connected to the view of *lex pacificatoria* as a developing set of practices on how the parties transiting from an armed conflict use legal norms to address their practical dilemmas of peace.[145] Therefore, both *jus post bellum* and *lex pacificatoria* frame the context of actors dealing with legal obligations in their search for peace, in a dynamic where their peace efforts are shaped by law and their peacemaking practice creates new legal norms.

Finally, one could say that while *jus post bellum* is more focused on the normative framework applicable to transition, *lex pacificatoria* is mainly concerned with the practice of peacemakers when applying such a framework. Nevertheless, if one understands *jus post bellum* as an interactional framework, where norms and practice of actors involved in transition apply and create law at the same time, then, there is no real difference between *jus post bellum* and *lex pacificatoria*. In consequence, being *jus post bellum* the most developed concept, adding a new name to designate the same phenomenon seems unnecessary and it does not help to reaching common ways to understand the complex interaction between law and transition from armed conflict to peace.

---

141   Bell, *On the Law of Peace*; Christine Bell, 'The "New Law" of Transitional Justice,' in *Building a Future on Peace and Justice: Studies on Transitional Justice, Conflict Resolution and Development: The Nuremberg Declaration on Peace and Justice*, ed. Kai Ambos, Judith Large, and Marieke Wierda (Berlin: Springer, 2009), 105–26; Christine Bell, 'Peace Settlements and International Law: From Lex Pacificatoria to *Jus Post Bellum*,' in *Research Handbook on International Conflict and Security Law. Jus Ad Bellum, Jus in Bello and Jus Post Bellum*, ed. Nigel White and Christian Henderson (499–546: Edward Elgar Publishing, 2013); Bell, 'Of *Jus Post Bellum* and Lex Pacificatoria: What's in a Name?'
142   Bell, 'Lex Pacificatoria Colombiana: Colombia's Peace Accord in Comparative Perspective.'
143   Kreß and Grover, 'International Criminal Law Restraints in Peace Talks to End Armed Conflicts of a Non-International Character,' 44.
144   Bell, 'Lex Pacificatoria Colombiana: Colombia's Peace Accord in Comparative Perspective,' 165.
145   Bell, *On the Law of Peace*, 287–88.

6   *Jus Post Bellum* in Non-international Armed Conflicts

Although the concept of *jus post bellum* emerged within the context of transition from IACs to peace, today there is a general opinion regarding its applicability to transition from NIACs.[146] However, few works have specifically analyzed the particular conditions of *jus post bellum* in contexts of internal transition.[147] Examining existing academic scholarship, only two articles are specifically devoted to assessing the application of the concept in NIACs.[148]

In one article, Bartels discusses the temporal scope of *jus in bello* and *jus post bellum*, seeking to determine when do NIACs end, and whether both regimes apply simultaneously.[149] Nonetheless, this contribution does not offer a systematic analysis of *jus post bellum* in NIACs, but only the temporal dimension of the concept regarding the end of internal conflicts.

In the second article, Boon has proposed the most specific analysis on the application of *jus post bellum* in NIACs that can be found in current academic scholarship in the field.[150] She departs from minimizing the distinction

---

[146]   See generally Stahn, '*Jus Post Bellum*: Mapping the Discipline(s),' 2008, 106; Österdahl and van Zadel, 'What Will *Jus Post Bellum* Mean? Of New Wine and Old Bottles,' 179; Bartels, 'From Jus in Bello to *Jus Post Bellum*: When Do Non-International Armed Conflicts End?'; Boon, 'The Application of *Jus Post Bellum* in Non-International Armed Conflicts'; Chetail, 'Introduction,' 18; Dieter Fleck, 'Legal Protection of the Environment. The Double Challenge of Non-International Armed Conflict and Post-Conflict Peacebuilding,' in *Environmental Protection and Transitions from Conflict to Peace: Clarifying Norms, Principles, and Practices*, ed. Carsten Stahn, Jens Iverson, and Jennifer Easterday (Oxford: Oxford University Press, 2017), 203–19; Matthew Gillett, 'Eco-Struggles: Using International Criminal Law to Protect the Environment During and After Non-International Armed Conflict,' in *Environmental Protection and Transitions from Conflict to Peace: Clarifying Norms, Principles, and Practices*, ed. Carsten Stahn, Jens Iverson, and Jennifer Easterday (Oxford: Oxford University Press, 2017), 221–22.

[147]   To highlight the specificities of making peace in contexts of NIACs, Stahn even uses the expression *"jus post bellum internum"*. Stahn, '*Jus Post Bellum*: Mapping the Discipline(s),' 2008, 106.

[148]   Bartels, 'From Jus in Bello to *Jus Post Bellum*: When Do Non-International Armed Conflicts End?'; Boon, 'The Application of *Jus Post Bellum* in Non-International Armed Conflicts.' Even if in the *Jus Post Bellum* Project's 2017 volume two articles address matters related to NIACs, they do not analyze the application of *jus post bellum* as such on those contexts, but the legal framework for the protection of environment in contexts of NIACs. These two works are: Fleck, Gillet (2017) Fleck, 'Legal Protection of the Environment. The Double Challenge of Non-International Armed Conflict and Post-Conflict Peacebuilding'; Gillett, 'Eco-Struggles: Using International Criminal Law to Protect the Environment During and After Non-International Armed Conflict.'

[149]   Bartels, 'From Jus in Bello to *Jus Post Bellum*: When Do Non-International Armed Conflicts End?'

[150]   Boon, 'The Application of *Jus Post Bellum* in Non-International Armed Conflicts.'

between international and non-international armed conflicts,[151] based on three reasons. First, many IHL norms have been qualified as customary rules applicable to both types of conflict. Second, the development of international criminal justice "has blurred the relevance of the international/internal divide" extending the protection of individuals at all levels. And third, the application of IHRL to internal conflicts is convergent with its application to IACs.[152] With these arguments, Boon suggests "the creation of a unified set of *jus post bellum* principles that would apply regardless of the nature of the conflict."[153]

However, she admits that a unified *jus post bellum* can be problematic regarding matters which are highly dependent on internal political conditions. In this sense, she points out:

> I make the case for a set of *jus post bellum* principles applicable to NIACs which would coincide with those applicable in IACs in areas governed by international humanitarian law, criminal law, and human rights, but which would differ with regards to rebuilding, reconstruction, and constitutional design. I argue that a narrower set of principles in these latter domains will improve the effectiveness and legitimacy of *jus post bellum* in the long run, and is justified by the principle of 'bounded discretion.'[154]

In other words, Boon proposes two levels of *jus post bellum* principles in the context of NIACs. A first set of principles is related to maters governed by IHRL, IHL, and ICL, which would be common for IACs and NIACs. A second set of principles would be specific for NIACs, regarding matters as reconstruction and political and institutional design, in which societies emerging from armed conflict need further leeway to find formulas according to their own dynamics. To apply this second set of principles she proposes the concept of "bounded discretion."

For her, the "bounded discretion" implies that *jus post bellum* should support the development of transitional instruments and structures under an

---

151 In the same way, Hofmann and Rapillard sustain that "The distinction between international armed conflict and NIAC has blurred over time. Nowadays, not only states, but also armed groups are considered to be holders of rights and obligations in internal conflict situations." Ursign Hofmann and Pascal Rapillard, 'Post-Conflict Mine Action: Environment and Law,' in *Environmental Protection and Transitions from Conflict to Peace: Clarifying Norms, Principles, and Practices*, ed. Carsten Stahn, Jens Iverson, and Jennifer Easterday (Oxford: Oxford University Press, 2017), 413.
152 Boon, 'The Application of *Jus Post Bellum* in Non-International Armed Conflicts,' 262–63.
153 Boon, 265.
154 Boon, 265.

international legal framework but leaving to local stakeholders the margin to define matters which are predominantly of domestic interest. In turn, the bounded discretion approach is supported by two principles: subsidiarity and margin of appreciation.[155] The principle of subsidiarity implies that *jus post bellum* should prefer local formulas regarding social, economic, and political issues, and it would limit its role to offering general guidance under international standards. In the same line, the margin of appreciation refers to the state's level of autonomy to interpret its international legal obligations according to its domestic context.[156]

Considering the elements of this discussion, *jus post bellum* is clearly relevant to transition from NIACs to peace, and empirical research is required to identify how the theorical developments of the concept—even if addressed mostly to IACs—are reflected or contested by the practice of internal transitions. As delineated since the Introduction, current armed conflicts in the world are mostly NIACs, and most of peace processes and agreements are related to this kind of conflicts.[157] Then, there are more practice on legal considerations around peacemaking and peacebuilding regarding NIACs than IACs to empirically assess *jus post bellum*.

On this point, translating the concept of *jus post bellum* to NIACs is a consequence of the increasing application of international legal elements to internal transitions, and not an assimilation of the automatic application of the three components of the law of armed force to both IACs and NIACs (because, for instance, *jus ad bellum* is not considered as applicable to NIACs). Then, through the analysis of the Colombian case as a concrete transition from a NIAC, in the next chapters we will see a normative framework based on international law guiding legal and political decisions in the process of ending armed conflict and building sustainable peace, which is the object of *jus post bellum*.

7 Conclusions

This chapter was devoted to the conceptual foundations of *jus post bellum*. Notwithstanding there is not consensual definition, three approaches have been proposed to understand the concept: 1) as a new legal regime; 2) as an ordering system; and 3) as an interpretative framework. The first approach has

---

155 Boon, 266.
156 Boon, 266–267.
157 Escola de Cultura de Pau, *Peace Talks in Focus 2018. Report on Trends and Scenarios*, 11–12. See, *supra*, Introdución, section 4.

been questioned by several authors, and such a conception of *jus post bellum* does not seem viable. However, the other two approaches offer useful elements for defining the content and scope of the concept, and they will be used as such in the next chapters of the book.

The notion of principles and the functional approach towards establishing sustainable peace helped to demarcate the object of *jus post bellum*. Such an object could be defined as offering a normative framework of principles guiding the transition from armed conflict to sustainable peace. In turn, sustainable peace has been conceived as composed by at least two conditions: addressing the root causes of the conflict, and observing international standards on human rights, IHL, and ICL. These elements define the rationale of *jus post bellum* and how it offers a more comprehensive legal framework for transition to peace than related concepts like *lex pacificatoria* and transitional justice.

Finally, *jus post bellum*, although mostly conceived from the perspective of IACs, is equally applicable to transition from NIACs. Regarding internal transition, the principles of *jus post bellum* require higher flexibility to address matters that are typically dependent on the specific political conditions of the context. Here, Boon suggests two levels of principles. First, principles dealing with violations of human rights and IHL, where international law provides more exigent standards. Second, principles regarding matters as reconstruction and institutional design, where international law only can provide general guidelines, leaving domestic actors enough leeway to adopt their own approaches. Based on this assumption, the next chapters assess how *jus post bellum* is relevant and applicable to NIACs, through the analysis of the Colombian case.

CHAPTER 2

International Law in the Colombian Transition

Colombia has assigned a central role to international law in its transition from armed conflict to peace. Even though this question became more visible since the recent peace process and the 2016 Peace Agreement concluded in the country, international law has been present in all the previous transitional mechanisms that Colombia has adopted since 2005. Colombia has a legal system widely receptive to international law, with a Constitution attributing to IHRL and IHL treaties duly ratified by the country the same normative level as the constitutional order.[1] This feature has been particularly relevant regarding the political and legal discussions on armed conflict and transition to peace in the country.

As such, this chapter examines how international law is reflected in transition in Colombia. The focus is given to the 2012–2016 peace process and the 2016 Final Agreement, but the analysis also incorporates elements from the previous transitional mechanisms designed in the country. The purpose of the chapter is to show how international law has shaped transition in Colombia, seeking empirical elements to assess how this case can be framed under *jus post bellum*. For that, Chapter 3 will overlap the conceptual framework offered in Chapter 1 with the practice exposed in this Chapter 2, to suggest how *jus post bellum* can be understood and applied from the perspective of the case study.

The chapter departs from offering a general overview of the Colombian armed conflict and its transition to peace. Such a background is important to better understand the complexities of this conflict, its root causes and dynamics, the different attempts to reach peace, and the challenges to implement an ambitious peace deal while armed conflict still persists in the country. Then, the chapter analyzes the main aspects in which international law has shaped the Colombian transition: the legal nature of the peace agreement, socioeconomic and political reforms, criminal justice, reparations, and inclusiveness. In each component, the chapter identifies the international legal framework relevant to the respective matter—including legal norms, legal discourses, and legal practices—, and then it analyzes how such a framework was applied in Colombia. On this point, it is important to clarify that even if the Colombian transition has involved several matters relevant to *jus post bellum*, the selection

---

1 Constitución Política de Colombia, 1991, Art. 93.

© CÉSAR ROJAS-OROZCO, 2021 | DOI:10.1163/9789004440531_004
This is an open access chapter distributed under the terms of the CC BY-NC 4.0 license.

of topics in this chapter is focused on the components in which the influence of international law is more specific and visible.

0 A General Overview of the Colombian Armed Conflict and Its Transition to Peace

This section summarizes the general elements to understand the origin, actors, and evolution of the Colombian armed conflict, as well as the main instruments and processes aimed at reaching peace in the country.

0.1 *Origin and Evolution of the Armed Conflict*

Since its independence and the configuration of the Republic in 1819, Colombia was politically divided into two traditional parties: liberals and conservatives. Both parties fought for power in different ways, leading to an intensive violent period known as *The Thousand Days War* (1899–1902).[2] Peace was agreed upon, but violence reappeared after several hegemonic conservative governments. In 1948 the presidential candidate by the Liberal Party was assassinated, which triggered a new civil war known as *La Violencia*. It lasted until 1958. That year, a settlement was reached between the Liberal and the Conservative Party, in which they agreed to alternate power for 16 years.[3]

Beyond those agreements among the two traditional parties, many people—mostly peasants and social leaders—did not feel represented by such a political system. Thus, some peasants organized movements demanding land access and rural development programs. Those demands were ignored by the government, who saw them as a communist threat in the global context of the Cold War. Repressive measures were the response, and organized peasants, together with communist militants, founded the left-wing guerrilla *Fuerzas Armadas Revolucionarias de Colombia* (FARC) in 1964, and later the *Ejército de Liberación Nacional* (ELN) the same year. Both groups—though different ideological approaches—claimed the use of arms to defend themselves from governmental repression and seek social justice under a communist thought.

The two guerrillas gained rapid expansion across the country, and other small guerilla groups appeared in the following two decades, owing a combination

---

2 See generally, Marco Palacios, *Entre la legitimidad y la violencia: Colombia 1875–1994*, (Bogota: Banco de la Republica, 1995).
3 See generally: Daniel Pécaut, *Crónica de cuatro décadas de política colombiana*, (Bogota: Norma, 2006).

of popular support and unsuccessful governmental strategies to reach a solution. In that scenario, in the early 1980s, some landowners organized themselves in a self-defense strategy against the guerrillas, which had used extortion and kidnaping as their main source of income. That process led to the conformation of paramilitary groups, gathered under the *Autodefensas Unidas de Colombia* (AUC) in the 1990s.[4] They received illegal support by different state agents, which intensified the armed confrontation around the country. Simultaneously, Colombia was experiencing an unprecedented growth in drug production and trafficking, which carried out alliances between traffickers and armed groups, adding new complexities to the armed conflict.

In 1991 a new Constitution was adopted, following peace negotiations with small guerrilla groups which appeared during the 1970s and 1980s. It opened democracy and gave people better mechanisms to protect their rights. However, in the mid-1990s, the lucrative traffic of illegal drugs and the struggle over territorial control intensified armed confrontation between the FARC and the ELN by one side, and the State and the paramilitary groups by the other. Several war crimes and crimes against humanity were committed by all actors, and Colombia entered the path of a failed state.[5]

A hope of peace appeared in 1998. A peace process with the FARC started, but four years later it failed after the guerrilla committed several abuses during the negotiations. In 2002 a new government initiated the most intensive military offensive against the guerrilla. At the time, a process for the demobilization of the paramilitary groups was implemented between 2003 and 2005, under a scheme of submission to the State in exchange for socio-economic and legal benefits. It brought a significant decrease in the armed confrontation.

However, after ten years of military offensive, the guerrillas were reduced but not defeated. In 2012 a new peace process started with the FARC, still the largest and oldest armed group in Colombia.[6] After four years of negotiations,

---

[4] See generally Centro Nacional de Memoria Histórica, *Paramilitarismo. Balance de la Contribución del CNMH al Esclarecimiento Histórico,* (Bogotá, Centro Nacional de Memoria Histórica, 2018).

[5] Gregoy Lobo, "Colombia, from Failing State to a Second Independence: The Politics and the Price", *International Journal of Cultural Studies* 16, no. 4 (2012): 351–366.

[6] Gobierno de Colombia and FARC, 'Acuerdo General Para La Terminación Del Conflicto y La Construcción de Una Paz Estable y Duradera,' 26 August 2012, http://www.altocomisionadoparalapaz.gov.co/procesos-y-conversaciones/acuerdo-general/Paginas/inicio.aspx (accessed on 5 March 2016).

a Final Peace Agreement was reached in 2016. Nevertheless, the other guerrilla group, the ELN, remains active, with low military capacity and several unsuccessful negotiations attempts.[7]

More than five decades of armed conflict have left millions of victims in Colombia. In 2011 the Unified Victim's Registry was created.[8] This tool registers victims who suffered any damage during the armed conflict since the 1st January 1985. Up to April 2019, 8.803.836 victims are registered,[9] which represents the 18% of the current Colombian population.[10] Most victims were affected by internal displacement (7.478.723), followed by homicide (269.650) and enforced disappearance (47.560).[11]

0.2 *Transitional Legal Mechanisms in the Ongoing Conflict*

During its protracted armed conflict, Colombia has developed several legal and constitutional instruments to protect and redress victims, to facilitate peace negotiations, and to reintegrate members of armed groups into civilian life. In 1997 a legal framework was adopted for assisting victims of internal displacement.[12] It was later complemented by the jurisprudence of the Constitutional Court,[13] offering not only humanitarian and socio-economic assistance but seeking also reparations and durable solutions. In 2005 the Justice and Peace Law[14] created a system of transitional justice for the demobilization of paramilitary groups, in talks with the government since 2003. The system was framed within the ordinary Colombian jurisdiction, offering to former fighters a trial with alternative punishment (5–8 years in prison) in exchange for their contribution to peace.

---

7   Julia Zulver, *¿Verá Colombia un acuerdo de paz con el ELN en 2019?*, Open Democracy, 7 January 2019, https://www.opendemocracy.net/es/democraciaabierta-es/ver-colombia-un-acuerdo-de-paz-con-el-eln-/ (accessed on 10 April 2019).
8   Congreso de la República de Colombia, Ley 1448 (Ley de Víctimas y Restitución de Tierras) Art. 154.
9   Registro Único de Víctimas, https://www.unidadvictimas.gov.co/es/registro-unico-de-victimas-ruv/37394 (accessed on 1 April 2019).
10 The total population of Colombia up to May 2019 is estimated in 48.2 million people. Source: http://www.dane.gov.co/index.php/estadisticas-por-tema/demografia-y-poblacion/censo-nacional-de-poblacion-y-vivienda-2018/cuantos-somos/ (accessed on 5 May 2019).
11 Registro Único de Víctimas, https://www.unidadvictimas.gov.co/es/registro-unico-de-victimas-ruv/37394 (accessed on 1 April 2019).
12 Congreso de la República de Colombia, 'Ley 387' (1997).
13 Corte Constitucional de Colombia, Sentencia T-025/04 (2004).
14 Congreso de la República de Colombia, 'Ley 975 (Ley de Justicia y Paz)' (2005).

Finally, and despite the ongoing armed conflict, in 2011 Colombia adopted the Law 1448,[15] known as Law of Victims and Land Restitution. Following international standards on reparation, this law set up an ambitious system to register all the victims of armed conflict since 1985 and to offer a comprehensive set of measures of restitution, compensation, rehabilitation, satisfaction, and guarantees of non-repetition.

0.3 Peace Process and Final Agreement (2012–2016)

The recent peace process with the FARC represents the most important attempt to achieve peace in Colombia. It advanced a negotiation scheme aimed not only at ending the armed conflict but also to address its root causes. After four years of negotiations[16] in Havana, Cuba, the parties signed a final agreement on 26 August 2016, which was later rejected in a plebiscite.[17] After a renegotiation following the requests of the main opposing leaders, a new agreement was reached on 24 November 2016, which was then approved by the Colombian Congress.[18]

The Agreement addresses six issues: 1) Rural development, improving land access and the productive capacities of peasants; 2) Political participation, expanding the democratic spectrum to new actors, including the former guerrilla; 3) End of the conflict, involving the laying down of arms and reintegration issues; 4) Solution to the problem of illicit drugs, as one of the fuels of the conflict; 5) Victims and transitional justice, establishing a comprehensive system of justice, truth, and reparation; and 6) An implementation and verification system with international support.

1 The Legal Status of the Peace Agreement

Since peace negotiations and peace agreements have become a highly "normatized" process,[19] determining the legal status of the resulting deal has been a

---

15 Congreso de la República de Colombia, Ley 1448 (Ley de Víctimas y Restitución de Tierras).
16 Although the process took four years, the peace negotiations in Colombia are considered the fastest moving peace talks in the world. Escola de Cultura de Pau, *Yearbook of Peace Processes 2015*, ed. Vicenç Fisas (Barcelona: Icaria, 2015), 9.
17 BBC News, *Colombia referendum: Voters reject Farc peace deal*, 3 October 2016, https://www.bbc.com/news/world-latin-america-37537252 (accessed on 10 April 2019).
18 Government of Colombia and FARC, 'Final Agreement to End the Armed Conflict and Build a Stable and Lasting Peace.'
19 Kastner, *Legal Normativity in the Resolution of Internal Armed Conflict*, 2.

matter of utmost importance. If the agreement is not seen as legally binding, the parties' confidence can be affected to the point that reaching an accord becomes difficult. This question is especially relevant in negotiations following NIACS. In such negotiations, the non-state actors are invariably concerned that the government will use its law-making powers to modify its commitments during the implementation phase.

In the Colombian case, such a concern was held by both the government and the FARC. Even if the government was committed to the implementation of the agreement during negotiation, there was a risk that a new government, the Congress or the Constitutional Court could modify what was agreed upon.

As such, the discussion on the legal nature of the peace agreement in Colombia was almost as central to the negotiation as those focused on substantial issues. The debate progressed from the intention to promote a new constitution integrating the peace deal to the idea of forming the agreement as an international legal document. The first option was rejected by the government, which insisted on adopting a deal under the existing constitutional framework. The FARC accepted such a position but remained apprehensive about the legal nature of the agreement. Subsequently, the idea of lending some form of international legal character to the accord prevailed as a means to guarantee that the State would not be able to amend it under domestic law.

In a joint communiqué issued on 12 May 2016, the parties announced a formula to grant legal certainty to the Final Agreement and guarantee compliance to it under both domestic and international law. The formula included two elements rooted in international law. First, declaring the Final Agreement as a special agreement in terms of Common Article 3 of the Geneva Conventions. Second, the formula involved a unilateral declaration by the Colombian State before the UN requesting that the Final Agreement be annexed to the UNSC Resolution 2261 (2016), which established a monitoring mission for the implementation of the peace agreement in Colombia.

Having said elements, this section is divided into three parts. The first part will focus on the discussion of the domestic or international legal status of internal peace agreements. The second part will present the two mechanisms agreed upon in Colombia to lend the peace agreement international legal value. The third part will analyze the potential effects of the use of international law to enhance the legal certainty of the peace deal in Colombia.

1.1 The Discussion on the Domestic or International Legal Status of Internal Peace Agreements

The legal-looking[20] structure and language used in peace agreements show the parties' intention to consider them as legally binding documents.[21] However, as a rule, these agreements are political documents that must be translated into a legal form for their implementation.[22] Nevertheless, internal peace agreements "do not easily fit within traditional international or domestic legal categories," because they entail a mix of state and non-state actors, and a combination of matters belonging to national and international spheres.[23]

In the case of agreements following NIACs, their legal status is typically given by domestic law in the form of a new constitution[24] or through constitutional amendments or new laws.[25] However, as Kastner highlights,

> Peace agreements can be understood as hybrid instruments between a state and nonstate actors to deal with a domestic situation, but which are often internationalized through references to international law. Such internationalization brings the agreement into the sphere of international legal norms and arguably confers additional legitimacy.[26]

---

20   Peace agreements are not legal documents in their own but their writing normally has a legal style.
21   Bell, 'Peace Agreements: Their Nature and Legal Status,' 378.
22   Colin Harvey, 'On Law, Politics and Contemporary Constitutionalism,' *Fordham International Law Journal* 26, no. 4 (2002): 999. Regarding the Colombian Peace Agreement, the Constitutional Court considered it as a mere political document (Sentence C-379/2016). Even the Court refrained from deciding a constitutionality action concerning the Peace Agreement, arguing that such a document does not have any normative, but only political character. Sentence C-171/2017.
23   Arist von Hehn, *The Internal Implementation of Peace Agreements after Violent Intrastate Conflict* (Leiden: Martinus Nijhoff, 2011), 50–51.
24   For example, South Africa, where the 1993 accord was written to serve as an "interim constitution" until the accord could be legally ratified as part of a final constitution. Peace Accords Matrix, https://peaceaccords.nd.edu/provision/ratification-mechanism-interim-constitution-accord, Kroc Institute for International Peace Studies, University of Notre Dame.
25   For example, the Northern Ireland Good Friday Agreement, in which it as agreed that if majorities were reached in the referendums on the agreement, "the Governments will then introduce and support, in their respective Parliaments, such legislation as may be necessary to give effect to all aspects of this agreement." Peace Accords Matrix, https://peaceaccords.nd.edu/provision/ratification-mechanism-northern-ireland-good-friday-agreement, Kroc Institute for International Peace Studies, University of Notre Dame.
26   Kastner, *Legal Normativity in the Resolution of Internal Armed Conflict*, 13.

In legal terms, this internationalization of internal peace agreements aims to protect the agreements from substantial variations during the domestic process of translating them into constitutional or legal forms. Indeed, when discussing the legal norms to implementing a deal, opposition groups could press the government or other actors to backtrack on commitments. To address these difficulties, Bell suggests that peace agreements "tend to include substantive reform of legislative and constitutional processes and institutions that make international law a key reference point and give international actors a role in what are normally domestic institutions."[27] However, it is not clear if such internationalization make an internal peace agreement to become an international legal instrument.

Article 2.1(a) of the 1969 Vienna Convention on the Law of Treaties (VCLT) defines a treaty as "an international agreement concluded between States in written form and governed by international law."[28] In this line, Article 2.1(a) of the 1986 Vienna Convention on the Law of Treaties between States and International Organizations or between International Organizations[29] extends the same definition to agreements concluded between states and international organizations or among these organizations. In these terms, agreements reached between a state and a non-state actor are not considered treaties.

However, Article 3 of both conventions specifies that the fact that they do not apply to agreements outside of the definition provided by Article 2.1 does not affect the legal value of those agreements. In particular, Article 3 of the 1986 Convention states that the fact that it does not apply "(i) to international agreements to which one or more States, one or more international organizations and *one or more subjects of international law other than States or organizations* are parties; [...] shall not affect: (a) the legal force of such agreements; (b) the application to them of any of the rules set forth in the present Convention to which they would be subject under international law independently of the Convention." (emphasis added).[30]

In consequence, both conventions make clear that in addition to treaties, other international agreements can exist. Given this, and considering that

---

27   Bell, 'Peace Agreements: Their Nature and Legal Status,' 405.
28   Vienna Convention on the Law of Treaties (1969).
29   Vienna Convention on the Law of Treaties between States and International Organizations or between International Organizations (1986). This Convention is not yet into force, as it has not reached the minimum of 35 state's ratifications established to this effect by its Article 85.
30   Vienna Convention on the Law of Treaties between States and International Organizations or between International Organizations (1986).

there is no legal definition for an international agreement other than a treaty, a systematic reading of both conventions could offer a solution. The conventional definitions of a treaty have three elements in common: first, the parties possess international legal subjectivity; second, the agreement should be governed by international law; and third, the agreement has a written form. This last condition is a formal one, and it does not entail major analytical challenges. However, the other two are substantial, and they could determine whether an agreement should be considered an international one even if it is beyond the scope of the Vienna Conventions.

By this logic, an agreement concluded between a state and a non-state armed group—as is the case with a peace agreement ending a NIAC—could be considered an international agreement, even though it is outside the scope of the Vienna Conventions on the Law of Treaties.[31] The two substantial conditions discussed above would be present in an internal peace agreement. On the first condition, as pointed out by Bell, in relation to peace agreements signed by armed opposition groups, those groups "can be argued to be 'subjects of international law'—based on international law's recognition of such groups, in particular through humanitarian law."[32] On the second condition, Common Article 3 to the 1949 Geneva Conventions allows the conclusion of special agreements with or between non-state armed groups in a NIAC, which will be governed by that international regime.

An analysis of these two elements in an internal peace agreement can be found in a 2004 decision of the Special Court for Sierra Leone, in which the Court denied the international legal nature of the 1999 Lomé Peace Agreement. On the one hand, the Court affirmed that even if "there is now no doubt that [Common Article 3 to the Geneva Conventions] is binding on States and insurgents alike and that insurgents are subject to international humanitarian law [...] [t]hat fact, however, does not by itself invest [a non-state armed group] with international personality under international law."[33] On the other hand, the Court stated that even though the Lomé Agreement put an end to an armed conflict and was welcomed by the international community acting

---

31   Bell, *On the Law of Peace*, 129; Laura Betancur, 'The Legal Status of the Colombian Peace Agreement,' *American Journal of International Law* 110 AJIL Unbound Symposium on the Colombian Peace Talks and International Law (2016): 189.

32   Bell, *On the Law of Peace*, 130. This subjectivity is generally recognized, despite the fact that governments have always tried to exclude non-state armed groups from international law. See generally, Andrew Clapham, 'Non-State Actors,' in *Post-Conflict Peacebuilding : A Lexicon*, ed. Vincent Chetail (Oxford: Oxford University Press, 2009), 201.

33   Special Court for Sierra Leone, The Appeals Chamber, Prosecutor v. Morris Kallon and Brima Bazzy Kamara (13 March 2004). para. 45.

through the UNSC, the agreement itself "created neither rights nor obligations capable of being regulated by international law."[34]

Nevertheless, in contrast to the position held by the Court, a different conclusion could be deducted from an analysis of the matter under IHL. Regarding the legal capacity of non-state armed actors to subscribe to international agreements, Bell points out that international legal subjectivity is different from international legal personality.[35] While the latter implies full capacity to exercise rights and obligations at an international level, the notion of legal subjectivity is limited. In this regard, as long as IHL recognizes the rights and duties of non-state armed groups, they enjoy international legal subjectivity under this regime. At the same time, as analyzed in the next part of this section, special agreements concluded by the parties in a NIAC under Common Article 3 of Geneva Conventions are indeed governed by IHL.

Therefore, a peace agreement ending a NIAC could potentially be considered an international legal accord and as such governed by international law. This question will be analyzed based on the Colombian case.

1.2 *Formulas of Normative Internationalization of the Colombian Peace Agreement*

As previously noted, even before a final agreement was reached, parties in Colombia defined two formulas aimed at giving international legal value to the resulting peace agreement: one, considering the Agreement as a special agreement under IHL; the other, making a unilateral declaration by the State expressing its international commitment to comply the peace deal. This item analyzes each of them.

1.2.1   The Peace Agreement as a Special Agreement under IHL

The first and most important mechanism used by the parties to give international legal status to the Peace Agreement in Colombia was to subscribe it as a special agreement under Common Article 3 of the Geneva Conventions. To do so, the parties agreed, even before the final deal was reached,[36] in a formula

---

34 Special Court for Sierra Leone, The Appeals Chamber, paragraph 42. para. 42. In a critic to this decision, Cassese points out that there was no need for the Court to discuss the domestic or international legal status of the agreement, but just to analyze the case regarding the prohibition on amnesties for international crimes. See Antonio Cassese, 'The Special Court and International Law The Decision Concerning the Lomé Agreement Amnesty,' *Journal of International Criminal Justice* 2, no. 4 (2004): 1130–40.

35 Bell, *On the Law of Peace*, 135.

36 Gobierno de Colombia and FARC, 'Comunicado Conjunto No. 69.'

that the Congress translated into a transitory article in the Constitution to qualify the Final Peace Agreement as a "Special Agreement in terms of Common Article 3 of the Geneva Conventions."[37] In addition, the amendment stated that once signed and entered into force, the Final Agreement would be part of the "constitutional block."[38]

This formula has important consequences under Colombian constitutional law. According to article 93 of the National Constitution, IHRL and IHL instruments duly ratified by Colombia prevail in the domestic order. This norm has been interpreted by the Constitutional Court as meaning that those norms have the same normative level as the Constitution itself and, in this way, form a constitutional block.[39] With this understanding, the constitutional amendment made explicit that the Final Agreement would have the same internal legal status as IHRL and IHL treaties.

This constitutional provision was strongly criticized by some sectors in Colombia through two main arguments. Critics argued that the IHL's mechanism of special agreements is reserved for strictly humanitarian issues and cannot be invoked for a document referring to various economic, political, and social matters. Other critics argued that a peace agreement cannot have the same internal legal status that the Constitution devotes to international human rights and IHL treaties.

Disregarding those critics, the parties subscribed the agreement signed on 24 August 2016 in the terms referred to above. However, after the agreement was rejected by a plebiscite a few weeks later, a renegotiation process took place, during which the opposing actors asked for a modification on this point.

The new Final Agreement reached on 24 November 2016 retained the formula of the special agreement in terms of Common Article 3 of the 1949 Geneva Conventions but added that it would be "to the effects of its international validity."[40] In this line, a copy of the Agreement was sent to the Swiss Federal Council as depositary of the Geneva Conventions.[41]

Because of this limitation on the scope of the formula of the Special Agreement, a new constitutional amendment was adopted to substitute the

---

37   Congreso de la República de Colombia, Acto Legislativo 01 de 2016.
38   Ibid.
39   Corte Constitucional de Colombia, Sentencia C-574 de 1992.
40   The parties stated in the Preamble of the Agreement that it was subscribed "as a Special Agreement pursuant to Article 3, common to the 1949 Geneva Conventions, as per its international standing." Government of Colombia and FARC, 'Final Agreement to End the Armed Conflict and Build a Stable and Lasting Peace,' 5.
41   Government of Colombia and FARC, 5.

previous one. This time, the reform introduced a transitory article to the Constitution stating that the contents of the Final Agreement "related to norms of international humanitarian law and fundamental rights [...] will be compulsory parameters of interpretation and a referent for the development and validity of the norms and laws developing and implementing the Final Agreement."[42] Additionally, it established that all the organs of the State must act according to what was agreed on, "preserving the contents, commitments, the spirit, and the principles of the Final Agreement."[43]

This new formula has two dimensions. For international effects, the parties considered the Final Agreement a special agreement under IHL. Domestically, the Final Agreement is no longer considered to have the same constitutional effect of IHRL and IHL treaties, but the elements related to IHL and fundamental rights are considered a parameter for the validity of the normative development of the Agreement.

To analyze this question, it is important to note that the mechanism of special agreements is enshrined by Common Article 3 to 1949 Geneva Conventions and applicable to NIACs. The final part of this Article is worded as follows: "The Parties to the conflict should further endeavour to bring into force, by means of special agreements, all or part of the other provisions of the present Convention. The application of the preceding provisions shall not affect the legal status of the Parties to the conflict."

This norm was conceived when NIACs were uncommon and unregulated by international law. Thus, in principle, special agreements were aimed at spreading the application of Geneva Conventions to NIACs beyond the minimum regulation of Common Article 3. In this sense, the 1952 ICRC Commentary on Geneva Convention I stated that "Although the only provisions which the individual Parties are bound to apply unilaterally are those contained in Article 3, they are nevertheless under an obligation to try to bring about a fuller application of the Convention by means of a bilateral agreement."[44]

Nevertheless, in the Colombian context the mechanism of special agreements "was used with a much broader objective: to increase legal certainty for the parties by reinforcing the deal's domestic and international effects."[45] Such a use of the mechanism by the parties in Colombia raises two questions. First,

---

42 Congreso de la República de Colombia, Acto Legislativo 02 de 2017. Available at: http://es.presidencia.gov.co/normativa/normativa/ACTO%20LEGISLATIVO%20N°%2002%20DE%2011%20DE%20MAYO%20DE%202017.pdf
43 Ibid.
44 ICRC, *Commentary I Geneva Convention*, (Geneva, 1952), 59.
45 Betancur, 'The Legal Status of the Colombian Peace Agreement,' 188.

what is the international normative character of special agreements? Second, can peace agreements be considered special agreements in terms of Common Article 3?

In 1995, assessing the constitutionality of Additional Protocol II as adopted by Colombia, the Constitutional Court referred to Common Article 3's mechanism of special agreements. The Court stated that those agreements are not, *stricto sensu*, treaties, as they are not established between subjects of public international law. However, the Court admitted that they are a valid legal mechanism to protect the victims of war, to foster consensus and increase reciprocal trust among the enemies for the pursuit of peace.[46]

On this point, as discussed above, special agreements are not treaties in terms of the 1969 and 1986 Vienna Conventions on the Law of Treaties. Since special agreements are formed between parties in a NIAC, at least one of those parties lacks the legal capacity to subscribe to treaties. Nevertheless, as discussed above, there are international agreements other than treaties, as long as they are subscribed by subjects of international law and susceptible to being regulated by this law. It is at this point where special agreements have international legal value.

As previously stated, non-state armed groups are subjects of IHL, a regime under which they are not only bound to respecting existing humanitarian rules but also allowed to create new ones through special agreements. In other words, non-state actors have a norm-creating power with respect to IHL,[47] though this fact does not give them any specific legal status.[48]

Additionally, as pointed out by Vierucci, since the notion and the content of special agreements are given by treaties of an international character (e.g., Geneva Conventions), the obligations they stipulate should also be regarded as international.[49] Thus it can be concluded that as long as special agreements create mutual obligations for the parties in a NIAC in terms of Common Article 3 and are binding for the parties under Geneva Conventions, these Agreements

---

46   Corte Constitucional de Colombia. Sentencia C-225/95 (18 May 1995), para. 17.
47   Anthea Roberts and Sandesh Sivakumaran, 'Lawmaking by Nonstate Actors: Engaging Armed Groups in the Creation of International Humanitarian Law,' *Yale Journal of International Law* 13, no. 1 (2012): 108.
48   Sandesh Sivakumaran, 'The Addressees of Common Article 3,' in *The 1949 Geneva Conventions. A Commentary*, ed. Andrew Clapham, Paola Gaeta, and Marco Sassòli (Oxford: Oxford University Press, 2015), 426.
49   Luisa Vierucci, 'Applicability of the Conventions by Means of Ad Hoc Agreements,' in *The 1949 Geneva Conventions. A Commentary*, ed. Andrew Clapham, Paola Gaeta, and Marco Sassòli (Oxford: Oxford University Press, 2015), 516.

should therefore have the same international legal value as the rest of their IHL obligations.

In this sense, special agreements face the same challenges related to enforceability as other IHL norms. On this topic, Heffes and Kotlik consider that as long as the parties assign greater legitimacy to the obligations created by themselves acting under international law, there are better "chances of voluntary compliance in the first place," at the time that the parties can create their own *ad hoc* enforceability mechanisms in the agreement.[50] Vierucci endorses this idea. However, she also mentions enforcement mechanisms through individual criminal responsibility (since the deal becomes a rule of IHL that could be considered a standard by a national or international court ruling over a war crime)[51] and state responsibility (since the special agreement creates international obligations for the state).[52]

Likewise, in discussing whether a peace agreement can be considered a special agreement, the answer is affirmative among the ICRC and the few scholars that have seized the matter. For Heffes and Kotlik, "ceasefire agreements and peace agreements could also be included within this category inasmuch as they bring into force humanitarian provisions, since they are concluded by the parties to the conflict."[53] Heffes and Kotlik support this idea based on the fact that many peace agreements include humanitarian provisions such as the return of displaced people, the location of landmines, the search of disappeared people, and other measures responding to the purpose of special agreements.

Along the same lines, in its 2016 Commentary on Geneva Convention I, the ICRC proposed a broad understanding of the content and form of special agreements as enshrined by Common Article 3. In such a case, there would be no need to name the agreement as a special agreement. For the ICRC, "What counts is that the provisions brought into force between the Parties serve to protect the victims of armed conflict."[54] On this point, the ICRC specifically stated that:

---

50 Ezequiel Heffes and Marcos Kotlik, 'Special Agreements as a Means of Enhancing Compliance with IHL in Non-International Armed Conflicts: An Inquiry into the Governing Legal Regime,' *International Review of the Red Cross* 96, no. 895/896 (2014): 1222.
51 See also Liesbeth Zegveld, *Accountability of Armed Opposition Groups in International Law* (Cambridge: Cambridge University Press, 2002), 28–30; Andrew Clapham, *Human Rights Obligations of Non-State Actors* (Oxford: Oxford University Press, 2006), 297. They note how special agreements create legally binding obligations for state and non-state actors that could give rise to individual international criminal responsibility.
52 Vierucci, 'Applicability of the Conventions by Means of Ad Hoc Agreements,' 518–20.
53 Heffes and Kotlik, 'Special Agreements as a Means of Enhancing Compliance with IHL in Non-International Armed Conflicts: An Inquiry into the Governing Legal Regime,' 1197.
54 ICRC, *Commentary on the First Geneva Convention*, 2nd ed. (Geneva, 2016), para. 847.

> A peace agreement, ceasefire or other accord may also constitute a special agreement for the purposes of common Article 3, or a means to implement common Article 3, if it contains clauses that bring into existence further obligations drawn from the Geneva Conventions and/or their Additional Protocols. In this respect, it should be recalled that 'peace agreements' concluded with a view to bringing an end to hostilities may contain provisions drawn from other humanitarian law treaties, such as the granting of an amnesty for fighters who have carried out their operations in accordance with the laws and customs of war, the release of all captured persons, or a commitment to search for the missing. If they contain provisions drawn from humanitarian law, or if they implement humanitarian law obligations already incumbent on the Parties, such agreements, or the relevant provisions as the case may be, may constitute special agreements under common Article 3. This is particularly important given that hostilities do not always come to an end with the conclusion of a peace agreement.[55]

According to these terms, the ICRC explicitly recognizes a broad scope to special agreements that can also include peace agreements. Even if the Colombian Peace Agreement is the first one in which the parties expressly claimed it to be regarded as a special agreement under Common Article 3, the ICRC has considered other peace deals to have the same character.[56] In these cases, the defining element of a special agreement is its inclusion of provisions governed by IHL, as in the case of amnesties and the search of missing people, for example. Based on this criterion, the Final Peace Agreement concluded by the Colombian government and the FARC in 2016 can be indeed considered a special agreement in terms of Common Article 3 to 1949 Geneva Conventions.

1.2.2   The Peace Agreement as a Document of the UN Security Council

The second mechanism aimed at giving international legal character to the Colombian Peace Agreement was its incorporation into a UNSC resolution. The parties agreed that the President of the Republic would make a unilateral declaration before the UN Secretary-General to request him to welcome

---

55   ICRC, *Commentary on the First Geneva Convention*, 2nd edition, 2016, para. 850.
56   The ICRC mentions here the Cotonou Agreement on Liberia (1993), ICRC, *Commentary on the First Geneva Convention*, n. 803. Heffes and Kotlick also include the example of the 2002 Cease Fire Agreement between the government of Angola and UNITA, Heffes and Kotlik, 'Special Agreements as a Means of Enhancing Compliance with IHL in Non-International Armed Conflicts: An Inquiry into the Governing Legal Regime,' n. 17.

the Peace Agreement and add it as an annex to UNSC Resolution 2261 (2016) in order to give it the character of an "official document of the Security Council."[57]

UNSC resolutions have been used to internationalize internal peace agreements in several cases. In general, the Security Council has shown support for internal peace agreements in cases where the UN had participated in the negotiation process. Examples include peace processes and agreements in Angola,[58] Afghanistan,[59] Nepal,[60] Ivory Coast,[61] Sudan,[62] and Libya.[63] In these cases, the Council endorsed or welcomed the agreement, encouraged the parties to cooperate toward its implementation, and created or extended the mandate of UN military or political missions in the respective country.

In the Colombian case, the Security Council has adopted several resolutions regarding the peace agreement. First, Resolution 2261 (2016) established a 12-month "political mission of unarmed international observers, responsible for the monitoring and verification of the laying down of arms."[64] Then, Resolution 2307 (2016) welcomed the Final Agreement reached on 24 August 2016 (which was later rejected by popular vote) and approved the deployment of the

---

57　Gobierno de Colombia and FARC, 'Comunicado Conjunto No. 69.'
58　UNSC Resolution 1127 (1997), UN. Doc. S/RES/1127 (1997).
59　UNSC Resolution 1383 (2001), UN. Doc. S/RES/1383 (2001). It *"Endorses* the Agreement on provisional arrangements in Afghanistan" concluded by the participants in the UN Talks on Afghanistan held in Bonn in December 2001. In this case, the negotiations were conducted under UN support, and the UNSC had previous resolutions and interventions on the matter.
60　UNSC Resolution 1740 (2007), UN. Doc. S/RES/1740 (2007), *"Welcoming* the signing on 21 November by the Government of Nepal and the Communist Party of Nepal (Maoist) of a Comprehensive Peace Agreement" and established a UN Political Mission in Nepal (UNMIN).
61　UNSC Resolution 1464 (2013), UN. Doc. S/RES/1464. It *"Endorses* the agreement signed by the Ivorian political forces in Linas-Marcoussis on 24 January 2003." A Conference of Heads of Stated on Côte d'Ivore was held in Paris right after the Agreement was concluded. This Conference was hosted by France, who, as permanent member of the UNSC sent an official letter to the Council submitting the peace agreement itself and the conclusions of the Conference of Heads of State in which they asked this endorsement.
62　UNSC Resolution 1590 (2005), UN. Doc. S/RES/1590 (2005), *"Welcoming* the signing of the Comprehensive Peace Agreement between the Government of Sudan (GOS) and the Sudan People's Liberation Movement/Army (SPLM/A) in Nairobi, Kenya on 9 January 2005" and establishes a UN Mission in Sudan (UNMIS) (with military component).
63　UNSC Resolution 2259 (2015), UN. Doc. S/RES/2259 (2015). It *"Welcomes* the signature on 17 December 2015 of the Libyan Political Agreement of Skhira", and *"Endorses* the Rome Communiqué of 13 December 2015 to support the Government of National Accord as the sole legitimate government of Libya."
64　UN Security Council, 'Resolution 2261 (2016),' Pub. L. No. S/RES/2261 (2016).

political monitoring mission created by Resolution 2261.[65] Later, Resolution 2366 (2017) welcomed the new Final Agreement signed on 24 November 2016 and established a new Verification Mission to monitor the reintegration process and the implementation of the Agreement.[66] Finally, through Resolutions 2377 (2017), 2381 (2017), 2435 (2018), and 2487 (2019) the Council defined operational aspects of the Verification Mission and expanded and renewed its mandate.

Additionally, as agreed in the Joint Communiqué No. 69, on 24 March 2017 Colombia deposited a letter before the UN Secretary-General in which the President of the Republic, after thanking the Organization for its support to the peace process, stated: "I would also like to officially express the Colombian Government's good faith through a unilateral State declaration, and herewith submit the full text of the Final Agreement."[67]

For some authors, UNSC resolutions lend international legal force to the agreements they support. For Bell, "Security Council resolutions can be used to bring the force of law to peace agreement commitments, establishing mechanisms for monitoring compliance that stand independently of the status of the agreement itself, which nevertheless forms their *raison d'être*."[68] Roucounas further affirms that through its incorporation in a Security Council resolution, the peace agreement becomes "an act of the international organization and operates as such towards the parties and towards the international community as a whole."[69]

An illustrative case for this discussion is given by the peace agreement between the Government of Angola and *União Nacional para a Independência Total de Angola* (UNITA). Under UN mediation, the parties signed two documents that were circulated as UN documents. UNITA failed to accomplish its obligations and consequently reactivated the risk of violence. In reaction, by Resolution 1127 (1997), the Security Council demanded UNITA to immediately implement its obligations under the peace agreement, invoking Chapter VII of the UN Charter.[70] Analyzing this case, Kooijmans argued:

---

65   UN Security Council, Resolution 2307 (2016).
66   UN Security Council, Resolution 2366 (2017).
67   UN Secretary-General, 'Letter Dated 29 March 2017 from the Secretary-General Addressed to the President of the Security Council,' 29 March 2017, https://colombia.unmissions.org/sites/default/files/s-2017-272_e.pdf Annex I.
68   Bell, 'Peace Agreements: Their Nature and Legal Status,' 394.
69   Emmanuel Roucounas, 'Peace Agreements as Instruments for the Resolution of Intrastate Conflicts,' in *Conflict Resolution: New Approaches and Methods*, by UNESCO (Paris: UNESCO, 2000), 120–21.
70   UNSC Resolution 1127 (1997), UN. Doc. S/RES/1127 (1997), section A.

> The fact that [the agreement] is concluded between a government and an insurrectionist party does not in itself detract from its international character. The United Nations as an organization of states has been deeply involved in the conflict, peace keeping forces have been deployed, the Secretary-General through his Special Representative has continuously mediated. If a settlement is reached which is co-signed by the Secretary-General's Representative, the non-state entity must be assumed not only to have committed itself to its counterpart, the Government but also to the United Nations.[71]

However, in opposition to Kooijmans' opinion, the Special Court of Sierra Leone concluded that in this case the "action taken by the Security Council upon failure of a party to implement the peace agreement derives from Chapter VII of the UN Charter and not from the peace agreement."[72] Indeed, the Security Council deemed that "the resulting situation in Angola constitutes a threat to international peace and security in the region" and cited this as the reason by which it acted "under Chapter VII of the Charter of the United Nations."[73] As such, the enforceability of the obligations agreed upon by the parties did not derive from the agreement itself but from the UN Charter. Nonetheless, the peace agreement was used by the Security Council as a reference to determine UNITA's noncompliance.

The Security Council's endorsement of a peace agreement therefore does not by itself lend international legal value to such a deal. However, its endorsement has at least two important consequences. First, on a political level, the Council's seizing of the agreement and involvement in its implementation—as in the case of Colombia through monitoring missions—raise international attention and can add pressure toward compliance. Second, on a legal level, in the case of a failure to meet the agreement obligations that raises a threat to international peace and security, the deal could be used as a parameter to determine obligations and eventual responsibilities before the Council acting under Chapter VII of the Charter.

Finally, the unilateral declaration made by the Colombian President at the time of depositing the Final Agreement before the Secretary-General requires

---

[71] P.H. Kooijmans, 'The Security Council and Non-State Entities as Parties to Conflicts,' in *International Law: Theory and Practice: Essays in Honour of Eric Suy*, ed. Eric Suy and Karell Wellens (The Hague: Martinus Nijhoff Publishers, 1998), 338.

[72] Special Court for Sierra Leone, The Appeals Chamber, Prosecutor v. Morris Kallon and Brima Bazzy Kamara, paragraph 39.

[73] UNSC Resolution 1127 (1997), UN. Doc. S/RES/1127 (1997), section B.

a special mention. In accordance with the Guiding Principles Applicable to Unilateral Declarations of States Capable of Creating Legal Obligations, which was adopted by the International Law Commission (ILC) in 2006, a public declaration made at the international level by the Head of State, Head of Government or Minister of Foreign Affairs, in which the will to be bound is expressed clearly and specifically, creates international legal obligations. The binding character of such a declaration is based on good faith, and other interested states "are entitled to require that such obligations be respected."[74] According to these terms, independent of the annexation of the Agreement to a UNSC Resolution, the unilateral declaration made by the President on behalf of the State generates international legal obligations for Colombia. The Agreement therefore also attained international legal character by this means.

1.3 Consequences of the Peace Agreement's International Legal Status

Despite the parties' intention to give the Peace Agreement legal certainty through its legal internationalization, the terms by which it was delimited following the plebiscite reduced the domestic effects of such a formula. As noted above, in Colombia duly ratified international treaties regarding IHRL and IHL have the same normative level as the Constitution, forming a constitutional block. However, the terms of Article 93 of the Colombian Constitution make clear that such a status is reserved to treaties *stricto sensu*.[75] As such, even if the Peace Agreement can be considered an international agreement, as per the above analysis, it does not have the character of a treaty under the VCLT. Legally, this is the reason why the first formula proposed by the Government and the FARC incorporating the agreement into the constitutional block was problematic. In contrast, the Final Agreement did not invoke such a constitutional feature but rather the status of special agreement for the purposes of "its international validity."[76]

The international character of the Peace Agreement as a special agreement therefore does not imply per se any legal constraint to its domestic modification. The legal certainty of the Final Agreement ultimately depends on the constitutional reforms introduced to protect it. To this effect, as mentioned above, a constitutional amendment was adopted stating that all organs of the

---

74　International Law Commission, Guiding Principles Applicable to Unilateral Declarations of States Capable of Creating Legal Obligations, 2006.
75　Constitución Política de Colombia, Art. 93.
76　Government of Colombia and FARC, 'Final Agreement to End the Armed Conflict and Build a Stable and Lasting Peace,' 5.

State must act according to what was agreed on, "preserving the contents, commitments, the spirit and the principles of the Final Agreement," and that this provision will be in force for three presidential terms.[77]

Additionally, the same amendment included a provision according to which the contents of the Agreement related to the norms of IHL and fundamental rights "will be compulsory parameters of interpretation and a referent for the development and validity of the norms and laws developing and implementing the Final Agreement."[78] Even if this provision did not give the Agreement an international effect at the domestic level, its content related to IHL and human rights became a parameter by which to interpret and develop the peace agreement.[79] For all the above reasons, Bell considers the Colombian Peace Agreement to be something " 'hybrid' between international and constitutional law."[80]

Nonetheless, at the international level, the international legal status of the Peace Agreement can have important political and legal effects. In political terms, defining the peace deal as an international agreement increases the "reputation costs" for the parties involved in the case of non-compliance.[81] In the Colombian case, the UNSC resolutions regarding the agreement have played a significant role, as the agreement has received the attention of the highest global body responsible for international peace and security. Though this cost could be higher for the State, the FARC also want to preserve the implicit degree of reputation and recognition attached to the legal status of the Peace Agreement.[82]

In legal terms, the international legal character of the Peace Agreement could have at least three consequences. First, the unilateral declaration made by the President on behalf of the Colombian State before the UN generated

---

77   Congreso de la República de Colombia, Acto Legislativo 02 de 2017, available at: http://es.presidencia.gov.co/normativa/normativa/ACTO%20LEGISLATIVO%20N°%2002%20DE%2011%20DE%20MAYO%20DE%202017.pdf.
78   Ibid.
79   This formula could capture the notion of "trans-textuality", proposed by Roucounas, according to which as peace agreements generally include obligations already enshrined by international law instruments, they will also become internationally binding. Roucounas, 'Peace Agreements as Instruments for the Resolution of Intrastate Conflicts,' 120–21.
80   Bell, 'Lex Pacificatoria Colombiana: Colombia's Peace Accord in Comparative Perspective,' 169.
81   Bell, *On the Law of Peace*, 139.
82   On the idea of the costs and benefits of the legal status of the peace agreement for non-state actors, see: von Hehn, *The Internal Implementation of Peace Agreements after Violent Intrastate Conflict*, 53.

legal obligations in terms of the Guiding Principles proposed by the ILC in 2006. To that effect, any interested state—for instance, the guarantor countries—could invoke international obligations contracted by Colombia in the Peace Agreement. An announcement made in 2018 by the new political party that emerged from the transition of the FARC to civilian life is illustrative of this point: the party asked the UN to request an International Court of Justice's advisory opinion on the scope and effects of the unilateral declaration made by the President of the Republic in March 2017 regarding the Peace Agreement.[83] Even though this request has not been followed, it shows the potential legal effects of such a unilateral declaration.

Second, as the special agreement constitutes a norm of IHL, the Agreement could eventually be considered as a parameter before the ICC in the case that a war crime was under its examination, and the commission of such a crime would have any relation with the agreement. This possibility is rare but theoretically conceivable.

Third, as a more likely consequence, the Peace Agreement can become a parameter by which to examine the State's responsibility before human rights bodies and courts. Regarding this point, von Hehn notes that "by including the applicability of human rights conventions in the peace package, countries also attract monitoring by the respective treaty bodies, enabling additional scrutiny of the implementation process outside of the main negotiations."[84] Along same lines, Verucci suggests that since a special agreement is an international norm, it could be used, for example, to evaluate a state under the Universal Periodic Review.[85]

With respect to this third consequence, a concrete example of the use of a peace agreement as a parameter by international bodies is given by the Inter-American Court of Human Rights. In the *El Mozote case*, the Court claimed that "when analyzing the compatibility of the Law of General Amnesty for the Consolidation of Peace with the international obligations arising from the American Convention and its application to the case," it is also necessary to consider "the provisions of Protocol II Additional to the 1949 Geneva Conventions, as well as of the specific terms in which it was agreed to end hostilities, which put an end to the conflict in El Salvador and, in particular, of

---

83   Caracol Radio. (2018). Farc pedirá opinión jurídica a la CIJ para implementación de los Acuerdos de Paz. Available at http://caracol.com.co/radio/2018/01/14/nacional/1515906848_061576.html (accessed on 20 February 2019).
84   von Hehn, *The Internal Implementation of Peace Agreements after Violent Intrastate Conflict*, 57.
85   Vierucci, 'Applicability of the Conventions by Means of Ad Hoc Agreements,' 520.

Chapter 1 ("Armed Forces"), section 5 ("End to impunity"), of the Peace Accord of January 16, 1992."[86] In this case, the Court used a domestic peace agreement as a parameter by which to evaluate the state's responsibility under IHRL.

2   Socioeconomic and Political Reforms

As presented in Chapter 1, the object of *jus post bellum* is not only about ending armed conflict but building sustainable peace. Regarding NIACS, both purposes usually demand socioeconomic and political reforms. First, ending armed conflict requires social, economic, and political measures for the reintegration of former fighters. Second, building sustainable peace involves both socioeconomic and institutional recovery from the damages caused by armed conflict, as well as addressing the root causes of confrontation, which are commonly related to socioeconomic and political matters. All those questions are present in the 2016 Colombian Peace Agreement.

This chapter departed from presenting a general overview of the Colombian armed conflict. As seen, the origin of armed conflict in the country was deeply related to socioeconomic and political reasons. Guerrilla groups have invoked land concentration, rural poverty, and political exclusion as the original causes of the conflict.[87] Additionally, the protracted confrontation brought other related elements such as the impact of forced displacement, landmines, and war economies—e.g. crops of illicit use. All those factors had to be addressed in a comprehensive way if parties wanted to negotiate a serious and lasting peace. And they did it.

This section is aimed at exploring how socioeconomic and political reforms adopted for transition in Colombia reveal legal and policy considerations responding to a framework of *jus post bellum*. Unlike the other sections of this chapter, which mainly assume a legal perspective, this one addresses policy aspects of peacebuilding related to removing the root causes of conflict and building a sustainable peace.

For that, the section presents the general international legal and policy framework applicable to socioeconomic and political reforms in transition. Then, it examines how those reforms are addressed in the Colombian Peace Agreement, broaching issues such as land access and rural development,

---

86   Inter-American Court of Human Rights, Case of the Massacres of El Mozote and nearby places v. El Salvador, Judgement of 25 October 2012 (2012), para. 284.
87   Government of Colombia and FARC, 'Final Agreement to End the Armed Conflict and Build a Stable and Lasting Peace,' 2.

environmental protection, demining, the problem of crops of illicit use, and the reintegration of former fighters.

2.1 Legal and Policy Framework on Socioeconomic and Political Reforms for Transition to Peace

Armed conflict affects social and economic development, deteriorates the environment, breaks social coexistence, and undermines democratic mechanisms and institutions. Moreover, in contexts of NIACs some of those problems existed before armed conflict started and, in most cases, they were the very cause of confrontation.

Therefore, addressing the root causes of armed conflict and building conditions for sustainable peace in transition from NIACs implies removing structural factors of exclusion and inequalities. As pointed out by Chetail, peacebuilding entails the responsibility "to free individuals not only from 'fear' but also from 'need'."[88] As such, "the concept of post-conflict peacebuilding is inextricably linked to the notion of a 'positive peace' describing a situation which is not only characterized by the absence of hostiles but by many other political, economic and social accomplishments."[89]

This aim of positive peace involves several social, economic, and political measures, all of which entail legal considerations. As Schaller argues, "the establishment of conditions for a positive and durable peace is also inseparably linked to effectively guaranteeing human rights."[90] In other words, building positive peace beyond the end of armed confrontation requires human rights-based reforms addressing matters as poverty, marginalization, development, and democratic participation.

Different international legal instruments enshrine provisions applicable to socioeconomic and political reform in transitional contexts, under a human rights perspective. In general terms, the International Covenant on Civil and Political Rights (ICCPR) establishes the state's obligation to ensure to all people under its jurisdiction the full enjoyment of their civil and political rights. It mainly includes, for the purpose of this section, the right to political and social participation.[91] Similarly, the International Covenant on Economic, Social, and

---

88   Chetail, 'Introduction,' 8.
89   Christian Schaller, 'Towards an International Legal Framework for Post-Conflict Peacebuilding,' *Research Paper, German Institute for International and Security Affairs* 3 (2009): 15.
90   Schaller, 15.
91   'International Covenant on Civil and Political Rights,' Pub. L. No. General Assembly Resolution 2200A (XXI), (1966) Art. 3 and 25.

Cultural Rights (ICESCR) enshrines the state's obligation to ensure the enjoyment of all economic, social, and cultural rights, and to adopt all appropriate means for that purpose.[92] Analogous provisions can be found in other regional human rights instruments.[93]

Regarding soft law documents, there are several instruments related to social, economic, and cultural rights relevant to the context of peacemaking and peacebuilding. The UN Declaration on the Right to Development establishes that "The right to development is an inalienable human right by virtue of which every human person and all peoples are entitled to participate in, contribute to, and enjoy economic, social, cultural and political development, in which all human rights and fundamental freedoms can be fully realized."[94] Additionally, it disposes that "Appropriate economic and social reforms should be carried out with a view to eradicating all social injustices."[95]

The UN Declaration on the Right to Peace underlines the positive dimension of peace as involving "mutual understanding, cooperation, and socioeconomic development," and for such a purpose recalls "the world commitment to eradicate poverty and to promote sustained economic growth, sustainable development and global prosperity for all, and the need to reduce inequalities within and among countries."[96] In this line, the 2030 Agenda for Sustainable Development states that "There can be no sustainable development without peace and no peace without sustainable development."[97]

More recently, the 2018 UN Declaration on the Rights of Peasants and Other People Working in Rural Areas[98] addressed the states' obligations under IHRL to ensure all human rights to people living in rural areas. This instrument is very revalent regarding peacemaking and peacebuilding in the contexts of NIACS, because of the special impact of armed conflict in the rural areas. At this regard, the Declaration states the right of peasants and rural people to

---

92 'International Covenant on Economic, Social and Cultural Rights,' Pub. L. No. General Assembly Resolution 2200A (XXI), (1966) Art. 2-3.

93 'European Convention for the Protection of Human Rights and Fundamental Freedoms' (1950); 'American Convention on Human Rights' (1969).

94 UN General Assembly, 'Declaration on the Right to Development,' Pub. L. No. A/RES/41/128 (1986) Art. 1.1.

95 UN General Assembly Art. 8.1.

96 UN General Assembly, 'Declaration on the Right to Peace,' Pub. L. No. A/HRC/RES/32/28 (2016), 2–3.

97 UN General Assembly, 'Transforming Our World: The 2030 Agenda for Sustainable Development,' Pub. L. No. A/RES/70/1 (2015), 3.

98 UN General Assembly, 'Declaration on the Rights of Peasants and Other People Working in Rural Areas,' Pub. L. No. A /RES/73/165 (2019).

have and "an adequate standard of living"[99] and to live in conditions of "peace and dignity."[100]

In terms of disarmament, demobilization, and reintegration (DDR), several UN documents provide policy and legal considerations relevant to *jus post bellum*. UN reports and resolutions have consistently stressed on DDR "as a key element of stabilization in post-conflict situations to facilitate a society's transition from conflict to development;"[101] the need to assume a comprehensive view of DDR programs[102] and to integrate them to other components of the peacebuilding framework;[103] and the adoption of differential considerations on DDR regarding women and children fighters.[104] In addition, the UN approach to DDR identifies several IHL and IHRL provisions as applicable to DDR, mainly regarding civil and political rights, promoting access to education, health, employment and other economic, social, and cultural rights without discrimination, and the duty to ensure special protection to women and children in all circumstances.[105]

According to such a general framework, different socioeconomic and institutional aspects must be addressed in transition to establishing a sustainable peace. For instance, reforms aimed at creating socioeconomic development are fundamental for employing former fighters and providing them with an alternative livelihood (a fundamental condition for an effective reintegration),[106] as well as for building conditions of wellbeing for the population, which can facilitate social integration and long-term stability. Similarly, institutional reforms aimed at empowering excluded groups and broadening civic and political participation are fundamental to reestablish civic trust, peaceful coexistence, and reconciliation.

Likewise, environmental protection is a fundamental dimension of peacebuilding.[107] Armed conflict usually impacts the environment, which is also

---

99   UN General Assembly Art. 17.1.
100 UN General Assembly Art. 24.1.
101 Secretary-General's report on The Role of UN Peacekeeping in Disarmament, Demobilization and Reintegration, S/2000/101, of 11 February 2000, paras. 2 and 8.
102 Statement by the President of the Security Council, S/PRST/2000/10, of 23 March 2000.
103 Report of the Panel on UN Peace Operations, A/55/305; S/2000/809, of 21 August 2000.
104 Security Council Resolution 1325 (2000) on *Women, Peace and Security*; and Resolutions 1379 (2001), 1460 (2003) and 1539 (2004) on *Children in Armed Conflict*.
105 United Nations Disarmament, Demobilization and Reintegration Resource Center, *The UN Approach to DDR*, 2006, pp. 18–19.
106 Achim Wennmann, 'Economic Provisions in Peace Agreements and Sustainable Peacebuilding,' *Négotiations* 1, no. 11 (2009): 46.
107 Carsten Stahn, 'R2P and *Jus Post Bellum*. Towards a Polycentric Approach,' in *Jus Post Bellum: Mapping the Normative Foundations*, ed. Carsten Stahn, Jennifer Easterday, and

irregularly exploited as a means to finance armed hostilities in the context of NIACs.[108] The environmental degradation caused by those situations can exacerbate violence, especially in contexts "where large parts of the population depend on land and renewable resources for their livelihood."[109] This situation imperils reconciliation and affects the conditions for effective post-conflict economic reconstruction.[110] For these reasons, "environmental protection and the sustainable management of resources are important pathways to consolidate peace and promote long-term development."[111]

Finally, mine action is another critical element in post conflict transition and post-conflict reconstruction.[112] In countries seriously affected by minefields during armed conflict, demining is a crucial element to restore livelihoods and contribute to peacebuilding.[113] It facilitates the reintegration of former fighters (when employed as deminers, for instance) and the return of refugees and internally displaced persons, promotes cooperation and confidence-building, and improves safety, security, and economic revitalization.[114]

All the above components of the post-conflict socioeconomic and political reconstruction have a legal base, mainly under IHRL and IHL, in addition to several UN and soft law documents related to the rights to peace and development, and to peacebuilding in general. In the next item, we will see how such an international legal framework shaped transitional formulas in Colombia on this matter.

Jens Iverson (Oxford: Oxford University Press, 2014), 118; Easterday, 'Peace Agreements as a Framework for *Jus Post Bellum*,' 409; Cymie Payne, 'The Norm of Environmental Integrity in Post-Conflict Legal Regimes,' in *Jus Post Bellum: Mapping the Normative Foundations*, ed. Carsten Stahn, Jennifer Easterday, and Jens Iverson (Oxford: Oxford University Press, 2014), 502–18; Stahn, Iverson, and Easterday, *Environmental Protection and Transitions from Conflict to Peace: Clarifying Norms, Principles, and Practices*.

108   Gillett, 'Eco-Struggles: Using International Criminal Law to Protect the Environment During and After Non-International Armed Conflict,' 223.
109   Jennifer Easterday and Hana Ivanhoe, 'Conflict, Cash, and Controversy: Protecting Environmental Rights in Post-Conflict Settings,' in *Environmental Protection and Transitions from Conflict to Peace: Clarifying Norms, Principles, and Practices*, ed. Carsten Stahn, Jens Iverson, and Jennifer Easterday (Oxford: Oxford University Press, 2017), 274.
110   Gillett, 'Eco-Struggles: Using International Criminal Law to Protect the Environment During and After Non-International Armed Conflict,' 249; Hofmann and Rapillard, 'Post-Conflict Mine Action: Environment and Law,' 404.
111   Hofmann and Rapillard, 'Post-Conflict Mine Action: Environment and Law,' 397.
112   Hofmann and Rapillard, 'Post-Conflict Mine Action: Environment and Law.'
113   Hofmann and Rapillard, 397.
114   Hofmann and Rapillard, 418–19.

2.2 Socioeconomic and Political Reforms in the Colombian Peace Agreement

The very name of the Final Agreement to End Armed Conflict and Build a Stable and Lasting Peace raises the parties' determination to address the root causes of the armed conflict, as a condition to build a sustainable peace in Colombia. In its introduction, the Agreement declares its rights-based approach, and its goal to contribute to greater territorial integration and greater social inclusion, as well as to strengthening democracy, bringing institutions to all over around the country, and ensuring that all the ideas can be expressed with full guarantees via politics and social conflicts can be resolved through institutional channels.[115] In this way, the Agreement states as its final aim the full realization of all human rights for all people,[116] and it considers itself as a guarantee of non-recurrence of violations of human rights.[117]

That explicit utterance of the rights-based approach to building sustainable peace is complemented with reiterated references to IHRL along the Agreement.[118] The parties explicitly defined a commitment to make effective all human rights, according to the Colombian Constitution, to the ICCPR, the ICESCR, and the other IHRL treaties ratified by Colombia.[119] As such, they openly attributed a role to international legal norms and standards to govern matters highly dependent on domestic political and practical considerations.

Having the elements presented above, the following are the main aspects referred to socioeconomic and political matters in the Colombian Peace Agreement.

First, the first chapter of the Peace Agreement is devoted to a comprehensive rural reform. This chapter understands rural problems in Colombia as a root cause of armed conflict, and the need to implement a comprehensive reform as a condition to build a sustainable peace. On this topic, the Agreement includes development programs for the structural transformation of the countryside, promoting an equitable relationship between rural and urban areas.[120] It includes an ambitious program of rural infrastructure, connectivity, health,

---

115 Government of Colombia and FARC, 'Final Agreement to End the Armed Conflict and Build a Stable and Lasting Peace,' 6.
116 Government of Colombia and FARC, 2.
117 Government of Colombia and FARC, 132.
118 The Agreement contains 14 specific references to IHRL. See Government of Colombia and FARC, 'Final Agreement to End the Armed Conflict and Build a Stable and Lasting Peace.'
119 Government of Colombia and FARC, 190.
120 Government of Colombia and FARC, 22.

education, housing, cooperative economy, income generation, progressive realization of the right to food, and land access.

Second, linked to rural development programs, the Agreement makes several references to environmental protection in the context of peacebuilding. In its preamble, the Agreement envisions a society in which peace allows to achieve sustainable development, protection of the environment, natural resources, and biodiversity.[121] Then, it offers special land access and other benefits for peasants, rural victims, and communities who work to protect the environment, substitute crops of illicit use, and improve food production.[122] Additionally, the deal calls for the protection of areas of special environmental interest with the participation of rural communities, looking for a sustainable development, in which the Agreement emphasizes on the special contribution of small-scale farmer and indigenous and Afro-descendent communities.[123]

Third, since political exclusion was at the heart of the root causes of armed conflict, in the same way as for the rural reform the parties dedicated a full chapter of the Agreement to political participation and democratic opening. Here, the parties agreed on rights and guarantees for the exercise of political opposition; a comprehensive security system for the exercise of politics; democratic mechanisms for citizen participation; guarantees for reconciliation, coexistence, and non-stigmatization; awareness-raising campaigns for non-discrimination, pluralism, and the free debate of ideas; promoting greater participation in politics among the most excluded social sectors; and the political participation of former members of the guerrilla.[124] This chapter also establishes a National Political Pact, aimed at reaching a commitment that arms will never again be used in politics and never again will violent organizations such as paramilitarism be promoted.[125]

Fourth, the Agreement contains a detailed and technical chapter on the ending of armed conflict, in which it describes the procedure for the laying down of arms and the socioeconomic and political reintegration of former fighters. It includes social, educational, and employment programs for demobilized persons, with special support for programs related to environmental conservation and demining.[126] Additionally, the Agreement established the creation of a new political party in which former guerrilla leaders could promote the

---

121 Government of Colombia and FARC, 3–4.
122 Government of Colombia and FARC, 15.
123 Government of Colombia and FARC, 11.
124 Government of Colombia and FARC, 37–55.
125 Government of Colombia and FARC, 80.
126 Government of Colombia and FARC, 75.

ideas they previously defended by arms.[127] On this point, it is important to mention that the guerrilla did not accept the use of the expressions *disarmament* and *demobilization*, as they saw them as a kind of capitulation. Instead, the Agreement systematically uses the expressions of laying down of arms, and social, political, and economic reintegration.

Fifth, since crops of illicit use and drug-trafficking became one of the main fuels of armed violence in the last decades in Colombia, the parties in negotiation dedicated a full chapter of the Agreement to this matter. They created a comprehensive program for substitution of crops used for illicit purposes, integrated to the comprehensive rural reform. The deal looks at promoting community-based plans and alternative agrarian development, ensuring economic and social rights.[128] Additionally, the Agreement promotes a human rights and public health-based approach to the problem of drugs, and the development of an international conference under the auspices of the UN to assess the policy counter drugs and discuss new approaches to the matter.

Sixth, being the FARC the main responsible of mine contamination in Colombia,[129] the Agreement establishes the cooperation of former guerrilla members with demining, and the State's commitment to clean the territory from landmines. Demining is presented as a condition for a safe return of internally displaced people and for rural development and substitution of crops of illicit use. Contribution to demining is among the possible restorative sanctions to be imposed to former fighters by the Special Jurisdiction for Peace.

In addition to those measures, the Agreement contains several references to economic, social, and cultural rights, the reparation for their violation,[130] and a Truth Commission's mandate to elucidate the impact of armed conflict over economic, social, and cultural rights.[131] The Agreement also states that

---

127 Government of Colombia and FARC, 69.
128 Government of Colombia and FARC, 106.
129 Colombia has the 15th position on extent of mine-contaminated land in the world up to the end of 2016, and the FARC were considered the main producer of antipersonnel landmines in Colombia until the signature of the Peace Agreement. See International Campaign to Ban Landmines. *Landmine Monitor 2017*, available at https://reliefweb.int/sites/reliefweb.int/files/resources/Landmine_Monitor_2017_Embargoed.pdf (accessed on 4 February 2019).
130 Government of Colombia and FARC, 'Final Agreement to End the Armed Conflict and Build a Stable and Lasting Peace,' 125.
131 Government of Colombia and FARC, 134. On this role of truth commissions addressing economic, social and cultural rights, see Lisa Laplante, 'Transitional Justice and Peace Building: Diagnosing and Addressing the Socioeconomic Roots of Violence through a Human Rights Framework,' *International Journal of Transitional Justice* 2, no. 3 (2008): 331–355.

all its socioeconomic and political measures seek the non-recurrence of the conflict and ensuring human rights for all. It indicates that the rural reform looks for the "guarantee of rights, including economic, social, cultural and environmental rights of the rural population," which "contributes to their well-being and quality of life."[132] As for the political reform, the Agreement seeks "the exercise of political rights, the promotion of a democratic culture and of human rights and guarantees for reconciliation, coexistence, tolerance, non-stigmatization, and the guarantees for the mobilization and social protest."[133] Finally, the Agreement refers to actions related to resolve the problem of drugs of illicit use as a way "to contribute to overcoming the conditions of poverty, marginalization and weak institutional presence" in the rural areas.[134]

As such, the Colombian Peace Agreement assumed a solid human rights-based approach to socioeconomic and political reforms aimed at building peace. In many cases the deal explicitly refers to IHRL obligations and, in the others, it involves substantial human rights issues, even though they are not necessarily expressed in the logic of international human rights instruments.[135] However, the most important element for the purpose of this analysis is the fact that the parties understood the need to address the root causes of the conflict and to create socioeconomic and political conditions for building sustainable peace, and that they did so acknowledging and invoking international human rights obligations. As such, the parties used an international frame of reference to design their specific approach, according to the conditions of their context, offering insights on the importance of a human rights-based approach to development and reconstruction in peacebuilding. These considerations offer elements to see the Colombian case as involving a principle of *jus post bellum* on reconstruction and transformation of the conditions for sustainable peace, as Chapter 3 will further analyze.

---

132   Government of Colombia and FARC, 'Final Agreement to End the Armed Conflict and Build a Stable and Lasting Peace,' 199.
133   Government of Colombia and FARC, 199.
134   Government of Colombia and FARC, 198.
135   On this point, Kastner sustains that "even though many agreements that do not explicitly refer to human rights deal, in their substance, with human rights issues. Provisions on power sharing, the electoral system and institutional reform, and access to natural resources typically address questions of injustice and inequality, without necessarily using the language and logic of international human rights instruments." Kastner, *Legal Normativity in the Resolution of Internal Armed Conflict*, 43. See also Christine Bell, *Peace Agreements and Human Rights* (Oxford: Oxford University Press, 2003), 302–3.

3 Criminal Justice

The most visible influence of international law in peacemaking is related to criminal responsibility for serious crimes committed during armed conflict. Traditionally, most peace negotiations had concluded with general amnesties for people responsible for such crimes. Then, South Africa introduced an internationally accepted mechanism of conditional amnesties to reach truth and reconciliation, with no criminal sanctions. However, since the paradigmatic development of ICL during the 1990s, this matter has progressively changed. Today, full amnesties are prohibited for crimes under international law, and conditional amnesties do not have any clear framework. This context carries out big challenges for countries emerging from internal armed conflicts through peace negotiations.

Colombia has assumed different approaches on this matter. During peace negotiations conducted in the late 1980s and early 1990s, blanket amnesties were granted to demobilized members of guerrillas. After the intensification of armed conflict during late 1990s and early 2000s, a demobilization process was agreed with paramilitary groups who accepted their submission to justice in exchange for lenient punishments. This model, created in 2005, looked at conciliating the international exigencies of justice with the practical needs of a negotiated demobilization. Now, after the 2012–2016 peace process with the FARC, a comprehensive model of transitional justice was agreed on by the parties, combining amnesties, criminal responsibility, and alternative punishments.

The 2016 Peace Agreement explicitly states that its transitional justice model is aimed at accomplishing the State's international obligations under IHL, IHRL, and ICL,[136] satisfying the victims' rights to truth, justice, and reparation. For that, a Special Jurisdiction for Peace was created to try armed conflict-related crimes under international and domestic law, when amnesty is not possible. However, the system adopts a restorative perspective and, in exchange of the accused's contribution to truth and reparation, sentences will determine alternative punishments primarily aimed at repairing victims and building peace.

This model of criminal responsibility has been welcomed by the ICC. The Court's Prosecutor "note[d], with satisfaction, that the final text of the peace agreement excludes amnesties and pardons for crimes against humanity and

---

136   Government of Colombia and FARC, 'Final Agreement to End the Armed Conflict and Build a Stable and Lasting Peace,' 2, 129.

war crimes under the Rome Statute."[137] Similarly, the President of the Court affirmed that the Colombian transitional justice model shows that peace and justice are not incompatible.[138]

Considering said elements, this section is divided into three parts. The first part presents the legal framework on amnesties at the end of NIACs and the duty to prosecute international crimes. The second part addresses the discussion on conciliating the needs of peace and the requirements of justice in transitional settings. And the third part explains the Colombian approach to criminal responsibility in a negotiated transition by observing applicable international legal standards.

3.1 Legal Framework on Amnesties and Criminal Responsibility

Both amnesty and criminal prosecution have international legal foundation. Amnesties are part of the instruments envisaged by IHL for the exit of armed conflict, but they cannot be used to evade the international legal obligation to prosecute serious crimes committed during armed conflict, which is a duty under IHL, IHRL, and ICL. As such, this item presents the legal framework on both amnesties and criminal responsibility for serious crimes, to then analyze its application in transition from armed conflict to peace and its application in the Colombian case.

3.1.1 Amnesties at the End of NIACs

Since the XVIII century, Kant stated that "the very concept of peace entails the idea of amnesty."[139] This notion has prevailed in most peace agreements ending armed conflicts in the following two centuries.

Regarding NIACs, Article 6(5) of 1977 Additional Protocol II to 1949 Geneva Conventions states that: "At the end of hostilities, the authorities in power shall endeavour to grant the broadest possible amnesty to persons who have participated in the armed conflict, or those deprived of their liberty for reasons related to the armed conflict, whether they are interned or detained." The ICRC considers this provision as a customary rule.[140]

---

137 Office of the ICC Prosecutor, 'Statement of ICC Prosecutor, Fatou Bensouda, on the Conclusion of the Peace Negotiations between the Government of Colombia and the Revolutionary Armed Forces of Colombia'.
138 'La Presidenta de La CPI: "Colombia Demuestra Que Paz y Justicia No Son Incompatibles"', *Agencia EFE*, 1 July 2017, https://www.efe.com/efe/america/portada/la-presidenta-de-cpi-colombia-demuestra-que-paz-y-justicia-no-son-incompatibles/20000064-3313655.
139 Kant, Immanuel. *Metaphysic of Morals*, 1797, § 58, quoted by Ambos, 'The Legal Framework of Transitional Justice,' 27.
140 Jean-Marie Henckaerts and Louise Doswald-Beck, *Customary International Humanitarian Law. Volume I: Rules* (Cambridge: Cambridge University Press, 2005). Rule 159.

Analyzing the rationale behind such a provision, Kreß and Grover point out that the norm looks at offering "an incentive for non-State fighters to conduct the hostilities in accordance with the law of non-international armed conflict."[141] Broomhall suggests that this provision "is intended primarily to discourage the prosecution under ordinary criminal law."[142] In a different view, Mégret affirms that encouraging amnesties for rebels goes beyond a humanitarian purpose and it raises "the difficult legal question of which rebellions more generally conform to a sort of non-state *jus ad bellum*, and would reward those that do."[143]

Nonetheless, in a more functional perspective, amnesties play a fundamental role in peacemaking. In its 1987 Commentary on Additional Protocol II, the ICRC considered that the object of this provision on amnesties "is to encourage gestures of reconciliation which can contribute to reestablishing normal relations in the life of a nation which has been divided."[144] Certainly, fighters who know that they will face a criminal "retribution will often consider that they have nothing to lose and fight to the end."[145] Thus, in contexts of NIACs waiver of punishment may be essential to restore peace and facilitate reconciliation.[146] As such, amnesties are mainly an incentive for rebels to agree to peace.

Pursuing that objective, the international community has encouraged and supported amnesties in several transitions from NIACs around the world.[147] In cases such as South Africa, Angola, Croatia, and Afghanistan the UN Security Council and the General Assembly explicitly called governments to grant amnesties or welcomed those that were agreed by the parties through

---

141   Kreß and Grover, 'International Criminal Law Restraints in Peace Talks to End Armed Conflicts of a Non-International Character,' 49.
142   Bruce Broomhall, *International Justice and the International Criminal Court: Between Sovereignty and the Rule of Law* (Oxford: Oxford University Press, 2003), 96.
143   Frédéric Mégret, 'Should Rebels Be Amnestied?,' in *Jus Post Bellum: Mapping the Normative Foundations*, ed. Carsten Stahn, Jennifer Easterday, and Jens Iverson (Oxford: Oxford University Press, 2014), 539.
144   ICRC, *Commentary of 1987 on Protocol Additional II* (Geneva, 1987), para. 4618.
145   Charles Garraway, 'The Relevance of *Jus Post Bellum*: A Practitioner's Perspective,' ed. Carsten Stahn and Jann Kleffner (The Hague: T.M.C. Asser Press, 2008), 159.
146   Gerhard Werle, *Principles of International Criminal Law* (Oxford: Oxford University Press, 2014), 89.
147   Michael Scharf, 'The Letter of the Law: The Scope of the International Legal Obligation to Prosecute Human Rights Crimes,' *Law and Contemporary Problems* 59, no. 4 (1996): 41. On this line, Jeffery describes the essentially political functional purpose of amnesties Renée Jeffery, *Amnesties, Accountability, and Human Rights* (Philadelphia: University of Pennsylvania Press, 2014), 35–49.

legislation or peace agreements.[148] In none of these cases the international community asked for conditions or limitations for those amnesties.

However, the UN approach to amnesties changed right after the conclusion of the 1998 ICC Statute. In 1999 the Lomé Peace Agreement in Sierra Leone included an unconditional and complete amnesty for the rebels.[149] The agreement was signed by international witnesses, including the Special Representative of the UN Secretary-General, who appended a disclosure stating that the UN would understand the amnesty provision contained in the agreement as not applicable to international crimes of genocide, crimes against humanity, and war crimes.[150] After a resumption of hostilities, and mediating a request from the government to the UN, the Special Court for Sierra Leone was set up in 2002 to try people responsible for international crimes committed during the armed conflict.[151]

On this point, the ICRC highlights that even though Article 6(5) of Additional Protocol II does not mention any exclusion, the provision "could not be construed to enable war criminals, or those guilty of crimes against humanity, to evade punishment."[152] As such, the customary rule on amnesties at the end of

---

148 See UN Security Council Resolutions 473 (1980), 1055 (1996), 1064 (1996), 1120 (1997); UN General Assembly Resolutions 47/141 (1992), 48/152 (1993), 49/207 (1994).

149 Art. IX.3 of the 19 May 1999 Lomé Agreement: "To consolidate the peace and promote the cause of national reconciliation, the Government of Sierra Leone shall ensure that no official or judicial action is taken against any member of the RUF, ex-AFRC, ex-SLA or CDF in respect of anything done by them in pursuit of their objectives as members of those organizations." Available at Peace Accords Matrix, https://peaceaccords.nd.edu/provision/amnesty-lom-peace-agreement.

150 In his Seventh Report on the UN Observer Mission in Sierra Leone, the Secretary-General stated that "I instructed my special representative to sing the agreement with the explicit proviso that the United Nations holds the understanding that the amnesty and pardon in article IX of the agreement shall not apply to international crimes of genocide, crimes against humanity, war crimes and other serious violations of humanitarian law" Seventh Report of the Secretary-General on the United Nations Observer Mission in Sierra Leona, Security Council, UN Doc. S/1999/836, 30 July 1999, para. 7. For a discussion on this UN disclosure see William Schabas, 'Amnesty, the Sierra Leone Truth and Reconciliation Commission and the Special Court for Sierra Leone,' *University of California Davis Journal of International Law and Policy* 11 (2004): 145–169; Simon Chesterman, 'Rough Justice: Establishing the Rule of Law in Post-Conflict Territories,' *Ohio State Journal on Dispute Resolution* 20, no. 1 (2005): 69–98.

151 UN Security Council Resolution 1315 (2000), UN. Doc. S/RES/1315 (2000).

152 Henckaerts and Doswald-Beck, *Customary International Humanitarian Law. Volume I: Rules*, 612. The ICRC endorses this opinion noting that it was expressed by the URSS delegation during the Diplomatic Conference leading to the adoption of the Additional Protocols on 7 June 1976.

NIACs must be in harmony with the customary duty to prosecute crimes prohibited under international law,[153] as the following items show.

3.1.2 The Duty to Prosecute International Crimes

Current international law has established a state's duty to prosecute serious violations of human rights and IHL. This obligation is explicitly enshrined by the 1949 Geneva Conventions,[154] the 1948 Genocide Convention,[155] the 1984 Convention against Torture,[156] and the 2006 Convention against Enforced Disappearance.[157] According to these conventions, states parties have the international obligation to bring to justice people under their jurisdiction who have committed conducts prohibited by those instruments.

The rationale behind this duty is that international crimes constitute offenses to humanity, and their prosecution is a matter of international concern to prevent impunity on those conducts.[158] As such, the UNSC created the

---

153 Henckaerts and Doswald-Beck, *Customary International Humanitarian Law. Volume I: Rules*. Rules 158 and 159. At this point, Rule 159 explicitly includes the exception: "At the end of hostilities, the authorities in power must endeavor to grant the broadest possible amnesty to persons who have participated in a non-international armed conflict, or those deprived of their liberty for reasons related to the armed conflict, with the exception of persons suspected of, accused of or sentenced for war crimes."

154 First Geneva Convention, Article 49; Second Geneva Convention, Article 50; Third Geneva Convention, Article 129; Fourth Geneva Convention, Article 146.

155 'Convention on the Prevention and Punishment of the Crime of Genocide' (1948). Articles 1 and 7.

156 'Convention against Torture and Other Cruel, Inhuman or Degrading Treatment or Punishment,' Pub. L. No. General Assembly Resolution 39/46 (1984). Article 7. At this point, the Committee against Torture has expressly affirmed the incompatibility of amnesty laws for acts of torture with the obligations enshrined by the Convention. See Conclusions and Recommendations Azerbaijan, A/55/44, para. 69 (17 November 1999); Peru, A/55/44, para. 61 (15 November 1999).

157 'International Convention for the Protection of All Persons from Enforced Disappearance' (2006). Articles 6, 7 and 11.

158 Grant Niemann, 'International Criminal Law Sentencing Objectives,' in *Criminal Justice in International Society*, ed. Willem de Lint, Marinella Marmo, and Nerida Chazal (New York: Routledge, 2014), 135. In this line, talking about crimes against humanity, the ICTY stated that: "Crimes against humanity are serious acts of violence which harm human beings by striking what is most essential to them: their life, liberty, physical welfare, health, and dignity. They are inhumane acts that by their extent and gravity go beyond the limits tolerable to the international community, which must perforce demand their punishment. But crimes against humanity also transcend the individual because when the individual is assaulted, humanity comes under attack and is negated. It is therefore the concept of humanity as victim which essentially characterises crimes against humanity." ICTY, Prosecutor v. Erdemovic, Sentencing Judgment, Case No. IT-96-22T (November 29, 1996), para. 28.

International Criminal Tribunals for former Yugoslavia[159] and for Rwanda[160] to prosecute international crimes committed in those contexts. Later, this idea was codified in a permanent way in the 1998 Statute of the ICC, to ensure that when the involved state does not prosecute international crimes, an international court will assume such a task.

Connecting this duty of prosecution with the prohibition to grant amnesties for serious violations of human rights and IHL has been a contribution of the jurisprudence of international human rights courts and bodies, which have considered such a prohibition as a part of the states' positive obligations under IHRL. Since 1992, the Inter-American System of Human Rights has developed a solid jurisprudence on the prohibition of domestic amnesties for serious crimes.[161] The Inter-American Commission on Human Rights has consistently concluded that laws granting amnesties for serious violations of human rights are incompatible with the Inter-American human rights instruments, deciding cases on Argentina,[162] Chile,[163] El Salvador,[164] Peru,[165] and Uruguay—where

---

159 UN Security Council. Resolution 823(1993), Pub. L. No. S/RES/827.
160 UN Security Council. Resolution 955(1994), Pub. L. No. S/RES/955.
161 As du Bois-Pedain highlights, this jurisprudence constitutes a "regional development that is reflected not only in the jurisprudence of treaty bodies under the American Convention of Human Rights, but also in decisions of the higher courts and in constitutional documents in the region that invalidate amnesty law for serious human rights violations." Antje du Bois-Pedain, *Transitional Amnesty in South Africa* (Cambridge: Cambridge University Press, 2007), 316. In the same line, taking about Latin America, Roht-Arriaza says: "Even if the evidence worldwide is more ambiguous, a rejection of amnesty seems to be the overwhelming trend in this region." Naomi Roht-Arriaza, 'After Amnesties Are Gone: Latin American National Courts and the New Contours of the Fight against Impunity,' *Human Rights Quarterly* 37 (2015): 344.
162 Inter-American Commission on Human Rights, Report No. 28/92, Cases 10.147, 10.181, 10.240, 10.262, 10.309 and 10.311 (Argentina), 2 October 1992.
163 Inter-American Commission on Human Rights, Report No. 34/96, Cases 11.228, 11.229, 11.231 and 11.282 (Chile), Report No. 36/96, Case 10.843, 15 October 1996, para. 105 (Chile), 15 October 1996; Report No. 25/98, Cases 11.505, 11.532, 11.541, 11.546, 11.549, 11.569, 11.572, 11.573, 11.585, 11.595, 11.562, 11.567 and 11.705 (Chile), 7 April 1998, para. 101.
164 Inter-American Commission on Human Rights, Report No. 26/92, Case 10.287, *Las Hojas Massacre* (El Salvador), 24 September 1992; Report No. 1/99, Case 10.480 *Lucio Parada and Others* (El Salvador), 27 January 1999 (In this case the Commission expressly rejected the application of amnesty for violations of IHL, referring that the provision on amnesty enshrined by Art. 6(5) of Additional Protocol I does not apply for violation of the laws of war, see para. 115-116); Report No. 136/99, Case 10.448, *Ignacio Ellacuria S.J. and Others* (El Salvador), 22 December 1999; Report No. 37/00, Case 11.481, *Monsignor Oscar Arnulfo Romero* (El Salvador), 13 April 2000.
165 Inter-American Commission on Human Rights, Report No. 1/96, Case 10.559, *Chumbivilcas* (Peru), 1 March 1996; Report no. 38/97, Case 10.548, *Hugo Bustos Saavedra* (Peru), 16

the law on amnesty was even previously declared constitutional by the Uruguayan Supreme Court and approved by a national referendum.[166] In all those cases, the Commission recommended to the respective states to adopt all necessary measures to clarify the facts and identify those responsible for human rights violations, reversing amnesty and pardon laws.

In 1998, the Inter-American Court of Human Rights defined impunity as "the total lack of investigation, prosecution, capture, trial and conviction of those responsible for violations of the rights protected by the American Convention," and reiterated the correspondent obligation of states to combat it by all legal means at their disposal.[167] Following this jurisprudence, in 2001 the Court concluded that an amnesty law precludes the "access to justice and prevents the victims and their next of kin from knowing the truth and receiving the corresponding reparation."[168] As such, the Court decided that "the said laws lack legal effect and may not continue to obstruct the investigation of the grounds on which this case is based or the identification and punishment of those responsible, nor can they have the same or a similar impact with regard to other cases that have occurred."[169] These decisions had domestic impacts and led states to derogate amnesty laws and prosecute former political and military leaders responsible for human rights abuses in Latin America.[170]

Although previous decisions on the matter were referred to post-dictatorial amnesties, in 2012 the Inter-American Court held the same view regarding amnesties after NIACS. In the case *Massacres of El Mozote* the Court considered that even though Additional Protocol II contemplates amnesties at the end of armed conflict, they cannot be applied to international crimes, as El Salvador

---

October 1997, para. 46-47; Report No. 42/97, Case 10.521, *Angel Escobar Jurador* (Peru), 19 February 1998, para. 32-33.

166 Inter-American Commission on Human Rights, Report 29/92, Cases 10.029, 10.036, 10.145, 10.305, 10.372, 10.373, 10.374 and 10.375 (Uruguay), 2 October 1992.

167 Inter-American Court of Human Rights, Paniagua Morales et al. Case, Judgment of 8 March 1998 (1998), para. 133.

168 Inter-American Court of Human Rights, Barrios Altos v. Peru, Judgement 25 November 2003 (2003), para. 43.

169 Inter-American Court of Human Rights, Judgement 25 November 2003 paragraph 44.

170 Some examples include Argentina (La Nacion, Diputados derogó la obediencia debida, 25 March 1998, https://www.lanacion.com.ar/politica/diputados-derogo-la-obediencia-debida-nid91500, accessed on 10 March 2017); Chile (Publico, Chile deroga el decreto ley de amnistía aprobado por la dictadura, 12 September 2014, https://www.publico.es/internacional/chile-deroga-decreto-ley-amnistia.html, accessed on 10 March 2017); El Salvador (El Nuevo Herald, Supremo salvadoreño deroga Ley de Amnistía, 10 July 2016, https://www.elnuevoherald.com/noticias/mundo/america-latina/article89949847.html, accessed on 10 March 2017).

did through a law of amnesty.[171] Similarly, the Human Rights Committee, in its concluding observations on Lebanon, expressed its concern for the amnesty granted to civilian and military personnel for human rights violations occurred during the civil war. For the Committee, "[s]uch a sweeping amnesty may prevent the appropriate investigation and punishment of the perpetrators of past human rights violations, undermine efforts to establish respect for human rights, and constitute an impediment to efforts undertaken to consolidate democracy."[172] This position was developed in General Comments 20[173] and 31,[174] where the Committee affirmed that failure to bring to justice perpetrators of human rights violations constitutes a separate breach of the ICCPR.

Owing to the consistent development of this obligation, the ICRC has identified the obligation to prosecute war crimes as a customary norm,[175] which has been extended to crimes of genocide and crimes against humanity.[176] Cassese even sustains that "international rules prohibiting and criminalizing a conduct that amounts to the most serious international crimes are peremptory in nature."[177]

These conventional, jurisprudential, and customary elements have therefore raised a prohibition to grant amnesties for international crimes in peace agreements. In his 2004 Report on the Rule of Law and Transitional Justice, the UN Secretary-General recommended: "that peace agreements and Security Council resolutions and mandates: [...] (c) Reject any endorsement of amnesty for genocide, war crimes, or crimes against humanity, [...] [and] ensure that

---

171 Inter-American Court of Human Rights, Case of the Massacres of El Mozote and nearby places v. El Salvador, Judgement of 25 October 2012 paragraphs 283–296, para. 283-296.
172 Human Rights Committee, Concluding Observations on Lebanon, CCPR/C/79/Add.78, 5 May 1997, para. 12.
173 Human Rights Committee, General Comment No. 20: Article 7 ICCPR (Prohibition of torture, or other cruel, inhuman or degrading treatment or punishment) (10 March 1992): "Some States have granted amnesty in respect of acts of torture. Amnesties are generally incompatible with the duty of States to investigate such acts; to guarantee freedom from such acts within their jurisdiction; and to ensure that thy do not occur in the future," para. 15.
174 Human Rights Committee, General Comment No. 31: The Nature of the General Legal Obligation Imposed on States Parties to the Covenant, CCPR/C/21/Rev.1/Add.13 (2004): "As with failure to investigate, failure to bring to justice perpetrators of such violations could in and of itself give raise to a separate breach of the Covenant," para. 18.
175 Henckaerts and Doswald-Beck, *Customary International Humanitarian Law. Volume I: Rules*. Rule 158.
176 Kreß and Grover, 'International Criminal Law Restraints in Peace Talks to End Armed Conflicts of a Non-International Character,' 47.
177 Cassese, 'The Special Court and International Law The Decision Concerning the Lomé Agreement Amnesty,' 1140.

no such amnesty previously granted is a bar to prosecution before any United Nations-created or assisted court."[178] This report reaffirmed the Secretary-General's disclosure regarding the 1999 Sierra Leone's Peace Agreement. Developing this notion, the 2005 UN Updated Set of Principles to Combat Impunity reiterated that: "[e]ven when intended to establish conditions conducive to a peace agreement or to foster national reconciliation, amnesty cannot benefit the perpetrators of serious crimes under international law."[179]

3.2 Conciliating Peace and Justice in Peace Negotiations

From the legal framework presented above, we can conclude that both amnesties at the end of NIACs and criminal accountability for international crimes are normatively supported and required in peace negotiations.[180] On the one hand, to negotiate peace some level of amnesty is necessary. On the other hand, to protect the rule of law and victim's rights, justice must be ensured for serious violations of human rights and IHL. Conciliating this tension in a negotiated transition from armed conflict to peace is a central challenge in NIACs.[181]

On this topic, the 2008 Nuremberg Declaration on Peace and Justice noted how the fight against impunity became a principle of international law that "has changed the parameters for the pursuit of peace."[182] However, the Declaration highlights that peace and justice must be complementary, and the "question can never be whether to pursue justice, but rather when and how." In a similar view, former UN Secretary-General Ban Ki-Moon pointed out in 2009 that: "the debate on how to 'reconcile' peace and justice or how to 'sequence' them has lasted more than a decade. Today, we have achieved a conceptual

---

178   UN Secretary-General, 'Report of the Secretary-General on the Rule of Law and Transitional Justice in Conflict and Post-Conflict Societies,' para. 64.
179   UN Commission on Human Rights, 'Updated Set of Principles for the Protection and Promotion of Human Rights through Action to Combat Impunity,' Pub. L. No. E/CN.4/2005/102/Add.1 (2005). Principle 24. On this line, Kulkarni presents an overview into the recent developments on criminal justice for conflict-related violations, noting that impunity continues to weaken due to a growing acceptance of the duty of states to prosecute international crimes, and the consideration of amnesties for such crimes as not legally valid. Anupma Kulkarni, 'Criminal Justice for Conflict-Related Violations. Developments during 2014,' in *Peace and Conflict 2016*, ed. David Backer, Ravi Bhavnani, and Paul Huth (New York: Routledge, 2016), 192–209.
180   Bell, *On the Law of Peace*, 241.
181   Negotiated transitions face many constraints. This book is mainly focused on the normative and political aspects to be considered. For an overview on other constraints influencing transitions, see Jon Elster, *Closing the Books: Transitional Justice in Historical Perspective* (Cambridge: Cambridge University Press, 2004), 188–215.
182   UN General Assembly, Nuremberg Declaration on Peace and Justice. Principle 2.

breakthrough: the debate is no longer between peace and justice but between peace and what kind of justice."[183]

Defining the levels and conditions of justice is a serious challenge in negotiated transitions. In a peace process ending a NIAC, four basic premises must be considered when deciding how to deal with crimes committed during the conflict. First, parties in negotiation, even if responsible for serious crimes, will hardly accept prison as a result of their talks.[184] Second, even if a state wanted to pursue all the crimes committed during the conflict, their dimension generally exceeds its prosecutorial capacities.[185] Third, amnesties are a fundamental legal instrument in transition, but at the current state of international law they only can be granted for offenses other than international crimes. Four, the multiplicity of actors and factors involved in a NIAC makes retributive justice insufficient for the needs of political and social reconciliation.

On this point, we could differentiate two levels of amnesty. For people involved in minor crimes related to armed conflict, full and unconditional amnesty is allowed. But in other cases, in principle, amnesties could only be admitted if they are conditioned to revealing truth and cooperating with reparation and reconciliation.[186] That was the South African approach, where

---

183   Ban Ki-Moon, 'Secretary-General's Remarks on the 60th Anniversary of the Geneva Conventions' (Ministerial Working Session hosted by the Government of Switzerland to mark the 60th Anniversary of the Geneva Conventions, Geneva, 26 September 2009), https://www.un.org/sg/en/content/sg/statement/2009-09-26/secretary-generals-remarks-ministerial-working-session-hosted (accessed on 15 June 2018).

184   Goldstone notes how negotiations would had been impossible in South Africa if those responsible for the apartheid had been expected to go to prison. Richard Goldstone, 'Past Human Rights Violations: Truth Commissions and Amnesties or Prosecutions,' *Northern Ireland Legal Quarterly* 51, no. 2 (2000): 168.

185   In this line, the Sierra Leone Truth and Reconciliation Commission notes that even if it would be desirable to prosecute perpetrators of serious human rights abuses, "amnesties should not be excluded entirely from the mechanisms available to those attempting to negotiate a cessation of hostilities after periods of brutal armed conflict. Disallowing amnesty in all cases would be to deny the reality of violent conflict and the urgent need to bring such strife and suffering to an end." Sierra Leone Truth and Reconciliation Commission Reports, vol. 3B, Chapter 6, "The TRC and the Special Court for Sierra Leone," p. 365, para. 11.

186   As noted by Braithwaite, "there is no objection in principle to amnesties following wars, so long as they are amnesties that contribute to the ending of war, so long as all stakeholders are given a voice in the amnesty negotiations, so long as those who benefit from amnesties are willing to show public remorse for their crimes and to commit to service to the new nation and its people to repair some of the harm they have done." John Braithwaite, *Restorative Justice & [and] Responsive Regulation* (Oxford: Oxford University Press, 2002), 203. In the same line, the Transitional Justice Institute notes that "*opinio juris* from domestic and hybrid courts together with state practice on amnesties does not reflect an

amnesties were internationally admitted because of their contribution to contain and prevent future human rights violations,[187] and to achieve full disclosure of all relevant facts.[188]

Following that experience, several transitional processes around the world have incorporated truth commissions to deal with past human rights violations, granting amnesties in exchange of contributing to truth and reconciliation.[189] This practice is grounded on the concept of restorative justice,[190] which proposes a comprehensive approach to justice aimed at restoring the relationships between the perpetrator, the victim, and the society, instead of just punishing the first.[191] At the time that consensus around the complementarity between peace and justice has been achieved, most authors agree that in post-conflict contexts judicial responses are insufficient.[192] As Freeman and

---

established, explicit and categorical customary prohibition of amnesties for international crimes;" and they are legitimate when offenders are required to contribute to truth, reparation, and reconciliation. Transitional Justice Institute, *The Belfast Guidelines on Amnesty and Accountability* (Belfast: University of Ulster, 2013), 12.

187   du Bois-Pedain, *Transitional Amnesty in South Africa*, 335.
188   Henckaerts and Doswald-Beck, *Customary International Humanitarian Law. Volume I: Rules*. Rule 159.
189   Kerry Clamp, *Restorative Justice in Transition* (London: Routledge, 2014), 71.
190   Porter points out that if the purpose is to achieve peace, restorative justice seems more adequate than retributive justice. This is the approach we should follow if the idea is to "give priority to victims in need of healing" and "building or restoring reconciled relationships" Elisabeth Porter, *Peacebuilding: Women in International Perspective* (London: Routledge, 2007), 20. In this line, Orozco Abad notes that in contexts of horizontal violence–where different actors are responsible of causing the violence, as it is the case of Colombia–, restorative mechanisms must prevail. Iván Orozco Abad, *Sobre Los Límites de La Conciencia Humanitaria: Dilemas de La Paz y La Justicia En América Latina* (Bogotá: Temis, 2005).
191   Rachel Kerr and Eirin Mobekk, *Peace and Justice: Seeking Accountability after War* (Cambridge: Polity, 2007); Porter, *Connecting Peace, Justice and Reconciliation*, 14. Ambos, 'The Legal Framework of Transitional Justice,' 23. On the idea of retributive justice as opposed to the needs of peace in transitional contexts, May notes that "Justice and peace are often discussed as opposed to each other. But the debate can be cashed out in terms of justice alone [...]. The justice that is sometimes opposed to peace is retributive justice." Larry May, 'Reparation, Restitution, and Transitional Justice,' in *Morality, Jus Post Bellum, and International Law*, ed. Larry May and Andrew Forcehimes (Cambridge: Cambridge University Press, 2012), 39.
192   As noted by Goldstone, "One must not expect too much from justice, for justice is merely one aspect of many-faceted approach needed to secure enduring peace in the transitional society." Richard Goldstone, 'Justice as a Tool for Peace-Making: Truth Commissions and International Criminal Tribunals,' *New York University Journal of International Law and Politics* 28, no. 3 (1996): 486. See also Sanam Anderlini, *Women Building Peace: What They Do, What It Matters* (Boulder: Lynne Rienner, 2007), 186.

Djukic argue, "transitional justice is about the pursuit of a responsible form of justice that takes into account the parallel need for peace, democracy, security, and economic growth, precisely in order to deliver a form of justice worthy of the appellation."[193] Pursuing this broad set of goals, criminal retribution has generally been excluded from peace agreements.

Some authors argue that conditional amnesties could even play the function of punishment, when they are aimed at contributing to reconciliation, restoration of the rule of law,[194] and creating a public record of past abuses.[195] For Mallinder, practice shows that international courts' rejection to amnesties has "focused on automatic, unconditional amnesties that aimed to prevent investigations into human rights violations," but it does not refer to conditional amnesties.[196]

However, at the current development of international law, the admissibility of conditional amnesties for serious crimes is not clear. A blanket amnesty will never satisfy the complementarity test before the ICC.[197] But it seems that, at present, not even a conditional amnesty will do so. In a letter sent in 2013 to the Colombian Constitutional Court during the exam of an amendment on transitional justice, the ICC Prosecutor affirmed that if a suspension of the criminal sanction implies that the most responsible for serious crimes do not spend time in prison, it would not satisfy the requirements of the ICC Statute.[198] Two years later, in a more moderated position, the ICC Deputy Prosecutor affirmed in a

---

193 Freeman and Djukic, '*Jus Post Bellum* and Transitional Justice,' 216.
194 Ruti Teitel, *Transitional Justice* (Oxford: Oxford University Press, 2000), 54.
195 du Bois-Pedain, *Transitional Amnesty in South Africa*, 322.
196 Louise Mallinder, 'Can Amnesties and International Justice Be Reconciled?,' *International Journal of Transitional Justice* 1 (2007): 228. In another view on this point, Jeffery notes that generally amnesties have been overturned, circumvented or annulled in contexts where such a decision does not represent a risk to bring back conflict. Jeffery, *Amnesties, Accountability, and Human Rights*, 169.
197 Kreß and Grover, 'International Criminal Law Restraints in Peace Talks to End Armed Conflicts of a Non-International Character,' 70.
198 Prosecutor of the ICC. Letter of 26 July 2013. Constitutional Court, of 26 July 2013, para. 3.16.1: "*En vista de que la suspensión de una pena de prisión significa que el acusado no pase tiempo encarcelado, deseo aconsejarle que esta sería manifiestamente inadecuada en el caso de quienes parecen ser los máximos responsables por la comisión de crímenes de guerra y comisión de lesa humanidad. Una decisión de suspender las penas de cárcel de estas personas podría sugerir que los procesos se llevaran a cabo, o bien con el propósito de sustraer a las personas de que se trate de su responsabilidad penal, de conformidad con los artículos 17(2)(a) y 20(3)(a) o alternativamente que los procesos hayan sido instruidos de manera que, dadas las circunstancias, fueren incompatibles con la intención de someter a las personas a la acción de la justicia, conforme a lo establecido en los artículos 17(2)(c) y 20 (3)(b)*".

conference in Colombia that in contexts of negotiated transitions alternative sentences could be applied. In this case, the complementarity test must consider, among other elements, "the type and degree of restrictions on liberty."[199]

Hence, even though the 2015 Deputy Prosecutor's position is softer than the 2013 Prosecutor's letter, both reflect that, in their opinion, an effective sanction is required by the ICC Statute, even mediating a peace negotiation. And, while for the Deputy Prosecutor prison time is not an indispensable punishment in transitional contexts, effective restrictions on liberty must be applied. As a result, those elements would mean that conditional amnesties, even if submitted to their recipients' contribution to truth and reparation, are no longer enough to satisfy the duty to prosecute international crimes.

In summary, according to the elements discussed above, rather than conditional amnesties current ICL would only admit alternative sanctions, conditioned on offenders contributing to truth, reparation, and reconciliation in transitional contexts.[200] Additionally, even if those sanctions assume a restorative approach, they would necessarily imply a restriction of liberty. And, to do so, a judicial process is required. In other words, regarding serious international crimes the practice of conditional amnesties generally granted through truth commissions would no longer be possible. A judicial process would be needed, in which a sentence is pronounced establishing restrictions on liberty—though not necessarily prison—in addition to restorative measures. This approach was adopted in Colombia, as the following item shows.

3.3 *The Colombian Approach: A Negotiated System of Criminal Justice*

During the late 1980s and early 1990s Colombia held peace negotiations with guerrilla groups who accepted demobilization in exchange for amnesties and political participation.[201] At that time, as the general practice around the

---

[199] James Stewart, Deputy ICC Prosecutor, 'Transitional Justice in Colombia and the Role of the International Criminal Court,' 13 May 2015, 13, https://www.icc-cpi.int/iccdocs/otp/otp-stat-13-05-2015-ENG.pdf (accessed on 8 February 2018).

[200] See on alternative sanctions Roht-Arriaza, 'After Amnesties Are Gone: Latin American National Courts and the New Contours of the Fight against Impunity,' 344; Louise Mallinder, 'The End of Amnesty or Regional Overreach? Interpreting the Erosion of South America's Amnesty Laws,' *International and Comparative Law Quarterly* 65, no. 3 (2016): 649.

[201] To have a look into these processes, see Marc Chernick, 'Negotiating Peace amid Multiple Forms of Violence: The Protracted Search for a Settlement to the Armed Conflicts in Colombia,' in *Comparative Peace Processes in Latin America*, ed. Cynthia Arnson (Stanford: Stanford University Press, 1999), 159–99.

world, amnesties were unconditional, regardless of the nature or scope of the crimes committed by their beneficiaries.

A new demobilization process with paramilitary groups occurred in 2003. By then, Colombia was already part of the ICC Statute, which, in combination with a consistent Inter-American jurisprudence against impunity, put pressure on the government to ensure higher criminal accountability. As a result, the 2005 Peace and Justice Law was adopted establishing a system of criminal responsibility with lenient prison sanctions in exchange for contributing to peace.

During the 2012–2016 peace negotiations between the government and the FARC guerrilla, the discussion on criminal justice was a complex matter. The ICL framework, the Inter-American jurisprudence on human rights, the precedent of the Justice and Peace Law, the political character of the guerrilla, and the active role played by the Office of the ICC Prosecutor and by national and international NGOs, led to an unprecedented and sophisticated system of criminal justice, set as a part of a comprehensive framework for truth, justice, and reparation.

This item will present a general overview into the precedent of the Justice and Peace Law, and then it will present the system of criminal justice set up by the 2016 Peace Agreement.

3.3.1   The Precedent of the Justice and Peace Law

Unlike the political character of the negotiations with the guerrilla in Colombia, the process involving paramilitary groups between 2003 and 2005 was basically a deal for demobilization in exchange for judicial and socio-economic benefits.[202] There was no discussion on the causes of conflict, or political, economic, and social reforms. At that time, the government in office did not even recognize the existence of an armed conflict in Colombia but just a terrorist threat against the State.[203]

Designing a legal framework for this process, in August 2003 the government presented to the Congress a law project on alternative penalties.[204] It

---

202   Alto Comisionado para la Paz, Acuerdo de Santa Fe de Ralito para Contribuir a la Paz de Colombia, 15 July 2003, http://www.altocomisionadoparalapaz.gov.co/acuerdos/acuerdos_t/jul_15_03.htm, accessed on 20 April 2017.

203   Hernando Salazar, "Colombia decide si reconoce la existencia de un conflicto armado," BBC Mundo, (11 May 2011), available at: http://www.bbc.com/mundo/noticias/2011/05/110511_colombia_impliaciones_reconocimiento_conflicto_armado_jrg (accessed on 6 August 2017).

204   Congreso de la República de Colombia, Gaceta Oficial, Proyecto de Ley Estatutaria 85 de 2003 Senado, accessed on 3 March 2017.

was not the outcome of a negotiation among the parties—the government and the paramilitaries—but an instrument proposed by the government to facilitate demobilization. The project established the conditional suspension of penalties to members of armed groups participating in peace talks by the discretional decision of the President of the Republic, on the condition of contributing to victims' reparation and informing changes of residence. There was no real mechanism of accountability but an incentive for demobilization. In Saffon and Uprimny's words, the project "consisted in a concession of legal pardons to all armed actors who accepted to demobilize, and was based on the restorative idea that criminal punishment did not contribute and could even become an obstacle for achieving reconciliation."[205]

Said project was largely criticized by human rights national and international organizations, which denounced it as an impunity bill.[206] As a result, the government withdrew the project from Congress.[207]

A new initiative was promoted by some congresspeople gathering views from academia, victims, and human rights sectors.[208] The new called Justice and Peace Law project "passed from one of absolute rejection of criminal punishment and total silence on victim's rights to an admission of the importance of achieving equilibrium between peace needs and justice requirements."[209] This law was approved in 2005,[210] and later passed the Constitutional Court's control, which balanced the law with constitutional and international standards.[211]

The Law created a system of criminal trial for demobilized not eligible for amnesty. The process included investigation, trial, and sentences according to ordinary criminal law, with penalties that could amount up to 60 years in prison. But because of the accused's contribution to peace, the sentence included an alternative punishment of prison between a minimum of 5 and a

---

205 Saffon and Uprimny, 'Uses and Abuses of Transitional Justice in Colombia,' 366.
206 For a comprehensive analysis on the project of alternative penalties and the main legal critics to it, see Catalina Botero, *La Ley de Alternatividad Penal y Justicia Transicional* (Bogota: DeJusticia, 2004).
207 Verdad Abierta, Procesos de Justicia y Paz, https://verdadabierta.com/la-historia/periodo4/justicia-y-paz (accessed on 10 February 2016).
208 Pablo Kalmanovitz, 'Introduction: Law and Politics in the Colombian Negotiations with Paramilitary Groups,' in *Law in Peace Negotiations*, ed. Morten Bergsmo and Pablo Kalmanovitz (Oslo: Torkel Opsahl Academic EPublisher, 2010), 4–5.
209 Saffon and Uprimny, 'Uses and Abuses of Transitional Justice in Colombia,' 366.
210 Congreso de la República de Colombia, 'Ley 975 (Ley de Justicia y Paz)' (2005).
211 Corte Constitucional de Colombia, Sentencia C-370/06 (18 May 2006).

maximum of 8 years in prison.[212] Thus, instead of conditional amnesties, the Law created a system of conditional reduced penalties.

From a total of 24.640 people demobilized under the process, 3.666 were submitted to this Law. At the end of 2015 more than 50.000 crimes had been admitted, but only 33 sentences had been pronounced in 10 years.[213] However, beyond the practical difficulties during the implementation of the Law, scholars generally admit that the system of conditional reduced penalties meets international standards on justice. Burbidge says that the rule of 5–8 years of prison seems balanced, as excessive sentences or excessive leniency could affect the intention of the perpetrators to continue in the negotiation in one side, and in the other make peace fragile. He also considers that the fact that the Law was approved by the Congress, controlled by the Constitutional Court, and the accused were judged and punished in due form, regardless of the duration of the sentence, makes an ICC intervention unlikely.[214] On this point, Ambos argues that the requirements of the complementarity test set by Article 17 of the ICC Statute were met, since the mitigation of punishment did not preclude neither an investigation nor a prosecution.[215]

This law set up a high standard of criminal accountability in Colombia, owing to the relevant international legal norms and discourses brought to the discussion by different actors. However, even if expected by most people, it was not possible to apply the same system to the guerrilla. As noted, the paramilitary groups demobilized under a framework of submission to justice in exchange for benefits. On the contrary, the guerrilla wanted a political deal, addressing the root causes of conflict, in which they defended the justness of their fight. As such, a new mechanism was necessary.

3.3.2   The Special Jurisdiction for Peace

In 2012 the Government and the FARC agreed on a negotiation agenda, in which no reference to justice or accountability was included. In item 3.3 the agenda said that the government would review the situation of members of the guerrilla detained or sentenced, and in item 4 the parties agreed to discuss the rights of victims.[216] Moreover, the guerrilla leaders openly rejected

---

212 Congreso de la República de Colombia, Ley 975 (Ley de Justicia y Paz), 2005 Article 29.
213 Verdad Abierta, '¿Qué Nos Dejan 10 Años de Justicia y Paz?,' Verdad Abierta, 2015, http://www.verdadabierta.com/especiales-v/2015/justicia-paz-10/ (accessed on 1 April 2018).
214 Peter Burbidge, 'Justice and Peace?—The Role of Law in Resolving Colombia's Civil Conflict,' *International Criminal Law Review* 8, no. 3 (2008): 576.
215 Ambos, 'The Legal Framework of Transitional Justice,' 80.
216 Gobierno de Colombia and FARC, 'Acuerdo General Para La Terminación Del Conflicto y La Construcción de Una Paz Estable y Duradera.'

any notion of individual responsibility. They claimed collective responsibility, and that if any form of justice had to be applied it should be social justice.[217] However, the guerrilla's position on this matter profoundly changed during the negotiation process. And it happened because of their understanding of applicable international standards, a task in which different national and international actors played a crucial role.[218]

As the guerrilla wanted an agreement grounded on international law, and even to be considered as an international legal accord, they finally understood that its content had to be substantially consistent with international legal standards. On this point, several elements and actors draw attention to relevant legal norms. First, the precedent of the Justice and Peace Law set up a high standard on criminal responsibility which was difficult to lower. Second, as noted above, the Office of the ICC Prosecutor actively reminded Colombia of its obligations under the ICC Statute to pursue international crimes. This pressure was reinforced by the fact that the Prosecutor has kept Colombia under preliminary examination since 2004.[219] Third, the participation of a UN Secretary-General's Special Representative during the negotiations should have brought to the table the UN position regarding the impossibility to grant amnesties for serious crimes, even in peace processes.[220] Forth, several human rights organizations widely insisted on the obligation to ensure victims' rights to truth, justice, and reparation.

As such, the Final Agreement developed a Comprehensive System of Truth, Justice, Reparation, and Non-Repetition, within its chapter on victims.[221] Regarding justice, a Special Jurisdiction for Peace was created. For that, the Agreement declared that according to international law, states emerging from armed conflict have the autonomy to adopt the mechanisms of justice that respond to the complexities of the context, provided that they respect international human rights parameters.[222] Then, the Agreement affirmed that the Special Jurisdiction for Peace was inspired by a restorative justice approach.[223]

---

217 Nelson Camilo Sanchez, 'Could the Colombian Peace Accord Trigger an ICC Investigation on Colombia?,' *American Journal of International Law* 110 AJIL Unbound Symposium on the Colombian Peace Talks and International Law (2016): 110.
218 A detailed analysis on the actors and discourses bringing international law elements to the peace process and its agreement will be offered in Chapter 3.
219 The Office of the Prosecutor, 'Report on Preliminary Examination Activities 2016' (The Hague: International Criminal Court, 2016), para. 231.
220 UN Secretary-General, 'Report of the Secretary-General on the Rule of Law and Transitional Justice in Conflict and Post-Conflict Societies,' para. 64.
221 Government of Colombia and FARC, 'Final Agreement to End the Armed Conflict and Build a Stable and Lasting Peace,' 132.
222 Government of Colombia and FARC, 144.
223 Government of Colombia and FARC, 144.

Defining the content and scope of the Special Jurisdiction, the Agreement invoked international law as the jurisdiction's main framework of reference.[224] The deal established that for the qualification and treatment of crimes under this jurisdiction, in addition to the Colombian Criminal Code, judges must consider the applicable norms of IHRL, IHL, and ICL.[225] As such, the Agreement invokes article 6(5) of Additional Protocol II restraining its application to conducts for which international law does not prohibit amnesty;[226] and following this line, the Agreement excluded from amnesty conducts defined as international crimes by the ICC Statute.[227]

The Special Jurisdiction for Peace has competence over guerrilla members, state agents, and civilians who directly or indirectly participated in the commission of crimes related to armed conflict.[228] Regarding sanctions when amnesty is not possible, the Tribunal can define different types of punishments, according to the accused's admission of truth and responsibility. Only those who fully cooperate with the process, provide truth and acknowledge responsibility, will receive restorative sanctions—e.g. working in demining, substitution of crops of illicit use, and construction of public infrastructure—accompanied by restrictions on liberty of movement and residence for a period of 2 to 8 years, depending on their level of responsibility. Those who do not provide the truth or accept responsibility, and are found guilty, will receive prison sentences.

This model of criminal accountability is the result of adapting to the context international legal norms, legal discourses, and related practices relevant to amnesty and criminal responsibility under international law. As seen in the Colombian case, no specific formula was taken as such from international law, but a particular model was designed interpreting and applying to the context the myriad of legal elements brought to the negotiations by several actors and considering the previous mechanisms of transitional justice adopted in the country. The frame in which such a normative process happens is *jus post bellum*.

---

[224] The Special Jurisdiction for Peace's statutory law states that its main framework of reference is given by IHRL and IHL. Cfr. Congreso de la República de Colombia, Ley 1957 de 2019, Art. 23: "[...] los marcos jurídicos de referencia incluyen principalmente el Derecho Internacional en materia de Derechos Humanos (DIDH) y el Derecho Internacional Humanitario (DIH)."

[225] Government of Colombia and FARC, 147.

[226] Government of Colombia and FARC, 148, 150.

[227] Government of Colombia and FARC, 151.

[228] A ruling of the Constitutional Court said later that civilians could be investigated and tried by this Special Jurisdiction only if they voluntarily decide so. Corte Constitucional, Sentencia C-674-17 (2017).

4 Reparations for Victims

Reparation for victims is a critical component of transition from armed conflict to peace. At least two reasons explain the relevance of reparations in transition. First, the growing development of IHRL has provided a clear framework on reparations for serious violations of human rights, applicable to contexts of armed conflict. Second, the shift from a retributive to a restorative approach to justice in transitions to peace enhanced the role of reparations. While a retributive approach to transition is mainly rooted in the punishment of the offender, a restorative approach focuses on the redress of victims.[229]

Colombia has made significant efforts to provide reparations for victims of armed conflict, even without any peace process ongoing. Before the 2012–2016 peace talks with the FARC, the government promoted, and the Congress adopted, the 2011 Law on Victims and Land Restitution, which is considered the most developed system of reparations ever conceived in the world.[230] Now, the 2016 Peace Agreement adopted a Comprehensive System of Truth, Justice, and Reparations, which incorporates the 2011 Law on Victims.[231] Both instruments are largely and explicitly based on international law.

In this way, this section is aimed at analyzing the role of international law regarding the development of a system of reparations for transition in Colombia. To this purpose, the section is divided into two parts. First, it presents the international legal framework on reparations for victims of armed conflict. Second, it discusses the Colombian system of reparations, and how it incorporates international standards notwithstanding the challenge of repairing several millions of victims.

4.1 *Legal Framework on Reparations for Victims of Armed Conflict*
This item presents the international legal framework on reparations, showing how reparations became an internationally-protected right for victims of violations of human rights and IHL, even in the context of damages occurred during armed conflict.

---

229 Ilaria Bottigliero, *Redress for Victims of Crimes under International Law* (Leiden: Nijhoff, 2004), 34.

230 Unidad de Atención y Reparación a Víctimas, *Universidad de Harvard destaca Política Integral de Reparación de Víctimas en Colombia*, 2015, available at: http://www.unidadvictimas.gov.co/es/valoraci%C3%B3n-y-registro/universidad-de-harvard-destaca-pol%C3%ADtica-integral-de-reparaci%C3%B3n-de-v%C3%ADctimas-en.

231 Government of Colombia and FARC, 'Final Agreement to End the Armed Conflict and Build a Stable and Lasting Peace,' 132.

4.1.1 The Right to Reparation in International Law

Since its paradigmatic decision in the *Chorzów Case*, the former Permanent Court of International Justice stated in 1927 that: "It is a principle of international law and even a general conception of law that any breach of an engagement involves an obligation to make reparation in an adequate form [...] Reparation is the indispensable complement of a failure to apply a convention and there is no necessity for this to be stated in the convention itself."[232]

This notion of reparation was basically referred to restitution and compensation and was historically seen as an inter-state measure.[233] However, the progressive development of IHRL extraordinarily expanded the scope of reparations and brought individuals to the international legal arena as subjects of reparation. Most international human rights treaties include reparation as a fundamental element of the state's obligation to guarantee human rights. Article 8 of the Universal Declaration of Human Rights enshrines the individual right to an effective remedy for any act violating the rights of the people.[234] This provision was translated into a binding instrument through the ICCPR,[235] whose Article 2(3) establishes the right to an effective remedy, which has been interpreted by the Human Rights Committee as involving reparation.[236] It has been similarly enshrined in Article 2(1) of the ICESCR,[237] Article 6 of the International Convention on the Elimination of All Forms of Racial Discrimination (ICERD),[238] Article 2(c) of the Convention on the Elimination of All Forms of Discrimination against Women,[239] Article 14 of the Convention against Torture and Other

---

232 Factory at Chorzów Case (Germany v. Poland), Jurisdiction, 1927, PCIJ, Ser. A, No. 9, p. 21.
233 Christine Evans, *The Right to Reparation in International Law for Victims of Armed Conflict* (Cambridge: Cambridge University Press, 2012), 29.
234 'Universal Declaration of Human Rights,' Pub. L. No. UN Doc. A/810 (1948).
235 International Covenant on Civil and Political Rights.
236 Human Rights Committee, General Comment No. 31, The Nature of General Legal Obligation Imposed on States Parties to the Covenant, CCPR/C/21/Rev.1/Add.13, 2004, para. 16.
237 International Covenant on Economic, Social and Cultural Rights. This Article does not proclaim expressly the right to a remedy in case of violation of the rights enshrined in the Covenant, but only calls states to adopt the measures to grant these rights. Nonetheless, the Committee on Economic, Social and Cultural Rights has interpreted that "[a]mong the measures which might be considered appropriate, in addition to legislation, is the provision of judicial remedies with respect to rights which may, in accordance with the national legal system, be considered justiciable." Committee on Economic, Social and Cultural Rights, General Comment No. 3: The nature of States parties' obligations (Art. 2, par.1) (14 December 1900) UN Doc. E/1991/23.
238 'International Convention on the Elimination of All Forms of Racial Discrimination,' Pub. L. No. General Assembly Resolution 2106 (XX) (1965).
239 'International Convention on the Elimination of All Forms of Discrimination against Women,' Pub. L. No. General Assembly Resolution 34/180 (1979).

INTERNATIONAL LAW IN THE COLOMBIAN TRANSITION 103

Cruel, Inhuman or Degrading Treatment or Punishment,[240] Articles 15(2) and 16(4–5) of the International Labor Organization (ILO) Convention 169,[241] Article 13 of the European Convention on Human Rights,[242] Articles 25 and 63 of the American Convention on Human Rights (AmCHR),[243] and Articles 7, 21, and 26 of the African Charter on Human Rights.[244]

Following such norms, the obligation to provide individual reparation for the violation of human rights has been consistently reaffirmed by different international courts and human rights bodies.[245] The aim behind this duty is related to the state's positive obligations regarding human rights. The violation of a human right entails the state's responsibility towards the individual, because of the state's obligation to respect, to prevent, and to ensure the rights of all people under its jurisdiction, including a remedy when respect and prevention have failed.

Based on human rights treaties and international practice, the UN General Assembly adopted the Basic Principles and Guidelines on the Right to a Remedy and Reparation for Victims of Gross Violations of International Human Rights Law and Serious Violations of International Humanitarian Law,[246] which identified the existing legal obligations in the matter.[247] According to these Basic

---

240 Convention against Torture and Other Cruel, Inhuman or Degrading Treatment or Punishment.
241 'Convention Concerning Indigenous and Tribal Peoples in Independent Countries C169,' § General Conference of the International Labour Organization (1989).
242 European Convention for the Protection of Human Rights and Fundamental Freedoms.
243 American Convention on Human Rights.
244 'African Charter on Human and Peoples' Rights' (1981).
245 See generally, European Court of Human Rights, *Case of Akkus v. Turkey*, Judgment of 9 July 1997; *Case of Kurt v. Turkey* (Merits and Just Satisfaction), Judgment of 25 May 1998; *Case of Doğan and others v. Turkey* (Merits and Just Satisfaction), Judgment of 29 June 2004. In the Inter-American Court of Human Rights, see *Case of Aloeboetoe et al. v. Suriname* (Reparations and Costs), Judgment of September 10, 1993; *Case of the Mayagna (Sumo) Awas Tingni Community v. Nicaragua* (Merits, Reparations and Costs), Judgment of August 31, 2001; *Case of the Moiwana Community v. Suriname* (Preliminary Objections, Merits, Reparations and Costs), Judgment of June 15, 2005; *Case of Yatama v. Nicaragua* (Preliminary Objections, Merits, Reparations and Costs), Judgment of Jun 23, 2005; *Case of the "Mapiripán Massacre" v. Colombia* (Merits, Reparations, and Costs), Judgment of September 15, 2005; *Case of the Yakye Axa Indigenous Community v. Paraguay* (Interpretation of the Judgment of Merits, Reparations and Costs), Judgment of Feb 6, 2006.
246 UN General Assembly, Basic Principles and Guidelines on the Right to a Remedy and Reparation for Victims of Gross Violations of International Human Rights Law and Serious Violations of International Humanitarian Law.
247 In their Preamble, the Basic Principles and Guidelines stress that they "do not entail new international or domestic legal obligations but identify mechanisms, modalities, procedures and methods for the implementation of existing legal obligations under international human rights law and international humanitarian law which are complementary though different as to their norms". UN General Assembly. It is also important to mention

Principles: "victims are persons who individually or collectively suffered harm [...], through acts or omissions that constitute gross violations of international human rights law, or serious violations of international humanitarian law."[248] Additionally, said Principles state that: "A person shall be considered a victim regardless of whether the perpetrator of the violation is identified."[249] The Basic Principles also derivate the right to reparation redressing the harm suffered by victims, from the general obligation to provide an effective remedy for violations of international law. Then, the Principles define reparation as composed by five elements: *restitution*, seeking to restore the victim to the original situation whenever possible;[250] *compensation*, through an economic assessment of the damage;[251] *rehabilitation*, including medical and psychological care as well as legal and social services;[252] *satisfaction*, aimed at restoring the dignity of victims through measures such as public apologies, truth disclosure, search of missing persons, etc.;[253] and *guarantees of non-repetition*, to prevent new violations.[254]

This comprehensive definition of reparation, developed through interpretation and application of different IHRL instruments, was enshrined in a legally binding instrument in the 2007 Convention for the Protection of All Persons from Enforced Disappearance.[255] Under IHL, the obligation to provide reparations has been considered a customary rule both in international and non-international armed conflicts.[256] The ICC Statute also provided that the Court "shall establish principles relating to reparations to, or in respect of, victims, including restitution, compensation, and rehabilitation."[257]

As such, based on the recognition of the right to reparation under different branches of international law, some authors have even argued the customary

---

the 2001 Draft Articles on Responsibility of States for Internationally Wrongful Acts, adopted by the ILC, which embodied the obligation to reparation and its modalities and conditions (see Articles 30-31 and 34-36).

248 UN General Assembly, para. 8.
249 UN General Assembly, para. 9.
250 UN General Assembly, para. 19.
251 UN General Assembly, para. 20.
252 UN General Assembly, para. 21.
253 UN General Assembly, para. 22.
254 UN General Assembly, para. 23.
255 International Convention for the Protection of All Persons from Enforced Disappearance Art. 24.
256 Henckaerts and Doswald-Beck, *Customary International Humanitarian Law. Volume I: Rules*, Rule 150.
257 'Rome Statute of the International Criminal Court' (1998) Art. 75.

character of reparations. For Evans, because of the "extensive recognition of the right of the individual to reparation in human rights and humanitarian law, as well as under general international law, it appears reasonable to state that this right has acquired a degree of recognition as forming part of customary law."[258]

4.1.2 Reparations for Armed Conflict-related Violations of Human Rights and IHL

International human rights norms on reparation were primarily conceived to address individual violations of rights on a case-by-case basis.[259] As noted by Carrillo, "they simply are not configured to deal with gross and systematic violations in the same way."[260] This is a major challenge faced by reparations in contexts of massive violations of human rights and IHL, such as during armed conflict. No state jurisdiction or international system would have the capacity to redress all the victims of armed conflict-related human rights violations under a judicial mechanism for reparation.

There are several factors involved when defining the mechanisms of redress for victims of armed conflict. One could mention the number of victims, their proportion within the total population, the economic situation of the country, the priority given to other transitional justice measures, among other factors. Additionally, the fact of having different actors involved in the conflict, where at least one is a non-state actor, poses challenges as who is responsible for reparations.

Regarding that point, the obligation to pay reparations has been traditionally assigned to the state. Nevertheless, the current development of ICL raised the responsibility of individuals for repairing the damages caused to their victims. It means that non-state armed actors in a NIAC should also pay reparations. The Basic Principles on Reparations establish that a state shall provide reparation to victims for acts or omissions which can be attributed to it, and that when a non-state actor is liable for reparation, such party should repair the victim or compensate the state if the state has already done it. But, again, the Basic Principles conclude that: "States should endeavour to establish national programmes for reparation and other assistance to victims in the

---

258 Evans, *The Right to Reparation in International Law for Victims of Armed Conflict*, 39.
259 Pablo De Greiff, 'Justice and Reparations,' in *The Handbook of Reparations*, ed. Pablo De Greiff (Oxford: Oxford University Press, 2006), 454.
260 Arturo Carrillo, 'Justice in Context: The Relevance of the Inter-American Human Rights Law and Practice to Repairing the Past,' in *The Handbook of Reparations*, ed. Pablo de Greiff (Oxford: Oxford University Press, 2006), 527.

event that the parties liable for the harm suffered are unable or unwilling to meet their obligations."[261]

On this point, the Inter-American Court of Human Rights declared, in the case *Mapiripan Massacre v. Colombia*, that the State was obligated to provide reparation, even if the massacre was committed by a non-state actor. This conclusion was based on the State's lack of due diligence to prevent the massacre, which was its positive obligation according to the AmCHR.[262]

Considering these particularities on reparation for victims of armed conflict, the Association of International Law adopted in 2010 a Declaration of International Law Principles on Reparation for Victims of Armed Conflict.[263] This document provides general guidelines on the matter, defining the holder of the right to reparation, its content, and the parties responsible to pay reparations.[264] On its Commentary to the Declaration, the Association stresses that the legal protection provided by international law to victims of human rights violations and breaches to IHL should not be reduced in contexts of armed conflict. However, the Association admitted that in case of massive violations of rights the conditions and amounts of reparations must regard the capacities of the liable state in post-conflict scenarios.[265] Later, in 2014 the Association adopted a Draft on Procedural Principles for Reparation Mechanisms[266] devoted to the access to effective redress mechanisms.

According to the elements discussed above, the victim's right to reparation must be ensured even when such a right emerges from violations caused within an armed conflict. However, the judicial approach to justice and reparation for individual violations of human rights is not feasible in cases of massive violations of human rights occurred during and armed conflict. In such contexts, systems of reparations must be designed in a way in which international standards are observed, at the time that reparations play a role in a broader

---

[261] UN General Assembly, Basic Principles and Guidelines on the Right to a Remedy and Reparation for Victims of Gross Violations of International Human Rights Law and Serious Violations of International Humanitarian Law, paras 15–16.
[262] Inter-American Court of Human Rights, Case of 'Mapiripán Massacre' v. Colombia, Judgment of 15 September 2005 (2005).
[263] International Law Association, 'Draft Declaration of International Law Principles on Reparation for Victims of Armed Conflict' (2010).
[264] International Law Association Article 5.
[265] See Commentary on Article 5. International Law Association.
[266] International Law Association, 'Draft Procedural Principles For Reparation Mechanisms' (2014).

political agenda, serving as a form of recognition to victims and helping to restore civic trust and reconciliation.[267]

4.2 *Colombian Approach to Reparations*

The international legal framework on reparations presented above has been developed in different ways in Colombia. From judicial to administrative systems of reparation, Colombia has assumed reparations as a victim's rights that must be addressed, regardless of a peace agreement. Since 1997, Colombia set up a program for administrative reparation addressed to victims of terrorism and other facts related to armed conflict.[268] In 2005 a judicial approach to reparation was incorporated into the Justice and Peace Law, which was later complemented with a norm on administrative reparations. Finally, a comprehensive system of reparations was implemented before the 2012–2016 peace negotiations, which could be even considered as an element facilitating the process and the participation of victims in those negotiations. As such, three dimensions of reparation for victims of armed conflict in Colombia must be considered as follows.

4.2.1   Judicial Reparation: Justice and Peace Law

As presented above in the section on criminal justice, in 2005 Colombia adopted the Justice and Peace Law for the demobilization of paramilitary groups. This instrument created a special system of criminal responsibility, granting reduced penalties in exchange for cooperation with justice and reparation to victims. According to Article 2 of this Law, all the system had to be interpreted and applied according to the Colombian Constitution and to international treaties duly ratified by Colombia.

Regarding reparations, the Law established a judicial mechanism of reparation in which reparation was addressed only to victims whose perpetrators were submitted to this judicial system. A Reparations Fund was created, composed by the illegally obtained assets delivered by the demobilized and limiting victim's reparation to the budget of the Fund. However, the Constitutional Court introduced two important changes on this point. First, it said that both legal and illegally obtained assets should be available for the reparation of victims.[269] Second, the Court ruled that no

---

267   De Greiff, 'Justice and Reparations,' 454.
268   Congreso de la República de Colombia, 'Ley 418' (1997).
269   Corte Constitucional de Colombia, Sentencia C-370/06, paragraph 6.2.4.1.11.

budgetary constraint could be used as a State's excuse for giving reparation to a victim.[270]

Nevertheless, such a system of judicial reparation was insufficient for redressing millions of victims affected by armed conflict. Only victims recognized within a criminal procedure were beneficiaries of reparation and it was to the judge to define forms and amounts on a case-by-case basis. For that reason, a program of administrative reparation was later created in 2008,[271] aimed at repairing victims beyond the criminal process through an administrative procedure. The new program allowed more victims to receive reparations. However, although the system predicated comprehensive reparation, it was focused on compensation.

4.2.2 Comprehensive Administrative Reparations: Law on Victims and Land Restitution

In 2011, with the presence of the UN Secretary-General, Colombia adopted an unprecedented Law on Victims and Land Restitution.[272] The Law established a comprehensive system of administrative reparation addressed to all the victims of armed conflict since 1985, which integrated the previous systems. The Law was largely inspired by international law. Its Article 3 defines victims as people who individually or collectively have suffered damage as a consequence of a violation of IHL or IHRL within the armed conflict.

Article 25 defines reparation in the same terms as the UN Basic Principles on Reparations. As such, the Law establishes measures of restitution, compensation, rehabilitation, satisfaction, and guarantees of non-repetition, entirely assumed by the State. To that purpose, the Law created a unified register of victims integrating existing registers and programs of reparation. Up to 1 April 2019, 8.803.836 victims were registered.[273] Additionally, a Unit for the Attention and Reparations of Victims was created, tasked to coordinate the implementation of the Law.

In 2014 the Carr Center for Human Rights Policy at the Harvard Kennedy School compared this system of reparation with other 31 mechanisms adopted

---

270 Corte Constitucional de Colombia, paragraph 6.2.4.3.3.2. For an analysis on this point in the Colombian case, see Julian Guerrero and Mariana Goetz, 'Reparations for Victims in Colombia: Colombia's Law on Justice and Peace,' in *Reparations for Victims of Genocide, War Crimes and Crimes against Humanity: Systems in Place and Systems in the Making*, ed. Carla Ferstman, Mariana Goetz, and Alan Stephens (Leiden: Martinus Nijhoff, 2009), 435–58.
271 Gobierno de Colombia, Decreto 1290 (2008).
272 Congreso de la República de Colombia, Ley 1448 (Ley de Víctimas y Restitución de Tierras).
273 Registro Único de Víctimas, https://www.unidadvictimas.gov.co/es/registro-unico-de-victimas-ruv/37394 (accessed on 1 April 2019).

around the world since 1979.[274] The study concluded that the Colombian system is the most complete ever adopted for reparation of victims of armed conflict in the world, though the Center warned on the challenges to implement it, considering the high number of victims.[275]

4.2.3 Reparations in the 2016 Peace Agreement

Since its preamble, the Agreement states its victim-centered approach and the importance given to the right to reparation, according to international law.[276] There is a chapter on victims, in which a system of truth, justice, and reparation was established. Regarding reparations, the Agreement considers them as a condition for peace, and adopts a comprehensive approach, following international standards on restitution, compensation, rehabilitation, satisfaction, and non-repetition.[277]

The Agreement recognized the existing system of reparations created by the 2011 Law on Victims. Nonetheless, the document proposed to adjust it in a participatory way, and according to the context and opportunities given by the end of armed conflict. Additionally, it stressed on the return of displaced people[278] and collective reparations,[279] where former guerilla members should contribute by doing community work, demining, and offering public apologies.[280] The guerrilla also assumed the obligation to give its assets for the reparation to victims.[281] On this point, reparation by the guerrilla, as a non-state actor, will be mainly related to the judicial procedures before the Special Jurisdiction for Peace, which, as part of the sanctions, will impose measures of reparations under a restorative justice approach.

---

274   Carr Center for Human Rights Policy, 2014. *Evaluation for the Unidad para las Víctimas: global and comparative benchmarking.* Available at http://wp.presidencia.gov.co/Noticias/2014/Octubre/Paginas/20141022_09-Estudio-de-Harvard-concluye-que-Colombia-lider-en-reparacion-victimas-revela-el-PresidenteSanto.aspx (accessed 20 November 2015).

275   The number of victims of armed conflict in Colombia represents around 18% of the total population of the country, which up to May 2019 was estimated in 48.2 million people. Source: http://www.dane.gov.co/index.php/estadisticas-por-tema/demografia-y-poblacion/censo-nacional-de-poblacion-y-vivenda-2018/cuantos-somos/ (accessed on 5 May 2019).

276   Government of Colombia and FARC, 'Final Agreement to End the Armed Conflict and Build a Stable and Lasting Peace,' 2.

277   Government of Colombia and FARC, 129–30.

278   Government of Colombia and FARC, 182.

279   Government of Colombia and FARC, 179.

280   Government of Colombia and FARC, 179.

281   Government of Colombia and FARC, 186.

Here, the Agreement adopted the approach of the offender's primary obligation to provide reparation, and the State's subsidiary role when there is no full reparation from the actor who caused the damage. Regarding this approach, the Agreement explicitly invokes the positive obligations of the State under IHRL.[282] However, on this point, the Colombian approach offers valuable insights on the growing discussion around the role of non-state armed actors regarding reparations in transitions from NIACs. International law is still too general on this matter, but legal basis exists, as seen in the legal framework presented here. Then, practice such as the Colombian would certainly contribute to better understand and apply the obligations of non-state actors on reparations, within and beyond judicial mechanisms.

Here, one can see how international law has framed the debate on reparations for victims of armed conflict in Colombia since 2005. Again, as for criminal responsibility, international law does not provide a specific general formula, but the normative elements that must be addressed to find the appropriate mechanism for a given context. As it will be further analyzed in Chapter 3, such a normative frame guiding the design of a concrete transitional mechanism is the display of *jus post bellum*.

5 Inclusive Transitions

Contemporary negotiations aimed at ending NIACs are no longer a matter to be decided only by the parties directly confronted. In general, the agreement resulting from a peace negotiation has impacts over different groups, and society at large. Thus, those groups should be heard, and their needs be addressed in a differential way in a peace deal. This inclusiveness is increasingly considered a condition of legitimacy, effectiveness, and sustainability of peace agreements.[283]

There are at least three reasons behind the need for inclusivity in transitions to peace. First, just as armed conflict has differential impacts on certain groups—e.g. women and ethnic communities—peace also does so. Second, transition from armed conflict to peace represents an opportunity to address structural discriminatory situations in society, which are generally at the base of the conflict or are exacerbated by it. Third, since parties in a peace process

---

282   Government of Colombia and FARC, 147.
283   Jennifer Easterday, "Peace Agreements as a Framework for *Jus Post Bellum*," in *Jus Post Bellum: Mapping the Normative Foundations*, ed. Carsten Stahn, Jennifer Easterday, and Jens Iverson (Oxford: Oxford University Press, 2014), 399.

discuss changes in the political and social order, it represents an opportunity for the incorporation of citizens into the polity, improving their engagement in the post-agreement scenario.[284]

Thus, given the importance of inclusiveness in peace processes, and the role of international law in peacemaking and peacebuilding, this section discusses if there is any normative obligation to hold inclusive transitions. On this matter, Kastner considers that the inclusion of social actors "is not only advisable from a pragmatic conflict resolution perspective; it has rather become part of the normative framework of peace negotiations and [...] is increasingly being internalized as a legal obligation."[285] Similarly, discussing on *jus post bellum*, Turner pleads for a principle of inclusivity in peace processes, given the requirements of human rights law regarding differential participation and inclusion of certain groups.[286]

This search for inclusivity has been present in transition from armed conflict to peace in Colombia in different ways. Since the normative framework on internally displaced persons, the Constitutional Court requested State institutions to adopt a differential approach in measures addressed to women, indigenous peoples, and Afro-descendants. Following this precedent, the 2011 Law on Victims incorporated a differential approach to women and ethnic communities. Finally, the 2012–2016 peace process with the FARC guerrilla developed unprecedented inclusive mechanisms, addressing different social groups.

This section analyzes to what extent Colombian practice reflects a legal obligation on inclusive transitions to peace, by associating international normativity related to inclusion and participation of certain social groups. For this purpose, it refers to international law provisions regarding both the general state's obligation to promote participation of people on matters of their interest, and the specific duty to include certain social groups in peace processes and agreements.

The section is divided into two parts. The first part presents the international legal framework to support inclusive peace transitions as a legal obligation, rather than a mere political choice. The second part assesses how Colombia

---

[284] Catherine O'Rourke, 'Transitioning to What? Transitional Justice and Gendered Citizenship in Chile and Colombia,' in *Gender in Transitional Justice*, ed. Susane Buckley-Zistel and Ruth Stanley (Basingstoke: Palgrave Macmillan, 2012), 152; Colleen Murphy and Linda Radzik, '*Jus Post Bellum* and Political Reconciliation,' in *Jus Post Bellum and Transitional Justice*, ed. Larry May and Elizabeth Edenberg (New York: Cambridge University Press, 2013), 317.
[285] Kastner, *Legal Normativity in the Resolution of Internal Armed Conflict*, 147.
[286] Turner, "Mapping a Norm of Inclusion in the *Jus Post Bellum*."

has implemented its obligations on inclusiveness when defining attention to victims of armed conflict, and the role that participation and the differential approach played in the 2012–2016 peace process.

5.1 *Legal Framework on Inclusiveness*

International law provides elements to support the demands of certain groups of people to be heard, and their concerns to be included, in peace processes and transitions. The most specific case is the legal regime related to the participation and inclusion of women in peace processes and agreements. However, general provisions are also applicable regarding other social groups, victims, and civil society in general. The following items examine the normative framework regarding these issues.

5.1.1 On Women and Gender Issues

Women suffer gender specific impacts because of armed conflict. Armed confrontation intensifies existing inequalities experienced globally by women and they are "specially affected by sexual violence, internal displacement, loss of family members, reinforced gender stereotypes, loss of social position and reduced access to essential supplies and services."[287] However, negotiating peace has been predominantly a male affair.[288] According to the 2016 Yearbook of Peace Processes, only 10.3% of people officially participating in peace talks were women.[289] This reality contradicts both the fact that women are one-half of the population, as well as that their gender-specific experiences and needs resulting from armed conflict are unlikely to be addressed without their participation in peace negotiation processes.[290]

The discussion on the specific impact of armed conflict on women only came to the international arena in the 1990s.[291] In 1992, the Committee

---

287 Judith Gardam and Michelle Jarvis, *Women, Armed Conflict, and International Law* (The Hague: Kluwer Law International, 2001), 21.

288 Christine Bell and Catherine O'Rourke, 'Does Feminism Need a Theory of Transitional Justice? An Introductory Essay,' *International Journal of Transitional Justice* 1, no. 1 (2007): 31. On the historical exclusion and inclusion of women in peace processes, and the potential role of their participation, see Anderlini, *Women Building Peace: What They Do, What It Matters*.

289 Escola de Cultura de Pau, *Yearbook of Peace Processes 2016*, ed. Vicenç Fisas (Barcelona: Icaria, 2016), 339.

290 Bell and O'Rourke, 'Does Feminism Need a Theory of Transitional Justice? An Introductory Essay,' 30.

291 According to Kastner, it was connected with the development of gender-related human rights considerations and the need to respond to gender-based violence. Kastner, *Legal Normativity in the Resolution of Internal Armed Conflict*, 62.

on the Elimination of Discrimination against Women adopted General Recommendation 19 related to violence against women. The Recommendation refers to the gender-based risks that women face in contexts of armed conflict and recommends states to take all necessary measures to protect them.[292] In 1995, the UN Fourth World Conference on Women, Action for Equality Development and Peace stated that "while entire communities suffer the consequences of armed conflict and terrorism, women and girls are particularly affected because of their status in society and their sex."[293] Then, the Beijing Declaration issued from such a Conference noted that "the equal access and full participation of women in power structures and their full involvement in all efforts for the prevention and resolution of conflicts are essential for the maintenance and promotion of peace and security."[294]

Following the Beijing Declaration's commitments, the UNSC adopted the crucial Resolution 1325 (2000) on Women, Peace, and Security. This Resolution urges states to increase representation of women at all decision-making levels for the prevention, management, and resolution of conflict.[295] It also requests the Secretary-General to appoint more women as special representatives in peace negotiations,[296] and to incorporate a gender perspective into peace operations.[297] Finally, the Resolution calls on all actors involved in peace agreements to adopt a gender perspective.[298]

This resolution introduced a specific international standard on women participation in peace negotiations. According to Ellerby, such a standard is composed by four elements of inclusion: representation (decision-making, quotas), incorporation (gender balance in everyday activities and institutions), protection (safety and equality, gender-based violence, access to resources, anti-discrimination), and recognition (gender perspective, special rights and needs, legal changes).[299]

---

[292] Committee on the Elimination of Discrimination against Women, General Recommendation No. 19 (1992), paras. 16 and 24(t).
[293] UN Fourth World Conference on Women, Action for Equality Development and Peace, 'Beijing Declaration and Platform for Action,' Pub. L. No. UN Doc A/Conf.177/20 (1995), para. 135.
[294] UN Fourth World Conference on Women, Action for Equality Development and Peace, 134.
[295] UN Security Council, Resolution 1325 (2000), para. 1.
[296] UN Security Council, para. 3.
[297] UN Security Council, paras 5–6.
[298] UN Security Council, para. 8.
[299] Kara Ellerby, '(En)Gendered Security? Gender Mainstreaming and Women's Inclusion in Peace Processes,' in *Gender, Peace and Security: Implementing UN Security Council Resolution 1325*, ed. Theodora-Ismene Gizelis and Louise Olsson (Abingdon: Routledge, 2015), 189.

For Bell and O'Rourke, Resolution 1325 provides a clear legal basis for addressing the role of women in the negotiation and implementation of peace agreements. For them, even though this resolution was adopted under Chapter VI of the UN Charter, "its legal authority has been accentuated by the fact that it was passed unanimously, and that the resolution uses the language of obligation."[300] Additionally, subsequent Security Council resolutions have followed and reinforced Resolution 1325's mandates.[301]

This resolution brought to the international practice a growing awareness on women participation and inclusion in peace negotiations and peace agreements. Anderlini notes that despite the difficulties in the implementation of Resolution 1325, "since it was passed, women's demands for inclusion have been heard more often in formal channels."[302] Bell and O'Rourke have found a "significant increase in references to women in peace agreements after Resolution 1325 was passed."[303] A similar conclusion was reached by Ellerby in 2015.[304]

In 2005, the Updated Principles to Combat Impunity adopted by the UN Commission on Human Rights[305] also called for the participation of women, minorities, victims, and civil society in peace processes. Principle 32 asked "to ensure that women and minority groups participate in public consultations aimed at developing, implementing, and assessing reparations programmes." Similarly, Principle 35 affirms that "adequate representation of women and minority groups in public institutions is essential to the achievement" of guarantees of non-repetition.

---

300 Christine Bell and Catherine O'Rourke, 'Peace Agreements or Pieces of Paper? The Impact of UNSC Resolution 1325 on Peace Processes and Their Agreements,' *International and Comparative Law Quarterly* 59, no. 4 (2010): 943.

301 See, for example, Resolution 1820 (2008) encouraging all parties in peace talks "to facilitate the equal and full participation of women at decision-making levels" (para. 12); Resolution 1888 (2009) urges that "issues of sexual violence be included in all United Nations-sponsored peace negotiations agendas" (para. 17); Resolution 1889 (2009) pointing out the underrepresentation of women in peace processes, and Resolution 2106 (2013) "reiterates the importance of addressing sexual violence in armed conflict whenever relevant, in mediation efforts, ceasefires and peace agreements" and it request to "engage on sexual violence issues, including with women, civil society, including women's organizations and survivors of sexual violence, and ensure that such concerns are reflected in specific provisions of peace agreements" (para. 12).

302 Anderlini, *Women Building Peace: What They Do, What It Matters*, 73.

303 Bell and O'Rourke, 'Peace Agreements or Pieces of Paper? The Impact of UNSC Resolution 1325 on Peace Processes and Their Agreements,' 956.

304 Ellerby, '(En)Gendered Security? Gender Mainstreaming and Women's Inclusion in Peace Processes,' 204.

305 UN Commission on Human Rights, "Updated Set of Principles for the Protection and Promotion of Human Rights through Action to Combat Impunity," Pub. L. No. E/CN.4/2005/102/Add.1 (2005).

Finally, the 2008 Nuremberg Declaration on Peace and Justice called for increased representation and active involvement of women in transitional processes. It recommends that "post-conflict legal orders should rectify legal and social discrimination based on gender."[306]

5.1.2   On Ethnic Minorities Issues

Like women, ethnic minorities can suffer specific impacts by armed conflict because of their ethnicity and their social and cultural conditions. In countries facing NIACs, traditionally marginalized groups could be exposed to higher risks than the rest of the population. Regarding ethnic minorities, armed conflict can cause specific impacts on their culture, their dynamics, their organization, and their territories.

However, unlike the case of women, there is not a specific international legal framework for the participation of ethnic minorities in peace processes, or for their specific needs to be included in peace agreements. Nevertheless, the rights of ethnic minorities have been addressed by several instruments of international law, which could be applied regarding peace processes.

In a general way, the ICERD provides a basis for the integration of racial and ethnic groups to achieve their advancement and full enjoyment of their rights.[307] Then, the 2001 Durban Declaration recognizes that racial discrimination is among both the root causes and the consequences of armed conflict and calls for the inclusion and participation of traditionally discriminated peoples when deciding matters of their concern.[308]

Regarding indigenous and tribal peoples, the most relevant instrument is the 1989 ILO Convention 169.[309] According to such an instrument, "the social,

---

306   UN General Assembly, Nuremberg Declaration on Peace and Justice. Recommendation 2.8.
307   International Convention on the Elimination of All Forms of Racial Discrimination.
308   World Conference against Racism, Racial Discrimination, Xenophobia and Related Intolerance, Declaration, Durban, South Africa, 8 September 2001.
309   General Conference of the International Labour Organisation, 'C169—Indigenous and Tribal Peoples Convention' (1989). According to its Article 1.1: "This Convention applies to:
   (a)   tribal peoples in independent countries whose social, cultural and economic conditions distinguish them from other sections of the national community, and whose status is regulated wholly or partially by their own customs or traditions or by special laws or regulations;
   (b)   peoples in independent countries who are regarded as indigenous on account of their descent from the populations which inhabited the country, or a geographical region to which the country belongs, at the time of conquest or colonisation or the establishment of present state boundaries and who, irrespective of their legal status, retain some or all of their own social, economic, cultural and political institutions."

cultural, religious and spiritual values and practices of these peoples shall be recognised and protected."[310] Additionally, indigenous and tribal peoples must be consulted and have the means to duly participate regarding "legislative or administrative measures which may affect them directly."[311] Lastly, the 2007 UN Declaration on Indigenous Peoples included some specific provisions regarding the right to be consulted on measures of relocation and reparations.[312]

5.1.3   On the Participation of Victims and Civil Society in General

The participation of victims and civil society actors in peace negotiations is getting increased attention in research and practice.[313] Since victims suffer the direct impact of armed conflict, they must have a voice, especially regarding the treatment of crimes committed against them and the corresponding reparations. As noted by Ambos, victims' "participation is indispensable to lend legitimacy to this process and make it socially acceptable."[314] Similarly, large participation of civil society, either directly—by public consultations or referendums—or through democratically-elected organs is essential to pave the way for national reconciliation.[315]

There is no specific legal basis for the participation of victims and civil society in peace negotiations. However, some general norms provide elements in that sense. General human rights instruments enshrine the right of every person to take part in public affairs (e.g., Article 25(a) of the ICCPR, and Article 23.1(a) of the AmCHR). A peace negotiation, whose outcome will have effects over people other than just the parties in talks, should be considered a public affair. According to Article 68.3 of the ICC Statute, the Court shall permit the views and concerns of the victims "to be presented and considered" at the proceedings. The right of victims to be heard and participate when asking for reparations can be found in the UN Basic Principles on Reparations.[316] A similar

---

310   Convention concerning Indigenous and Tribal Peoples in Independent Countries C169 Art. 5.
311   Convention concerning Indigenous and Tribal Peoples in Independent Countries C169 Art. 6.
312   UN General Assembly, 'United Nations Declaration on the Rights of Indigenous Peoples,' Pub. L. No. Resolution 61/295 (2007). Arts. 10, 28.
313   Thania Paffenholz, 'Civil Society,' in *Post-Conflict Peacebuilding: A Lexicon*, ed. Vincent Chetail (Oxford: Oxford University Press, 2009), 64.
314   Ambos, 'The Legal Framework of Transitional Justice,' 40.
315   Ambos, 40; UN Secretary-General, 'Report of the Secretary-General on the Rule of Law and Transitional Justice in Conflict and Post-Conflict Societies,' para. 16.
316   UN General Assembly, Basic Principles and Guidelines on the Right to a Remedy and Reparation for Victims of Gross Violations of International Human Rights Law and Serious Violations of International Humanitarian Law Preamble and Chapter VIII.

view is found in the Updated Set of Principles to Combat Impunity, providing for the consultation of victims and other sectors of civil society when defining guarantees of non-recurrence of human rights violations.[317] All those elements were gathered by the 2008 Nuremberg Declaration on Peace and Justice, whose Principle 3 promotes a victim-centered approach in peace negotiations and recommends broader consultations with victims, civil society, and women.[318]

The UN Secretary-General pointed out that inclusivity "increases the legitimacy and national ownership of the peace agreement and its implementation," at the time that it "reduces the likelihood of excluded actors undermining the process."[319] This position is emphasized by Kastner, who sustains that the UN "has manifestly internalized an obligation *vis-à-vis* the participation of civil society actors in peace negotiations that involves normative considerations and that goes beyond merely reaching out and consulting civil society."[320]

5.2 The Colombian Approach

This item presents three mechanisms by which Colombia has assumed and implemented an inclusive and differential perspective in its transition from armed conflict to peace.

5.2.1 Differential Approach for the Attention and Reparation of Victims of Armed Conflict

In 1997, Colombia adopted a law on internal displacement,[321] which included some provisions on the special attention to internally displaced women. However, in 2008 the Constitutional Court found a gender gap in this Law and ordered a series of measures to address the special needs and risks faced by women victims of displacement. The Court referred to international obligations applicable to the matter, with a special emphasis to CEDAW General Recommendation 19 and UNSC Resolution 1325. Under those elements, the Court ordered to different institutions a series of measures to meet the specific needs of displaced women ensuring their participation in the definition and implementation of those actions.[322]

---

317 UN Commission on Human Rights, Updated Set of Principles for the Protection and Promotion of Human Rights through Action to Combat Impunity. Principle 35.
318 UN General Assembly, Nuremberg Declaration on Peace and Justice Principle 3 and Recommendation 1.3.
319 UN Secretary-General, 'Strengthening the Role of Mediation in the Peaceful Settlement of Disputes, Conflict Prevention and Resolution,' para. 29.
320 Kastner, *Legal Normativity in the Resolution of Internal Armed Conflict*, 148.
321 Congreso de la República de Colombia, Ley 387.
322 Corte Constitucional de Colombia, Auto 092/08 (2008).

A year later, the same gaps were found regarding indigenous peoples[323] and Afro-descendants.[324] For the Court, Colombia was internationally obligated to adopt specific measures regarding the protection of ethnic groups affected by armed conflict. As such, the Court invoked, among other instruments, Article 26 of the ICESCR regarding ethnic minorities and ILO Convention 169.

The Constitutional Court opened a public follow-up system for those decisions, in which the concerned institutions should inform the measures adopted for the differential attention to these groups of victims.[325] This situation created a positive environment for women and ethnic organizations to promote a public agenda on their specific needs as victims of armed conflict, since they also have the possibility to submit reports to the Court and to participate in their discussion.

These jurisprudential standards were incorporated by the 2011 Law on Victims and Land Restitution. According to this instrument, differential approach regarding gender, ethnicity, sexual orientation, age, and physical conditions is a central principle of the whole system for the attention and reparation of victims.[326] As such, the Law created a unified register of victims including differential categories. Up to 1 April 2019, from a total of 8.803.836 victims registered,[327] 4.218.519 were women, 4.211.087 men, 3.367 LGBTI people, 218.657 indigenous, 776.861 Afro-Colombians, and 41.838 Roma and other ethnic minorities.[328] To address the conditions of these groups in a differential way, specific norms were adopted regulating special measures regarding ethnic minorities. Additionally, a differential approach subsystem was established to coordinate the adoption of differential measures for victims at all the levels, in which representatives from each population group are present.

5.2.2 Participation of Victims and Civil Society in the Peace Negotiations

Armed conflict in Colombia has impacted more than eight million people. It represents around 18% of the country's total population.[329] Such an impact

---

323 Corte Constitucional de Colombia, Auto 004/09 (2009).
324 Corte Constitucional de Colombia, Auto 005/09 (2009).
325 Corte Constitucional de Colombia, Sentencia T-025/04 (2004).
326 Congreso de Colombia, Ley 1448 (2011), Art. 13. Additionally, it is important to mention that the Law explicitly indicates that its provisions must be interpreted and applied according to IHL and IHRL treaties ratified by Colombia (Art. 27).
327 Registro Único de Víctimas, https://www.unidadvictimas.gov.co/es/registro-unico-de-victimas-ruv/37394 (accessed on 1 April 2019).
328 Registro Único de Víctimas.
329 The total population of Colombia up to May 2019 was estimated in 48.2 million people. Source: http://www.dane.gov.co/index.php/estadisticas-por-tema/demografia-y-poblacion/censo-nacional-de-poblacion-y-vivenda-2018/cuantos-somos/ (accessed on 5 May 2019).

has made armed conflict a constant element in the life of millions of people and their communities. Thus, the participation of victims and civil society in general in the negotiation table and the inclusion of their interests and views in the peace agreement were a must.

The Agreement explicitly states its victim-centered approach.[330] Additionally, the preceding legal and jurisprudential developments on victims empowered them to claim a significant role in the process. As a result, 60 victims representing different regions, groups, and victimizing facts, participated in the negotiation table in Havana. Moreover, looking for the largest social acceptance of the Agreement, the parties agreed on a mechanism of open participation, in which 3.000 people gave their opinions through UN-led forums around the country, and 17.000 proposals were received through the internet.[331] These mechanisms and figures express a decisive openness of the parties, and their recognition of victims and civil society's participation as a matter of rights; which is in contrast with the traditional approach to involve victims only after the agreement is reached, mainly before truth commissions.

5.2.3   Differential Gender and Ethnic Approaches in the Peace Agreement

The inclusion of a differential perspective to gender and ethnic minorities is considered as one of the major victories for human rights advocates in the Colombian peace process. The Agreement invokes the incorporation of a differential approach as an expression of the right to equality and non-discrimination enshrined by international law.[332]

Regarding gender, the preceding legislative and jurisprudential developments derived from international law inspired women and other gender-related groups to ask for their participation and inclusion during the negotiation process. In addition, the UN representatives explicitly called for all the Agreement to incorporate a gender approach and to ensure women participation.[333] In this way, in September 2014 the parties set up a Gender Sub-commission whose purpose was to "provide recommendations to the Table in order to enable an appropriate

---

330   Government of Colombia and FARC, 'Final Agreement to End the Armed Conflict and Build a Stable and Lasting Peace,' 8.
331   Government of Colombia and FARC, 126–28.
332   Government of Colombia and FARC, 'Final Agreement to End the Armed Conflict and Build a Stable and Lasting Peace,' 3.
333   Government of Colombia and FARC, 144.

gender approach, particularly in relation with women and the LGBTI community."[334]

On this topic, the parties went beyond women issues and included a LGBTI-gender related perspective in the Agreement, which is unprecedented in other processes. It was more a consequence of domestic developments on LGBTI issues,[335] and the acknowledgment of the specific impacts that LGBTI people suffered because of armed conflict.[336] As such, the parties extended the international law appropriation of gender as related to women to a point in which other gender issues were covered. As Céspedes points out, during the negotiation "women's issues were at the center and LGBT's followed in their path."[337]

In general, the Agreement includes equality, gender approach, and ethnic diversity as guiding principles;[338] calls for the empowerment of women[339] and the political participation of different identity groups;[340] highlights the role of women as peacebuilders;[341] establishes the necessity to ensure a differential approach regarding reincorporated women;[342] looks for strengthening the administration of justice concerning gender-based violence;[343] and defines the incorporation of a differential gender and ethnic approach over the system of truth, justice, and reparation.[344]

According to the parties, these measures aim to "create conditions for women, and people with diverse sexual orientation, to access in equal conditions to the benefits of a country without armed conflict."[345] For the negotiators, "the inclusion of a gender approach in a peace process such as this one

---

334   Gobierno de Colombia and FARC, 'Joint Communiqué,' 11 September 2014, https://www.ambitojuridico.com/BancoMedios/Documentos%20PDF/comunicado11-09-14.pdf.
335   See, for instance: Corte Constitucional, Sentencia SU-617-2014, C-071-2015, SU-214-2016.
336   The Colombia's National Centre for Historical Memory elaborated a report on the specific impacts of armed conflict on LGBT people. Centro Nacional de Memoria Histórica, *Aniquilar la diferencia*, Lesbianas, gays, bisexuales y transgeneristas en el marco del conflicto armado colombiano, 2015, available at: http://www.centrodememoriahistorica.gov.co/descargas/informes2015/aniquilar-la-diferencia/aniquilar-la-diferencia.pdf (accessed on 20 January 2018).
337   Céspedes-Báez, 'Gender Panic and the Failure of a Peace Agreement,' 186.
338   Government of Colombia and FARC, 'Final Agreement to End the Armed Conflict and Build a Stable and Lasting Peace,' 12.
339   Government of Colombia and FARC, 31.
340   Government of Colombia and FARC, 54.
341   Government of Colombia and FARC, 55.
342   Government of Colombia and FARC, 69.
343   Government of Colombia and FARC, 79, 85.
344   Government of Colombia and FARC, 128.
345   Gobierno de Colombia and FARC, 'Joint Communiqué No. 82,' 24 July 2016, http://es.presidencia.gov.co/noticia/160724-Comunicado-conjunto-82.

INTERNATIONAL LAW IN THE COLOMBIAN TRANSITION 121

has no precedents in the world, and sets a milestone in the construction of the agreements already reached and yet to be reached."[346]

Regarding ethnic issues, the parties heard a civil society ethnic commission providing recommendations to incorporate a differential ethnic approach into the Peace Agreement. As a result, the Final Agreement included an Ethnic Chapter,[347] in which it recognizes the serious impacts that armed conflict had on indigenous and Afro-Colombian communities, and the necessity to assume a differential ethnic approach to reach peace. To this effect, the Agreement indicates that it must be interpreted and applied in a way that respects and incorporates the specific needs, concerns, and dynamics of ethnic minorities, according to international and domestic law. On this point, the Agreement invokes the ICESCR, the ICERD, the ILO Convention 169, the Durban Declaration for Action, and the UN Declaration on Indigenous Peoples.[348]

As such, the Agreement established measures as the fundamental right to previous, informed, and free consent regarding the implementation of the peace deal in matters related to ethnic groups; special consideration of ethnic communities' needs on rural development; the restitution of collective ethnic territories and return of displaced ethnic communities; the coordination of the Special Jurisdiction for Peace with the special indigenous jurisdiction;[349] and a commission to follow-up the observance of the ethnic approach in the implementation of the Agreement.[350]

In all of these matters, the Colombian approach to inclusiveness in its different transitional instruments has consistently been inspired by international law, following legal norms and the discourses and requests of differential groups to ensure international legal standards. As Chapter 3 will analyze, such a normative landscape can be framed by *jus post bellum*.

6   Conclusions

This chapter examined how international law has shaped the Colombian transition in different matters and by different ways. At least three reasons explain

---

346   Gobierno de Colombia and FARC, 'Joint Communiqué.'
347   Government of Colombia and FARC, 'Final Agreement to End the Armed Conflict and Build a Stable and Lasting Peace,' 206–9.
348   Government of Colombia and FARC, 206.
349   According to Article 246 of the Colombian Constitution, indigenous authorities can exercise their own jurisdiction within their territories.
350   Government of Colombia and FARC, 'Final Agreement to End the Armed Conflict and Build a Stable and Lasting Peace,' 207–9.

such an influence of international law in this case. First, the growing development of IHRL, IHL, and ICL has established standards to protect individual rights, even beyond domestic political decisions by states and parties in peace negotiations. As such, the legal developments explored in this chapter showed to the parties in negotiation their inescapable obligation to follow international standards, and it gave legal arguments to actors claiming for their rights and interests to be considered in the negotiations. Second, Colombia has a constitutional system particularly receptive to international law, establishing that duly ratified IHRL and IHL treaties have the same normative level as the Constitution. Thus, the negotiators knew that international law was a parameter to control the constitutionality of the mechanisms designed in the negotiation. For that reason, those mechanisms had to be in conformity with international law. Third, the involvement of international actors in the process and the parties' intention to have an agreement internationally accepted, created a favorable environment for the active role played by international law in the process.

In this way, legal obligations, discourses, and comparative practices created a normative framework in which parties moved to reach their own formulas.

Regarding the legal nature of the agreement, the parties showed a creative use of international law for shielding the accord from domestic political or legal changes. In this case, they framed the peace deal as a special agreement under IHL and through a unilateral declaration by the Colombian State before the UN.

Pursuing a sustainable peace, a broad set of socioeconomic, political, and institutional questions had to be addressed. On this matter, the parties treated the problems related to rural development, political participation, environmental protection, and crops of illicit use under a human rights approach. As such, the parties used an international legal frame of reference, invoking instruments such as the ICCPR and the ICESCR to delineate socioeconomic and political reforms as a matter of rights rather than mere political decisions.

On criminal responsibility, international legal obligations set up a framework with clear conditions to be observed: no amnesty for international crimes, formal prosecution and trials were required, and effective restrictions on liberty had to be imposed as a part of the criminal sanctions. With those elements, the parties created a special system of justice, with formal judges and procedures, trials and sentences, imposing restorative sanctions but including effective restrictions on liberty. Here, the legal obligations enshrined by ICL, IHL, and IHRL regarding amnesties and prosecution of international crimes, together with comparative practices and the discourses of actors such as the Office of the ICC Prosecutor and the Inter-American System of Human Rights, defined a normative bargaining zone within which the negotiators created their formula to deal with criminal responsibility for past crimes related to the armed conflict.

Similarly, regarding reparations, the Colombian case shows that it is possible to develop a comprehensive system of reparation even in the context of massive violations of human rights and IHL within an armed conflict. No previous transition from conflict to peace has recognized such a larger number of victims as Colombia did. Although victims of armed conflict represent around 18% of the total population, the country assumed the comprehensive concept of reparation set by international law, which was defined by reference to international legal norms.

Finally, the participation and inclusion of different groups of people has been assumed not only as a political condition of legitimacy, but as a legal obligation. The parties in negotiation, and several social and institutional actors, have invoked international legal elements to support inclusiveness in transition in Colombia, both in the process of negotiation and in the content of the Agreement, leading to special provisions to address structural factors of discrimination and exclusion.

Therefore, as presented in this chapter, the international legal obligations binding both the Colombian State and the guerilla, the precedents regarding matters as amnesties in other contexts around the world, and the discourses of relevant actors (e.g., guarantor countries, UN agents, the ICC, and other domestic and international institutional and civil society actors) were decisive for the way in which negotiations were conducted and for the very content of the Peace Agreement. In consequence, this chapter showed how practice in Colombia proves the existence of an international normative framework shaping transition from armed conflict to peace. This framework is what the book considers *jus post bellum*.

CHAPTER 3

Jus Post Bellum Viewed from the Colombian Transition

This chapter aims to connect the previous two. Chapter 1 explored the concept of *jus post bellum* as the analytical framework for framing the role of international law governing transition from armed conflict to peace. Chapter 2 examined the role played by international law in different areas of the Colombian transition, identifying the relevant legal framework and how it has shaped several transitional instruments in the country. This third chapter assesses the concept of *jus post bellum* from the perspective of the Colombian experience to identify how theory is reflected in practice and how the Colombian practice offers new insights on the content and the scope of *jus post bellum* as the normative framework for transitioning from armed conflict to sustainable peace.

The main argument of this chapter is that the way in which international law has molded transition in Colombia reflects most of the theoretical elaborations on *jus post bellum*. As such, considering that no previous work has analyzed *jus post bellum* comprehensively through a case study, this chapter suggests empirical insights to delineate the definition, the content, the formation, the actors, and the functions of *jus post bellum*, contrasting the theoretical basis introduced in Chapter 1 to the Colombian case presented in Chapter 2.

This chapter thus refers back to the approaches to defining *jus post bellum* discussed in the first chapter to address whether they work in practice and what definition could be proposed in light of the experience in Colombia. Then, by using concrete examples in the Colombian process, the chapter analyses how *jus post bellum* is permanently built through practice, because of the dual process of application and creation of law occurring in negotiations and transitions to peace. The chapter also readdresses the discussion on principles of *jus post bellum* presented in the first chapter to explain why they constitute the substantive content of the concept and to suggest a series of principles that can be identified in the Colombian case. The chapter thus analyzes how the variety of actors involved in the normative internationalization of the Colombian transition shows the broad spectrum of potential actors of *jus post bellum*, which are not limited to the parties in negotiation. Finally, the chapter assesses the functions played by international law in the Colombian transition, suggesting the potential functions that *jus post bellum* can serve as

© CÉSAR ROJAS-OROZCO, 2021 | DOI:10.1163/9789004440531_005
This is an open access chapter distributed under the terms of the CC BY-NC 4.0 license.

the normative framework guiding successful transition from armed conflict to sustainable peace.

1   A Definition of *Jus Post Bellum* from the Colombian Experience

Assessing the elements from theory and practice discussed in the previous chapters, it can be observed that, at present, *jus post bellum* is still a concept of scholarly use. It is not yet used in the official UN and state language and does not have a recognized normative standing on its own. At the time of writing only one mention to the concept was found in a UN document, consisting in the 2016 ILC's Special Rapporteur Marie Jacobsson's Third Report on the Protection of the Environment in Relation to Armed Conflicts.[1] However, the Special Rapporteur mentioned the concept to mean that she was not going to address the "legal-political discussion" on *jus post bellum* in her report, because, in her opinion, "this concept is wider than positive law and has a clear connection to just war theories."[2] Even though her reasons are inaccurate, since transition to peace necessarily involves more than positive law and the concept of *jus post bellum* already has a legal development beyond its original conception within the just war theory,[3] the Special Rapporteur's statement not to address the concept in her report shows the challenges from bringing the concept into the official practice.

In that sense, it is clear that even if the parties in a peace process are aware of existing legal considerations shaping their negotiation and the resulting agreement, they do not identify these elements as belonging to or constituting a specific legal framework for transition. Nevertheless, though the concept of *jus post bellum* is not yet officially used in practice, it offers an effective framework for designating the legal norms, discourses, and practices that apply to the transition from armed conflict to sustainable peace.

The different definitions discussed in Chapter 1 offer useful elements to build an integrative approach. As analyzed in that chapter, existing definitions can be grouped under three approaches to *jus post bellum*: 1) as a new legal regime; 2) as an ordering system; and 3) as an interpretative framework.[4]

---

1 Marie Jacobsson Special Rapporteur, 'Third Report on the Protection of the Environment in Relation to Armed Conflicts' (Geneva: International Law Commission, 2016).
2 Jacobsson, para. 10.
3 See Introduction, Sections 3 and 8.
4 Stahn, '*Jus Post Bellum* and the Justice of Peace: Some Preliminary Reflections.'

Regarding *jus post bellum* as a new legal regime, in addition to the criticism exposed in Chapter 1, practice in Colombia confirms that such a formal regime would not be possible nor consistent with the inner flexibility of peacemaking. The negotiators and other actors involved in the process took norms from different international legal instruments and branches of law, based on the matters in negotiation. Those matters could be significantly different in other transitional contexts, and the relevant actors could even use or apply the same norms in a different way. Even in Colombia, the application of ICL standards to sanctions for people responsible for serious armed conflict-related crimes was different in the 2005 Justice and Peace Law compared to the 2016 Peace Agreement. As such, *jus post bellum* must be open, flexible, and able to combine different legal and political considerations according to the needs of the context.

However, the two other approaches to defining *jus post bellum* can be supported in practice. *Jus post bellum* can work as a framework ordering legal norms, discourses, and practices defining the normative bargaining zone in which parties can move to create their own transitional formulas. At the same time, such a framework can offer interpretative elements on how those norms should be understood and applied to the specific context. Two examples illustrate this argument in Colombia. One example is the way in which the system of criminal justice negotiated by the parties was influenced by IHL and ICL norms regarding amnesties and prosecution for international crimes, by the ICC Prosecutor's discourses on how to ensure sanctions compatible with ICL, and by comparative practices on transitional justice.[5] A second example can be found in the way in which international standards on women's participation in peace processes set by UNSC Resolution 1325 came together with different discourses on inclusiveness, leading to a broad approach to participation involving not only women but also LGBTI and ethnic groups.[6] In both cases, one can see that legal norms, discourses,[7] and comparative practices framed a zone of negotiation showing the parties' limits and possibilities in coordinating, interpreting, and applying the international legal framework relevant to their transition to peace.

Considering said ideas, a definition of *jus post bellum* from practice is based on four elements. The first is the possible content of *jus post bellum*. Here, a

---

5 See Chapter 2, Section 3.
6 See Chapter 2, Section 5.
7 Regarding the value of legal discourses, Kastner argues: "that discourse is not only illustrative but constitutive of the normative framework." Kastner, *Legal Normativity in the Resolution of Internal Armed Conflict*, 32.

set of principles seems more appropriate than a formal legal regime. In the Colombian transition, legal norms from different branches of international law defined matters of the peace negotiation and of the previous transitional instruments. However, those norms were not applied in a linear process; rather, the parties took elements from legal discourses, comparative experiences, and the practical needs of the context to define a way to interpret and apply legal norms in a manner consistent with the pursuit of peace. Thus, the parties were guided by principles defining a framework on the legal and the political considerations to be addressed.[8]

The second element is the object of *jus post bellum*, which, as discussed in Chapter 1, consists in contributing to establish a sustainable peace.[9] This book has argued that sustainable peace requires at least two conditions: first, addressing the root causes of armed conflict, which is the only way to promote reconciliation and prevent the recurrence of violence; and second, observing adherence to relevant standards of international law, which are essential to ensure the rule of law, respect for human rights, democratic governance, and international legitimacy. In the Colombian case, transition has entailed not only ending armed confrontation but also building peace,[10] seeking to remove the causes of the conflict, meeting victim's rights, and encouraging reconciliation under an international legal framework.

The third element is a functional rather than a temporal approach. *Jus post bellum* is not a regime with starting and ending benchmarks. It is a framework providing guidance during any phase when efforts are put in place to end armed conflict and to establish sustainable peace.[11] As seen in Chapter 2, Colombia is an example on the use of normative principles of criminal justice[12] and reparations[13] even before having a peace process. Moreover, despite a comprehensive peace agreement in the country, armed conflict is still ongoing with another

---

[8]   Easterday, 'Peace Agreements as a Framework for *Jus Post Bellum*,' 386.
[9]   See Chapter 1, Section 4.
[10] It can be seen even since the name of the agreement, called Final Agreement to End the Armed Conflict and Build a Stable and Lasting Peace. Government of Colombia and FARC, 'Final Agreement to End the Armed Conflict and Build a Stable and Lasting Peace.'
[11] At this regard, the book follows Larry May's approach, who, as noted in Chapter 1, Section 3, suggests that *"jus post bellum* refers to any principles that govern the mopping up efforts, namely the efforts at the end and after the end of war that lead into a position of peace." May, *After War Ends*, 3.
[12] Congreso de la República de Colombia, Ley 975 (Ley de Justicia y Paz), 2005.
[13] Congreso de la República de Colombia, Ley 1448 (Ley de Víctimas y Restitución de Tierras).

rebel group.[14] Thus, the case study showed that *jus post bellum* applies because of the function it plays in the transition from armed conflict to peace, rather than to a specific moment of such a transition.[15]

Fourth, *jus post bellum* is a matter of international law, even regarding NIACs.[16] *Jus post bellum* has been mainly developed in relation to IACs, in which the norms involved are international. So far, the few works addressing *jus post bellum* in NIACs[17] have not analyzed the concrete application of legal norms. However, even though *jus post bellum* involves the interaction of international and domestic law,[18] it is based on international law. There are at least three reasons explaining this argument in the context of NIACs. First, the transition from armed conflict to peace became a matter of international legal interest because it relates to international values such as human rights, justice, and the rule of law. Second, in a global legal world, states are bound by several international obligations covering most of the matters treated in peace processes. Third, and possibly the most substantial reason, because of the intrinsic asymmetry between the state and the non-state actors involved in a NIAC, domestic law would hardly be seen as an impartial framework to hold peace negotiations, and non-state actors would be more reluctant to accept conditions derived from the institutional order they are fighting against.

In conclusion, considering the elements discussed above, *jus post bellum* can be understood as a normative framework of principles—grouping legal norms, discourses, and practices—that offers a space of contextualized interpretation and application of relevant international law to the transition from armed conflict to sustainable peace. This framework offers guidance on the standards that should be observed, but its precise content is built through the practice of actors involved in transitional processes, in the way they integrate, interpret, and apply international legal norms, discourses, and practices

---

14 As seen in Chapter 2, the ELN guerilla keeps in armed confrontation in Colombia. See Chapter 2, Section o.

15 See Chapter 1, Section 3, on the discussion on the temporal or fuctional approach to *jus post bellum*.

16 Even though existing definitions do not explicitly describe *jus post bellum* as being international law, all of them refer to international legal norms. However, in a literature review on peacebuilding, Chetail and Jütersonke refer to a previous Chetail's article to define *jus post bellum* as "norms of international law that are applicable in a post-conflict environment." Chetail and Jütersonke, 'Peacebuilding: A Review of the Academic Literature,' 5.

17 See Introduction, Section 4.

18 See, for instance, Stahn, '*Jus Post Bellum*: Mapping the Discipline(s),' 2008, 102; Payne, 'The Norm of Environmental Integrity in Post-Conflict Legal Regimes,' 118. Easterday, 'Peace Agreements as a Framework for *Jus Post Bellum*,' 380.

from other processes to their specific context. As such, the principles comprising *jus post bellum* are in permanent evolution, incorporating new rules, discourses, and practices according to the dynamics of the actors involved in the application and creation of law through peacemaking and peacebuilding.

2 The Formation and Operation of *Jus Post Bellum*

Jus post bellum is a framework in continual development. Sari sustains that conceiving *jus post bellum* as a normative process "rather than just as a set of norms, emphasizes that the legal standards applicable in post-conflict environments are not static but evolutionary. This is both a factual and a normative claim."[19] Indeed, theory and practice coincide in demonstrating that the complexity and context-specificity of transition from armed conflict to peace require a level of flexibility that cannot be provided by an imperative legal regime. Instead, *jus post bellum* should offer a framework containing legal constraints, possible options, and guidelines for parties to make their own normative decisions. Thus, it is a process of continual construction involving both the application and creation of new norms.[20]

In Kastner's words, "Law shapes peace negotiations, and peace negotiations generate legal normativity."[21] This is so since norms and obligations associated with transition "are rooted in the social interaction between the actors involved and are constantly reassessed and renegotiated."[22] In this sense, more than prescriptive, these norms are "purposive and aspirational in character."[23]

This idea is expressed more generally by Brunée and Toope, who sustain that "law can help to shape interactions in international society, and is in turn modified by those interactions."[24] Following Fuller, this is due to the fact that law is a process, and legal norms are never a completed project.[25] On this topic, Bell points out that,

---

[19] Sari, 'The Status of Foreign Armed Forces Deployed in Post-Conflict Environments: A Search for Basic Principles,' 500.
[20] Kreß and Grover, 'International Criminal Law Restraints in Peace Talks to End Armed Conflicts of a Non-International Character,' 46.
[21] Kastner, *Legal Normativity in the Resolution of Internal Armed Conflict*, 182.
[22] Kastner, 2.
[23] Kastner, 3.
[24] Jutta Brunnée and Stephen Toope, *Legitimacy and Legality in International Law: An Interactional Account* (Cambridge: Cambridge University Press, 2010), 354.
[25] Lon Fuller, *The Morality of Law* (New Heaven: Yale University Press, 1969), 106, as referred by Kastner, *Legal Normativity in the Resolution of Internal Armed Conflict*, 32.

> [P]eace agreements can be argued to have evolved and shaped the same international legal developments that promoted them as a conflict resolution tool [...] The relationship of international law to peace agreements cannot be simply pulled apart as one of cause and effect. [...] [P]eace agreements as legalized documents shape not just particularized conflicts but also the international legal order itself.[26]

This double process of normative application and creation of law is given by the fact that the practice of peace negotiations involves taking elements from applicable international law as well as from comparative practice in other processes, and adapting these elements to the concrete context, generating new forms of interpretation and application of the corresponding norms. Kastner notes that through their discourses and practices, "the respective actors constantly create and redevelop the legal-normative framework of peace negotiations. While crafted in a specific context, this framework is not entirely spontaneous or self-sufficient but influenced by international legal norms and the experiences and lessons from other peace negotiation contexts."[27]

At least three examples from the peace negotiations in Colombia can illustrate the formative process of *jus post bellum*. One is the use given by the parties to the IHL's mechanism of special agreements and to unilateral declarations before the UN to provide legal certainty to the peace agreement. Given that there is no specific legal regulation on the normative status of domestic peace agreements, the parties took elements from international positive law and practice to declare the international legal character of their peace agreement. This will likely serve as a precedent for other peace processes around the world.

A second example is the way in which the transitional justice model was created, taking legal discourses and legal practices to interpret and apply relevant legal obligations. The statements by the Office of the ICC Prosecutor, UN agents and civil society organizations, and previous rulings of the Constitutional Court created a framework on the scope, limits, and possibilities of interpreting and applying both the IHL's provision on amnesties at the end of armed conflict and the ICL's prohibition on those amnesties regarding serious international crimes.

The third example is the inclusive approach of the peace process that expanded the mandate of UNSC Resolution 1325 on women's participation and

---

26 Bell, *On the Law of Peace*, 44–45.
27 Kastner, *Legal Normativity in the Resolution of Internal Armed Conflict*, 83–84.

inclusion to other groups such as LGBTI and ethnic peoples, as the result of strategic advocacy by human rights organizations. This advocacy was based on international law, drawing on positive and soft law instruments to build a discourse defending inclusiveness as a legal obligation rather than a political choice.

All three examples illustrate how the confluence of legal norms, discourses, and practices, which involved different actors at different levels, formed and operated a framework to coordinate, interpret, and apply legal normativity that was not specifically designed for transitional contexts. Such a framework is *jus post bellum*.

Based on this logic, in the transition from armed conflict to peace international law does not work by imposing external imperative norms on the parties. On the contrary, it works as a framework providing guidance on the issues to address and the rights that must be respected, allowing the parties to devise their own way of dealing with them. This process implies a new vision of the role of international law and its interaction with domestic transition. According to Kastner,

> The still-prevalent emphasis on existing international law that is seen as imposing rigid standards and a certain conduct from 'above' should be supplanted by the view that law can also facilitate, offer guidance, reflect mutual commitments and serve to stabilize expectations. [...] Recognizing the norm creative capacity of the actors involved in peace negotiations is one avenue to use legal norms more constructively and effectively in the context of the negotiated resolution of internal armed conflicts.[28]

Along this line, then, "the legal obligations operate, again, rather as 'framework' obligations whose precise normative content must be specified in every context."[29] This is evident in the Colombian transition. General international legal obligations defined a framework on the fundamental issues that the parties had to consider, as well as the rights and conditions to be ensured.[30] Additionally, legal discourses and comparative practices on these matters demarcated the ways and conditions in which to apply those norms. However, such a framework was opened to the concrete requirements of the context.

---

28   Kastner, 83–84.
29   Kastner, 169.
30   E.g.: the prohibition on amnesties for international crimes and victim's rights, as presented in Chapter 2.

The parties understood that they had to find a way to balance international legal obligations with the political needs of peace. In this way, such a process, in which the parties negotiated and defined formulas aimed at establishing sustainable peace in their concrete context, expresses how *jus post bellum* works in practice.

3   Principles of *Jus Post Bellum* Identified in the Colombian Case

As discussed in Chapter 1, most authors working on *jus post bellum* have proposed principles as the way to define the content of the concept. For Stahn, *jus post bellum* should allow the identification of normative principles guiding "legal policy choices in situations of transition."[31] Easterday refers to overarching principles "focused on sustainable peace against which laws and policies can be interpreted."[32] De Brabandere understands the concept as "a normative set of principles" based on existing international law to interpret applicable "rules in function of the identified overarching principles."[33] And though Bell does not use the concept of *jus post bellum*, she advocates for a "set of programmatic standards that provide guidance [...] as to how the dilemmas of peace [...] can be resolved concomitantly with the requirements of international law."[34]

Following the above views, and as discussed in Chapter 1, it can be concluded that principles are the substantive content of *jus post bellum*. May suggests six principles: building and rebuilding, retribution, restitution, reparation, reconciliation, and proportionality.[35] His proposal is endorsed by the University of Leiden's *Jus Post Bellum* Project as a solid basis for defining the content of the concept.[36]

Regarding this matter in NIACS, Boon argues that there are at least two kinds of principles of *jus post bellum*.[37] One kind entails principles guiding matters governed by IHRL, IHL, and ICL, where international law establishes

---

31   Stahn, '*Jus Post Bellum*: Mapping the Discipline(s),' 2008, 101–2.
32   Easterday, 'Peace Agreements as a Framework for *Jus Post Bellum*,' 385.
33   De Brabandere, 'The Concept of *Jus Post Bellum* in International Law: A Normative Critique,' 137.
34   Bell, 'Of *Jus Post Bellum* and Lex Pacificatoria: What's in a Name?,' 192.
35   May, *After War Ends*, 5.
36   Easterday, Iverson, and Stahn, 'Exploring the Normative Foundations of *Jus Post Bellum*: An Introduction,' 1; Stahn, '*Jus Post Bellum* and the Justice of Peace: Some Preliminary Reflections.'
37   Boon, 'The Application of *Jus Post Bellum* in Non-International Armed Conflicts.'

more exigent standards to observe. Another kind refers to principles guiding matters such as socio-economic reconstruction and institutional design, where international law provides only general elements, giving greater leeway to the parties in defining their own formulas.

Having these elements, this section explores the principles of *jus post bellum* in the Colombian case. Toward this aim, we depart from May's proposal (because they are the most widely accepted principles among scholars working in this field) but reformulate some of his principles, uses references to other authors' principles, and adds new ones. Furthermore, this section will consider Boon's proposal on the scope of these principles in the context of NIACs. In any case, it is important to make clear that the principles referred to in this section are far from being exhaustive, and other matters are susceptible to be also considered as principles. However, this selection expresses the components of the Colombian transition that were most influenced by international legal considerations, and, consequently, closer to the purpose of illustrating an international normative framework guiding transitions through general normative principles.

3.1   *Reconstruction and Transformation*

May argues that there is an obligation to rebuild the capacity to protect human rights and to promote the rule of law, as well as to build such a capacity where it did not exist prior to the conflict.[38] In a similar approach, Patterson formulates this principle as order, including the obligation to ensure security needs, the guarantee of rights, and reconstruction both in terms of infrastructure damaged by armed conflict and institutional capacities.[39] Williams and Caldwell also discuss the restoration of order and economic reconstruction from a human rights perspective.[40] For them, *jus post bellum* should lead to a peace where human rights "are more secure than they were before war."[41] Also on this topic, Orend proposes a principle of rehabilitation of the capacities affected by conflict,[42] Coady a principle of rebuilding and reconstruction,[43]

---

38   May, *After War Ends*, 19.
39   Eric Patterson, 'Conclusion. Toward a Twenty-First Century *Jus Post Bellum*,' in *Ethics Beyond War's End*, ed. Eric Patterson (Washington: Georgetown University Press, 2012), 221–29.
40   Williams and Caldwell, '*Jus Post Bellum*: Just War Theory and the Principles of Just Peace,' 318.
41   Williams and Caldwell, 316.
42   Orend, '*Jus Post Bellum*: A Just War Theory Perspective,' 38–41.
43   Coady, 'The *Jus Post Bellum*.'

and De Brabandere a principle of reconstruction for the benefit of the population.[44]

This principle embodies two kinds of obligations: first, the obligation to reconstruct physical infrastructure and institutional capacities affected during the hostilities; and second, the obligation to address the root causes of conflict and transform the conditions that led to armed confrontation. As such, the principle conveys the idea of both reconstruction and transformation. The principle calls for a certain level of restoration of the *status quo ante*,[45] but it also calls for transformation when that *status quo* was the very cause of the conflict, as it is often the case in NIACS. On this line, Kastner sustains that internal peace "negotiations typically introduce novelty, seeking not to reestablish but to alter the *status quo ante*."[46]

This principle is related to the notion of positive peace.[47] *Jus post bellum* looks at integrating standards not only for ending conflict but also for creating or recovering the conditions to ensure an adequate level of living.[48] As pointed out by Chetail, peacebuilding means "to free individuals not only from 'fear' but also from 'need',"[49] and Benson refers to "post-conflict economic reconstruction and development" as a central goal of *jus post bellum*.[50] In that way, peace negotiations and peace agreements represent an opportunity for discussing and addressing structural issues in society,[51] and then this principle embodies such an opportunity also as a legal obligation.[52]

In this way, this principle offers a space to integrate international legal obligations into the political and socio-economic structure of transition. Looking at the Colombian experience, the principle is expressed in the way in which the parties conceived the agenda of peace negotiations. The objective was not only to end armed confrontation but also to address its structural causes. As seen in Chapter 2, Colombia comprehensively addressed matters such as

---

44 De Brabandere, 'The Concept of *Jus Post Bellum* in International Law: A Normative Critique,' 137–38.
45 Bass, '*Jus Post Bellum*,' 384.
46 Kastner, *Legal Normativity in the Resolution of Internal Armed Conflict*, 6.
47 Galtung, 'Violence, Peace, and Peace Research.'
48 See Chapter 1, Section 4, on the object of *jus post bellum*.
49 Chetail, 'Introduction,' 8.
50 Christina Benson, '*Jus Post Bellum* in Iraq: The Development of Emerging Norms for Economic Reform in Post Conflict Countries,' *Richmond Journal of Global Law & Business* 11, no. 4 (2012): 350–51.
51 Bell, *Peace Agreements and Human Rights*, 229–30; Easterday, 'Peace Agreements as a Framework for *Jus Post Bellum*,' 401–4.
52 See Chapter 2, Section 2.1., on the legal framework related to socioeconomic and political reforms in transition from armed conflict to peace.

socioeconomic rural development, alternatives to crops of illicit use, political participation, and opportunities for new political expressions, among others.[53] The lack of these conditions has been considered a root cause of the conflict,[54] making clear that for the parties such an element was a departing point to envisage a sustainable peace.

Following Boon's proposal, this is one of the principles of *jus post bellum* regarding which international law can only offer general guidelines, leaving the parties enough margin of appreciation to define their own arrangements. The 2016 Colombian Peace Agreement exhibits a deep grounding on international law in all its matters, including references to the international framework on economic, social, and cultural rights to adopt socioeconomic and political reforms,[55] but the concrete formulas on this matter were mostly based on policy and domestic law.[56]

Here, one can see the parties' understanding of the existence of international legal obligations guiding socioeconomic, political, and institutional affairs, and their will to ground reforms on those matters on such an international legal framework. However, unlike other components of the negotiation, in this matter the parties did not follow a clear legal standard but responded to the concrete causes and circumstances of armed conflict in Colombia. For example, the parties agreed on formulas on rural development or political participation, framing them under international law, but the specific measures on land access, reintegration programs, or the conditions for the creation of a political party were primarily policy-based. However, it is worth to note how the references to international law as a framework for the negotiations on those matters gave a human-rights-based approach to socioeconomic and political reforms.

As such, the Colombian experience displays reconstruction and transformation as an authentic normative principle of *jus post bellum*. In this way, the political discussions around addressing the root causes of armed conflict, implementing socioeconomic and political reforms, and promoting reintegration of former fighters and rural development, had an international legal framework of reference guiding relevant actors in their negotiation and definition of formulas according to the needs and conditions of their context. Then,

---

53 See Chapter 2, Section 2.2.
54 Government of Colombia and FARC, 'Final Agreement to End the Armed Conflict and Build a Stable and Lasting Peace,' 2.
55 Government of Colombia and FARC, 199.
56 Government of Colombia and FARC, 125, 134, 199.

this principle offers a normative space of discussion on matters that by their nature are more a question of policy and socioeconomic debate.

3.2 Criminal Accountability

May refers to this principle as retribution, denoting criminal justice for wrong-doings during armed conflict.[57] However, since retributive justice is not the most common form of justice in contexts of transition, this principle can be better named as criminal accountability. This principle is proposed by most authors in the field, even though different terms are used. Stahn talks about individual responsibility for wrongs committed during the conflict.[58] Orend,[59] Coady,[60] and Williams and Caldwell[61] refer to the principle as punishment for human rights violations. Gallen,[62] De Brabandere,[63] and Boon[64] refer to a principle of accountability.

As pointed out by May, trials constitute a fundamental step in restoring the rule of law.[65] However, in transitions from conflict to peace, this principle should be understood as the exigency of a certain form of justice, though not necessarily a retributive one.[66] Affirming this idea, May later sustained that "the justice of *jus post bellum* is secured not through giving to people what is their due in the short run, but in securing what is good for societies that seek to return to a lasting peace."[67]

This perspective expresses the nature and function of *jus post bellum* principles. Though criminal accountability is a fundamental component of transition from conflict to peace, the levels and forms of criminal justice must be determined through balancing this duty with other principles of *jus post bellum*. On this point, Peperkamp claims that the moral and legal obligation of punishment should not prevail over the concrete needs of peace, even if there is no agreement on what should be the outcome of this collision of

---

57　May, *After War Ends*, 20.
58　Stahn, '"Jus Ad Bellum", "jus in Bello" … "*Jus Post Bellum*"?—Rethinking the Conception of the Law of Armed Force,' 938–41.
59　Orend, '*Jus Post Bellum*: A Just War Theory Perspective,' 38–41.
60　Coady, 'The *Jus Post Bellum*.'
61　Williams and Caldwell, '*Jus Post Bellum*: Just War Theory and the Principles of Just Peace.'
62　Gallen, '*Jus Post Bellum*: An Interpretive Framework.'
63　De Brabandere, 'The Concept of *Jus Post Bellum* in International Law: A Normative Critique,' 137–38.
64　Boon, 'Legislative Reform in Post-Conflict Zones: *Jus Post Bellum* and the Contemporary Occupant's Law-Making Powers.'
65　May, *After War Ends*, 78.
66　May, 'Reparation, Restitution, and Transitional Justice,' 39.
67　May, '*Jus Post Bellum*, Grotius, and Meionexia,' 21.

values.[68] May warns that one of the problems of this principle "is that since retribution is backward-looking and most of the other *jus post bellum* principles are forward-looking, pursuit of a just and lasting peace tends to favor the forward-looking principles."[69] Bass and Walzer even claim that the duty of peace and reconciliation prevails over the duty of justice.[70]

Looking at those elements, it is here where principles offer a space of coordination and balance for interpreting and applying legal obligations consistently with respect to the exigencies of peace. As seen in Chapter 2, criminal justice is one of the most sophisticated components of the Colombian Peace Agreement.[71] Since 2005 Colombia developed a system of transitional justice for the demobilization of paramilitary groups, which offered an innovative way to reconcile the requirements of international law with the practical needs of peace. The Justice and Peace Law balanced the prohibition on amnesties for serious violations of human rights and IHL against the fact that members of armed groups in negotiation would not accept regular criminal sanctions.[72] Thus, such a law established a system of justice in which those responsible for the most serious crimes were tried and sentenced, but given reduced penalties in exchange for their contribution to peace.

In the 2012–2016 peace negotiations, the conditions were more complicated. Unlike paramilitary groups, the guerilla claimed the political character of their fight, and as such they were not willing to accept the same conditions that were offered by the 2005 Justice and Peace Law. As seen in Chapter 2, the guerrilla was even resistant to including an item on justice in the agenda of negotiations.[73] However, as they accepted a chapter on victims, they understood that criminal justice was a victim's right and an exigence of international law. Here, again, a discussion on the balance between peace and justice emerged. And this is where *jus post bellum* offers a space of coordination and interpretation: a principle of accountability, including criminal responsibility, exists in international law and is a necessity in peace negotiations; however, the conditions of the context require it to be interpreted and applied according to the specific needs of peace.

---

68 Peperkamp, '*Jus Post Bellum*: A Case of Minimalism versus Maximalism?,' 261.
69 May, *After War Ends*, 79.
70 Bass, '*Jus Post Bellum*,' 405; Walzer, 'The Aftermath of War. Reflections on *Jus Post Bellum*,' 45.
71 See Chapter 2, Section 3.3.
72 See Chapter 2, Section 3.3.1.
73 See Chapter 2, Section 3.

In this case, new elements emerged for the interpretative balance. Colombia had the precedent of the 2005 system of reduced penalties. As examined in Chapter 2, the final version of that law was the result of different actors' claims around the international legal prohibition on amnesties for serious crimes. The parties in the 2012–2016 peace process departed from the fact that no amnesty was possible for those crimes. However, the guerilla was not willing to accept any kind of prison sanctions. At the same time, the Office of the ICC Prosecutor insisted on the obligation to prosecute serious crimes committed during the conflict. Furthermore, the Prosecutor added a new element specifying that even if restorative sanctions were possible in the context of a peace process, they should include effective restrictions on liberty. All these elements finally carried out a Special Jurisdiction for Peace tasked with investigating and trying people responsible for the most serious crimes. These individuals should fully cooperate with truth and reparation, and in exchange they will receive restorative sanctions accompanied by effective restrictions on liberty as defined by their judges.

As such, compared to the other principles, for the principle of criminal accountability international law sets stronger standards and exigences that must be observed in the transition from armed conflict to peace. This is in accordance with Boon's argument that in matters dealing with past human rights and IHL violations, principles offer a lower margin of appreciation to the parties.

Therefore, in the way this principle worked in Colombia, we can see a clear example on the role of international law as a framework offering to the parties limits and possibilities, expressed in legal norms, discourses, and practices, in which they moved to create a transitional justice model conciliating the exigences of international law with their practical needs of peace.

3.3 *Reparation*

Contemporary armed conflicts occur in a way such that civilians suffer most of the damages caused by the confrontation. NIACs usually entail degradation of violence, where forced displacement, killings, sexual violence, enforced disappearance, and many other violations of human rights and IHL occur. This situation evinces the state's failure to fulfill its international obligation of respecting and guaranteeing the rights of its people. Therefore, the legal obligation to provide reparation for these damages emerges.[74]

---

74 See the legal framework on reparations presented in Chapter 2, Section 4.1.

On this issue, May proposes the principles of restitution and reparation, while Stahn[75] and Coady[76] propose just reparation, and Orend compensation.[77] For May, "restitution is the restoring to the rightful owner what has been lost or taken away," whereas "reparation is the restoring to good condition of something that has been damaged."[78] In any case, both concepts are grounded in the idea of restoration, which he defines as "a kind of rectification or compensation."[79] However, such a distinction appears unnecessary as restitution is a modality of reparation. This is the view of the UN Basic Principles and Guidelines on the Right to a Remedy and Reparation for Victims, Principle 18 of which states:

> In accordance with domestic law and international law, and taking account of individual circumstances, victims of gross violations of international human rights law and serious violations of international humanitarian law should, as appropriate and proportional to the gravity of the violation and the circumstances of each case, be provided with full and effective reparation [...], which include the following forms: restitution, compensation, rehabilitation, satisfaction and guarantees of non-repetition.[80]

The victim's right to reparation is enshrined in several instruments under IHRL, IHL, and ICL.[81] However, as mentioned in the previous paragraph, reparations must take consideration of the specific circumstances in which the violations of human rights or IHL have occurred. This is especially the case in the context of armed conflict, where victimization is widespread and is committed by different state and non-state actors.[82] This principle thus offers the space and

---

75 Stahn, ' "Jus Ad Bellum", "jus in Bello" ... "*Jus Post Bellum*"?—Rethinking the Conception of the Law of Armed Force,' 938–41.
76 Coady, 'The *Jus Post Bellum*.'
77 Orend, '*Jus Post Bellum*: A Just War Theory Perspective,' 37–42.
78 May, *After War Ends*, 183.
79 May, 'Reparation, Restitution, and Transitional Justice,' 32.
80 UN General Assembly, Basic Principles and Guidelines on the Right to a Remedy and Reparation for Victims of Gross Violations of International Human Rights Law and Serious Violations of International Humanitarian Law.
81 See Chapter 2, Section 4.1., for the international legal framework on reparations.
82 At this regard, the International Law Association has proposed two resolutions on the specific conditions of reparation for victims or armed conflict, in an effort to advance the discussion on the issue both in substantive and procedural terms. International Law Association, Draft Declaration of International Law Principles on Reparation for Victims of Armed Conflict; International Law Association, Draft Procedural Principles For Reparation Mechanisms.

the elements to coordinate and interpret international standards vis-à-vis the concrete circumstances of a given transitional scenario.

The principle of reparation has been a core element in the Colombian transition. As seen in Chapter 2, in 2011 the country adopted what is internationally considered the most developed system of comprehensive reparations to victims of armed conflict.[83] Such a milestone imposed on the parties involved in the 2012–2016 peace process the duty of placing victims at the center of the negotiation.[84] The awareness regarding this principle of reparation in Colombia has been a significant element in developing the negotiations and is reflected in the Final Agreement. Additionally, the aim to grant remedies to victims led the parties to include other elements in the Agreement, through the development of a comprehensive system of truth, justice, and reparations.[85]

The principle of reparation in Colombia has played a vital role in transition, and this case offers insightful elements for other transitional contexts around the world. Reparation for victims of armed conflict is a must not only as a legal duty under international law, but as a condition to make peace sustainable and reconciliation effective. From this case, one can conclude that the normative principle of reparation has a solid international legal basis as well as valuable comparative practice showing to actors involved in trasitions the way to make reparation possible and effective, following international standards and considering the limits and conditions imposed by their context. Additionally, an important contribution of the Colombian approach is given by the way in which it addresses reparations by non-state actors. As seen in Chapter 2, international law and legal scholarship are increasingly discussing this matter, and practice from Colombia will certainly offer new insights, mainly regarding the role of reparation by those actors whitin the judicial process before the Special Jurisdiction for Peace, as well as beyond judicial mechanisms through acts of public apologies and contribution to truth and reconciliation.

3.4   *Reconciliation*

The principle of reconciliation expresses the main political challenge of peacemaking and peacebuilding. It is aimed at bringing people together to

---

83 Unidad de Atención y Reparación a Víctimas, *Universidad de Harvard destaca Política Integral de Reparación de Víctimas en Colombia*, 2015, available at: http://www.unidadvictimas.gov.co/es/valoraci%C3%B3n-y-registro/universidad-de-harvard-destaca-pol%C3%ADtica-integral-de-reparaci%C3%B3n-de-v%C3%ADctimas-en (accessed on 1 April 2018).

84 Government of Colombia and FARC, 'Final Agreement to End the Armed Conflict and Build a Stable and Lasting Peace,' 8.

85 Government of Colombia and FARC, 132.

live peacefully, which is an expression of sustainable peace.[86] Reconciliation seeks "to create relationships of respect, trust, and friendship,"[87] as well as to "bring emotional healing to the victims of war."[88] However, as May argues, "the *jus post bellum* principle of reconciliation is often one of the hardest things to achieve," as it involves a *modus vivendi* in which people are able to not only respect each other but also reach cooperation.[89] This principle is equally proposed by Stahn[90] and by Patterson.[91]

Due to its highly political content, this principle is the most difficult to delineate in a legal perspective. May says that reconciliation is often viewed as "too amorphous a category to count as *jus post bellum* normative principle."[92] Nonetheless, the principle of reconciliation can find different legal bases. First, it is an expression of the state's general obligation to promote peaceful societies and ensure respect for people's rights.[93] Second, reconciliation is a condition to guarantee the non-repetition of human rights violations, which embodies the positive obligations of prevention and reparation.[94] And, third, reconciliation is closely related to the right to truth, both for victims and society.[95]

Based on these considerations, the principle of reconciliation attains legal value. Although reconciliation seems more a goal of transition than a principle guiding the coordination and interpretation of legal norms, such a goal

---

86   See Chapter 1, Section 4, for the discussion on the role of reparations as part of the object of *jus post bellum* in building a sustainable peace.
87   Peperkamp, '*Jus Post Bellum*: A Case of Minimalism versus Maximalism?,' 269.
88   Mark Allman and Tobias Winright, *After the Smoke Clears: The Just War Tradition and Post War Justice* (New York: Orbis, 2010), 102.
89   May, *After War Ends*, 75.
90   Stahn, ' "Jus Ad Bellum", "jus in Bello" ... "*Jus Post Bellum*"?—Rethinking the Conception of the Law of Armed Force,' 938–41.
91   Eric Patterson, *Ending Wars Well: Order, Justice, and Conciliation in Contemporary Post-Conflict* (New Haven: Yale University Press, 2012), 102.
92   May, *After War Ends*, 85.
93   UN General Assembly, Declaration on the Right to Peace; International Covenant on Civil and Political Rights Art. 2.
94   Inter-American Court of Human Rights, Case of the Massacres of El Mozote and nearby places v. El Salvador, Judgement of 25 October 2012 Concurrent Opinion Judge Diego García-Sayán et. al., para. 23. See also Juana Acosta-Lopez, 'The Inter-American Human Rights System and the Colombian Peace: Redefining the Fight Against Impunity,' *American Journal of International Law* 110 AJIL Unbound Symposium on the Colombian Peace Talks and International Law (2016): 179.
95   UN Commission on Human Rights, 'Study on the Right to the Truth, Report of the Office of the United Nations High Commissioner for Human Rights,' Pub. L. No. E/CN.4/2006/91 (2006); Yasmin Naqvi, 'The Right to the Truth in International Law: Fact or Fiction?,' *International Review of the Red Cross* 88, no. 862 (2006): 245–73.

is present in the process of balancing legal obligations against the political needs and aims of peace. In other words, if reconciliation is a condition necessary for building sustainable peace, it becomes a crucial consideration for the application of the normative framework of *jus post bellum*, and any measure or instrument designed for transition should contribute to that aim of social reconciliation. Therefore, reconciliation is a principle of *jus post bellum*.

Reconciliation has been a vital principle in the Colombian transition. In the recent peace process, this principle is expressed in several ways. Addressing the root causes of the conflict related to inequality and political exclusion contributes to reconciliation.[96] The search for truth is a measure aimed at healing people and rebuilding the social fabric. The reparation of victims is also a reconciliation-oriented measure, including actions of reparation by non-state armed actors.[97] Similarly, the mechanism of restorative sanctions for those responsible for serious crimes—which included contributing to rural development and demining as well as participating in social programs—is aimed at integrating former fighters into their communities to foster peaceful coexistence.[98] All of these aims could be considered to be playing a role in balancing international legal requirements with the interests of the parties and the expectations of victims and society as a whole.

Nevertheless, the political dimension of this principle does not allow international law to define specific conditions or standards, but general elements for guiding parties in the transition. Here, in accordance with Boon's proposal, there is a general obligation for states to promote peaceful coexistence and rebuild the social fabric after armed conflict, responding to the *jus post bellum*'s objective of attaining sustainable peace, but it must be met in accordance to the concrete conditions of the context. However, from the case study one can see how this principle has a normative standing to be integrated not only as a goal, but also as component of the normative framework guiding the legal and political decisions for transition to peace.

3.5 *Proportionality*

This principle has the larger consensus among authors. Alongside May, Orend, Gallen, De Brabandere, and Boon include proportionality as a principle of *jus*

---

96 See Chapter 2, Section 2.2. on socioeconomic and political reforms included in the Peace Agreement in Colombia for addressing the root causes for armed conflict.
97 See Chapter 2, Section 4.2. on the approach to reparations in the Colombian transition.
98 See Chapter 2, Sections 2.2 and 3.3 on the mechanisms of transitional justice in Colombia, and how restorative santions play also a role in the social reintegration of former rebels.

post bellum.[99] May describes proportionality as a "meta-principle" over the others. In his words, proportionality "urges that we think about the harm that is caused by the post war application of the other normative principles. In this way, the proportionality principle could be written into each of the principles as a modification of them."[100] The idea behind proportionality is "to consider whether the operation of these other *post bellum* principles might not do more harm than good."[101]

Proportionality is a general requirement of international law that can be considered to be implicit in the other principles of *jus post bellum*. However, it has relevance in *jus post bellum* as long as it guides the parties' balances and decisions within the bargaining zone defined by the other principles. For instance, proportionality plays a role in defining the balance between the retributive dimension of criminal responsibility required by ICL and the need to adopt a restorative approach in a transitional process.[102] On this point, the following analysis presented in a concurrent opinion of an Inter-American Court of Human Rights' judgement is relevant:

> 38. Thus, in certain transitional situations between armed conflicts and peace, it can happen that a State is not in a position to implement fully and simultaneously, the various international rights and obligations it has assumed. In these circumstances, taking into consideration that none of those rights and obligations is of an absolute nature, it is legitimate that they be weighed in such a way that the satisfaction of some does not affect the exercise of the others disproportionately. Thus, the degree of justice that can be achieved is not an isolated component from which legitimate frustrations and dissatisfactions can arise, but part of an ambitious process of transition towards mutual tolerance and peace.[103]

This principle of proportionality is expressed in different components in the Colombian transition. For instance, regarding criminal responsibility,

---

99 Boon, 'Legislative Reform in Post-Conflict Zones: *Jus Post Bellum* and the Contemporary Occupant's Law-Making Powers'; Orend, '*Jus Post Bellum*: A Just War Theory Perspective'; May, *After War Ends*; Gallen, '*Jus Post Bellum*: An Interpretive Framework'; De Brabandere, 'The Concept of *Jus Post Bellum* in International Law: A Normative Critique.'
100 May, *After War Ends*, 22.
101 May, '*Jus Post Bellum*, Grotius, and Meionexia,' 18.
102 See Chapter 2, Section 3.3.
103 Inter-American Court of Human Rights, Case of the Massacres of El Mozote and nearby places v. El Salvador, Judgement of 25 October 2012 Concurrent Opinion of Judge Diego García-Sayan, suscribed by four of the seven judges, para. 38.

the parties balanced ICL's exigences and the ICC Prosecutor's messages on the need to impose effective restrictions of liberty, on the one hand, against the practical need of offering restorative rather than retributive sanctions after a peace negotiation, on the other. As a result, the parties found an intermediate formula that established formal trials and judicial sanctions alongside restorative measures accompanied by restrictions of liberty. This was the result of a proportional balance between legal standards, values, and political requirements of peacemaking. Another example can be seen in the component of reparations, for which international legal standards needed to be measured against the extensive number of victims requiring reparation.[104] A proportional balance was thus required that took into account the comprehensive approach to reparations established by international law, the number of victims, and the State's financial constraints, giving as a result an administrative system of comprehensive reparations offering standard measures according to the kind of damage suffered by the victims. In this way, balances of proportionality from the case study offer elements and examples on how this principle works as a component of the normative framework for transition and how it could be applied in other contexts.

3.6 *Inclusiveness*

The broad participation of different social sectors, as well as the consideration of their particular needs in peace processes and agreements, is gaining increasing importance around the world. As presented in Chapter 2, international law enshrines the right of traditionally marginalized groups to be consulted on issues of their interest, as it is the case of indigenous and tribal peoples.[105] Similarly, the UN has consistently advocated for women's participation and inclusion in peace processes and agreements.[106] Although this principle was not envisaged by May, practice provides elements for considering participation and inclusion as a principle of *jus post bellum*.

Stahn refers to this principle as "fairness and inclusiveness of peace settlements," arguing that sustainable peace requires all interests to be represented, including those of "groups and minorities protected by international law."[107] Along the same line, Turner highlights that inclusion of groups such as women

---

[104] See Chapter 2, Section 4.2.
[105] See Chapter 2, section 5.1.2.
[106] See Chapter 2, section 5.1.1.
[107] Stahn, ' "Jus Ad Bellum", "jus in Bello" ... *"Jus Post Bellum"*?—Rethinking the Conception of the Law of Armed Force,' 938.

and indigenous peoples is being considered by parties in peace negotiations as a legal obligation.[108]

Ensuring specific participation in peace processes to certain groups is based on the idea that armed conflict does not impact all people in the same way. Different affected sectors should have a voice in peace negotiations and be differentially included in the resulting agreement. For this reason, this principle involves both a procedural and a substantive dimension. It is not just about granting participation in the peace negotiation process but also about ensuring that the specific needs of the involved sectors are adequately addressed in the peace agreement.

On this idea, Ní Aoláin and Haynes sustain that "countries emerging from conflict provide multiple opportunities for transformation on many different levels, opportunities uncommon in stable and non-transitional societies."[109] For them, this opportunity is especially important for social groups traditionally "marginalized, underrepresented, and discriminated against."[110] Transitional moments have great transformative potential, and this is why they must be made an opportunity to evaluate the situation of marginalized groups in society.

In this sense, this principle should be understood in a broad sense, as including the participation of victims and civil society as well as the specific interests of differential groups. Building sustainable peace after a NIAC does not only depend on the parties in conflict or the state. It must be the result of social dialogue involving a broad participation of different sectors. This is a crucial element for reaching lasting peace,[111] increasing societal acceptance, and reducing the likelihood of excluded actors undermining the process.[112] As such, it must be considered a *jus post bellum* principle guiding transition.

A principle of inclusiveness is notable in the Colombian peace process and its Final Agreement. As analyzed in Chapter 2, inspired by the UNSC Resolution 1325 on women's participation and inclusion in peace processes, Colombia devoted significant attention to women and gender issues in the

---

108   Catherine Turner, "Mapping a Norm of Inclusion in the *Jus Post Bellum*," in *Just Peace After Conflict. Jus Post Bellum and the Justice of Peace*, ed. Carsten Stahn and Jens Iverson (Oxford: Oxford University Press, 2020), 130–146.

109   Ní Aoláin and Haynes, 'The Compatibility of Justice for Women with *Jus Post Bellum* Analysis,' 161.

110   Ní Aoláin and Haynes, 161.

111   Anthony Wanis-St. John and Darren Kew, 'Civil Society and Peace Negotiations: Confronting Exclusion,' *International Negotiation* 13 (2008): 14.

112   *Strengthening the Role of Mediation in the Peaceful Settlement of Disputes, Conflict Prevention and Resolution, Report of the Secretary-General*, UN Doc. A/66/811 (25 June 2012), Annex I, para. 29.

negotiations.[113] Following this path, the parties extended the gender dimension to LGBTI people, who also participated in the process and are referred to in the Agreement. Regarding ethnic minorities, the negotiators accepted the participation of indigenous and Afro-Colombian representatives, invoking ILO Convention 169 and other related instruments, and an ethnic chapter was included in the Agreement.[114] Finally, under a victim-centered approach, a large delegation of victims participated in the negotiations, while other civil society actors were heard in different scenarios.[115] In all of these cases, as exposed in Chapter 2, these social groups invoked international law to support their claims for participation and inclusion in the process. In this way, they were able to present the discussion on inclusiveness as not merely a question of legitimacy but an international legal requirement.

The experience in Colombia shows the normative power of this principle and it creates precedents for other processes around the world. Inclusiveness is a condition to make peace effective, sustainable, and transformative. As such, it cannot be left to the leeway of the parties, but it must be embodied as a normative principle for transition. Insightful elements are offered by this case study, and this principle can be considered as one of the most promising components of *jus post bellum*.

3.7 Environmental Protection

Armed conflict usually impacts the environment in different ways. In some cases, natural resources are exploited as a means to finance war, and in others, armed confrontation has direct or collateral effects on the environment.[116] Thus, restoring and ensuring a healthy environment is a condition for building sustainable peace.[117] Since 2014 Stahn has affirmed that *jus post bellum* needs to "encourage fresh thinking" on environmental damage related to armed conflict,[118] which Easterday describes as a matter typically "ignored or superficially treated in peace agreements."[119] Accordingly, Payne proposes a principle of environmental integrity as a component of *jus post bellum*,[120] and the 2017 publication of the University of Leiden's *Jus Post Bellum* Project was devoted to

---

113 See Chapter 2, Section 5.2.3.
114 See Chapter 2, Section 5.2.3.
115 See Chapter 2, section 5.2.2.
116 Gillett, 'Eco-Struggles: Using International Criminal Law to Protect the Environment During and After Non-International Armed Conflict,' 223.
117 Stahn, '*Jus Post Bellum* and the Justice of Peace: Some Preliminary Reflections,' 16.
118 Stahn, 'R2P and *Jus Post Bellum*. Towards a Polycentric Approach,' 118.
119 Easterday, 'Peace Agreements as a Framework for *Jus Post Bellum*,' 409.
120 Payne, 'The Norm of Environmental Integrity in Post-Conflict Legal Regimes.'

the question of environmental protection and transition from armed conflict to peace.[121]

For Payne, the principle of environmental integrity ensures the soundness of natural resources, including human life and certain properties such as religious and cultural objects.[122] She claims,

> Three intertwined elements of *jus post bellum* are necessary to realizing environmental integrity. One is reparations, which provide means for reconstruction, create a record of what happened, and may provide disincentive for repetition of unlawful acts. A second is collective concern, which is a basis for community action on several fronts to contribute to reconstruction of war-torn states. The third is reconstruction itself.[123]

As analyzed in Chapter 2, damages to the environment can affect reconciliation,[124] reconstruction, and socioeconomic development in post-conflict scenarios,[125] making "environmental protection and the sustainable management of resources [...] important pathways to consolidate peace and promote long-term development."[126] For that reason, a principle of environmental protection must be part of *jus post bellum*, both in terms of the restoration of damages caused by armed conflict,[127] and the promotion of the sustainable management of natural resources as a condition for lasting peace and development.

Regarding this issue, the ILC designated a Drafting Committee on the Protection of the Environment in Relation to Armed Conflicts, which

---

121 Stahn, Iverson, and Easterday, *Environmental Protection and Transitions from Conflict to Peace: Clarifying Norms, Principles, and Practices*.
122 Payne, 'The Norm of Environmental Integrity in Post-Conflict Legal Regimes,' 506. This broad view of environmental protection looks at overcoming the traditional anthropocentric frame given to environmental concern. Such an idea was later sustained by Payne in: Cymie Payne, 'Defining the Environment: Environmental Integrity,' in *Environmental Protection and Transitions from Conflict to Peace: Clarifying Norms, Principles, and Practices*, ed. Carsten Stahn, Jens Iverson, and Jennifer Easterday (Oxford: Oxford University Press, 2017), 62.
123 Payne, 'The Norm of Environmental Integrity in Post-Conflict Legal Regimes,' 514.
124 Gillett, 'Eco-Struggles: Using International Criminal Law to Protect the Environment During and After Non-International Armed Conflict,' 249; Hofmann and Rapillard, 'Post-Conflict Mine Action: Environment and Law,' 404.
125 Easterday and Ivanhoe, 'Conflict, Cash, and Controversy: Protecting Environmental Rights in Post-Conflict Settings,' 274.
126 Hofmann and Rapillard, 'Post-Conflict Mine Action: Environment and Law,' 397.
127 Douglas Lackey, 'Postwar Environmental Damage: A Study in *Jus Post Bellum*,' in *International Criminal Law and Philosophy*, ed. Larry May and Zachary Hoskins (Cambridge: Cambridge University Press, 2010), 141.

elaborated a Draft Principles on the matter in 2016. Draft Principle 14 states that: "Parties to an armed conflict should, as part of the peace process, including where appropriate in peace agreements, address matters relating to the restoration and protection of the environment damaged by the conflict."[128] This principle is drawn from different branches of international law related to environmental protection.[129] It includes provisions from IHL,[130] IHRL,[131] and ICL.[132]

Having such a normative reference, the principle of environmental protection can be seen in different aspects of the Colombian Peace Agreement.[133] As analyzed in Chapter 2, in its preamble the Agreement relates peace to sustainable development and the protection of the environment, natural resources, and biodiversity.[134] Then, in the component on rural development, the Agreement discusses the "environmental rights of the rural population,"[135] and offers special land access and other benefits to communities who work to protect the environment, substitute crops of illicit use, and improve food production.[136] Similarly, the Agreement establishes the protection of areas of special environmental interest, seeking a sustainable development involving rural and ethnic communities.[137] Furthermore, there are environmental protection-related provisions regarding the substitution of crops of illicit use and demining.

In this way, the Colombian case shows the negotiators' awareness on the duty to address environmental protection in their peace talks and to include related provisions in the Final Agreement. As such, this practice constitutes an expression of a *jus post bellum* principle of environmental protection in the

---

128 Report of the International Law Commission to the General Assembly, Seventy-first session, 2 May-10 June and 4 July-12 August 2016, UN Doc. A/71/10, http://legal.un.org/docs/?path=../ilc/reports/2016/english/a_71_10.pdf&lang=EFSRAC, 309.
129 Fleck, 'Legal Protection of the Environment. The Double Challenge of Non-International Armed Conflict and Post-Conflict Peacebuilding,' 203.
130 See, for instance, Henckaerts and Doswald-Beck, *Customary International Humanitarian Law. Volume I: Rules*. Rule 44.
131 See Report of the Special Rapporteur on the issue of human rights obligations relating to the enjoyment of a safe, clean, healthy and sustainable environment, A/HRC/31/53, 28 December 2015.
132 Rome Statute of the International Criminal Court. Article 8(b)(iv).
133 See Chapter 2, Section 2.2.
134 Government of Colombia and FARC, 'Final Agreement to End the Armed Conflict and Build a Stable and Lasting Peace,' 3–4.
135 Government of Colombia and FARC, 199.
136 Government of Colombia and FARC, 15.
137 Government of Colombia and FARC, 11.

transition from armed conflict to peace, in which international law is attracting increasing attention, evident in the recent work by the ILC[138] and legal scholarship.[139] Then, this experice offers new elements from practice that contribute to the legal grounding of a principle of environmental protection in transition for future processes around the world.

4 The Actors of *Jus Post Bellum* in Colombia

Both *jus ad bellum* and *jus in bello* have relatively clear addressees. In *jus ad bellum*, the UN Charter defined the conditions and actors to allow the legal use of force. In *jus in bello*, IHL is addressed to the fighting parties in armed conflict. However, the transition from armed conflict to peace is a complex process involving a variety of actors at all levels, both domestically and internationally.

For Patterson, defining who is an actor of *jus post bellum* means identifying "*who* has the obligation to do *what*?"[140] In this sense, *jus post bellum* would involve any actor with obligations in the transition from armed conflict to sustainable peace. Thus, it would go beyond merely the parties in conflict or in negotiation. As May argues, the addressees of *jus post bellum* are not only the parties in the peace negotiations and the political leaders, but also all the citizens.[141]

Under the understanding of *jus post bellum* proposed in this chapter, its actors cannot be limited to the direct addressees of legal obligations, but involve all actors invoking, interpreting, or applying legal norms, discourses, and comparative practices with a view to achieve a sustainable transition from armed conflict to peace. This standpoint is clear in the Colombian case. In addition to the parties' commitment to international law during peace negotiations, a broad range of external and domestic actors has played a role in the normative internationalization of transition in the country. This section presents these actors and their contribution to incorporating principles of *jus*

---

138 Jacobsson, 'Third Report on the Protection of the Environment in Relation to Armed Conflicts.' And, Report of the International Law Commission to the General Assembly, Seventy-first session, 2 May-10 June and 4 July-12 August 2016, UN Doc. A/71/10, http://legal.un.org/docs/?path=../ilc/reports/2016/english/a_71_10.pdf&lang=EFSRAC, 309.
139 Stahn, Iverson, and Easterday, *Environmental Protection and Transitions from Conflict to Peace: Clarifying Norms, Principles, and Practices*.
140 Patterson, 'Conclusion. Toward a Twenty-First Century *Jus Post Bellum*,' 222.
141 Larry May, '*Jus Post Bellum*, Proportionality and the Fog of War,' *European Journal of International Law* 24, no. 1 (2013): 318–19.

post bellum in the Colombian transition, offering insights for understanding the variety of actors that can play a role in *jus post bellum* in general.

4.1 The Parties in Negotiation

Within the context of a peace process, the parties in negotiation are the main actors of *jus post bellum*. In the case of a NIAC, the state has the primary duty to observe its international obligations applicable to matters in negotiation. However, non-state actors could also have an interest in following those obligations, pursuing international acceptability and legal grounding for the resulting agreement.

Unlike most peace processes, where negotiators are rarely preoccupied with international law and want to be free of legal restraints,[142] in Colombia the parties in negotiation deliberately seized international law as a parameter for their talks and for their agreement. Even though the negotiation agenda did not include any specific reference to international law, the development of negotiations, the regular joint communiqués, and the Final Agreement consistently involved several international legal references. In this way, the parties showed their acknowledgment of international law, accepting the existence of unavoidable international legal obligations as well as the opportunity to frame the negotiation and the agreement under such a regime.

Indeed, both the Colombian government and the FARC wanted an agreement that would be internationally accepted. The government was responsible for ensuring the conformity of the peace deal with the State's international legal obligations. The FARC wanted to obtain legal certainty beyond the domestic order. Those elements not only eased their acceptance of external guidelines but also their search for reconciling international legal standards with the political needs of peace. Thus, in the Agreement the parties explicitly affirmed their determination to reach peace within the parameters of international law,[143] which is then reflected in many aspects of the document, as analyzed in the Chapter 2.

4.2 External Guarantors

As noted by Bell, external backing and mediation in peace negotiations and agreements is the rule rather than the exception.[144] Such a rule has been present in the 2012–2016 peace negotiations in Colombia. However, rather

---

142 Kastner, *Legal Normativity in the Resolution of Internal Armed Conflict*, 68–69.
143 Government of Colombia and FARC, 'Final Agreement to End the Armed Conflict and Build a Stable and Lasting Peace,' 144.
144 Bell, *On the Law of Peace*, 66.

than mediation, the parties assigned to external actors the role of guarantors (Cuba and Norway) and partner states (Chile and Venezuela).[145] A similar role was assigned to the UN, which participated in the talks through a Secretary-General's Special Representative and received a monitoring mandate for the implementation phase.[146]

In normative terms, these external actors have played an essential role in bringing international law standards to the negotiation process and to the Agreement. Regarding this topic, Kastner highlights that external actors "not only assist the negotiation parties in generating their proper normative framework but are also norm promoter and norm creators who may introduce predominantly external norms into the negotiations."[147] This was the case in Colombia.

During the negotiations, Norway, as a guarantor, offered and sponsored a group of experts in international law and transitional justice to counsel the parties during the process. The group was chaired by Morten Bergsmo, a prestigious professor of international law and former advisor to the ICC and the ICTY. The group was tasked with advising on the legal limits that the peace agreement could have *vis-à-vis* Colombia's international legal obligations.[148]

Because of the confidentiality of the negotiations, it is difficult to know the terms in which that external legal advice was presented and assumed by the parties around the table. However, considering the international legal consistency of the Final Agreement, one could deduce that the role played by those external actors was vital for such an outcome. In addition to the technical legal advice provided by the experts in the negotiation, the external guarantors likely claimed for the observance of international standards. It is difficult to imagine that the same result could have been achieved without an independent party advising on the legal limits of the agreement. If those limits had been brought to the table only by the government, the guerrilla would have shown more resistance to accept them.

Finally, regarding the role of the UN Representative for the negotiations, his influence could be measured in terms of the inclusion of relevant UN guidelines in the Final Agreement. In particular, the 2004 Secretary-General Report

---

145 Government of Colombia and FARC, 'Final Agreement to End the Armed Conflict and Build a Stable and Lasting Peace,' 1.
146 Government of Colombia and FARC, 214–16.
147 Kastner, *Legal Normativity in the Resolution of Internal Armed Conflict*, 129.
148 Hugo García and Juan David Laverde. Los arquitectos del acuerdo. *El Espectador*, 26 September 2015, https://www.elespectador.com/noticias/politica/los-arquitectos-del-acuerdo-articulo-588936 (accessed on 1 April 2018).

on Transitional Justice[149] recommended a series of measures to be incorporated in peace agreements, especially those regarding victims' rights, the prohibition on amnesties, and the safeguard of the rule of law.[150] Something similar could be said regarding UNSC Resolution 1325 and the participation and inclusion of women in the negotiation process and the Agreement. It is because of these elements that one can conclude that the UN considered the Agreement to have satisfied international and UN standards, and that the Security Council not only welcomed the deal but also assumed its monitoring and verification.[151]

4.3 The Colombian Constitutional Court

Colombia has a very influential Constitutional Court, which has the mandate to control the constitutionality of constitutional reforms and of any law. To do so, in addition to the Constitution, the Court must use IHRL and IHL as a parameter of constitutional control. It is because according to Article 93 of the Constitution, international human rights treaties duly ratified by Colombia are prevalent in the domestic order. This provision has been interpreted by the Court to mean that these international norms integrate a constitutional block that has the same legal status as the Constitution itself.[152]

As such, all the transitional norms adopted in Colombia are under the control of the Constitutional Court, both under the Constitution and under IHRL and IHL. For this reason, the Court has played an essential role in bringing international law to the discussion around the transition to peace in the country. This can be observed in at least three instances.

One instance is the constitutional exam of the 2005 Justice and Peace Law created for the demobilization of paramilitary groups. In its main decision regarding this Law, the Court used several international instruments to assess

---

149 UN Secretary-General, 'Report of the Secretary-General on the Rule of Law and Transitional Justice in Conflict and Post-Conflict Societies,' para. 64.
150 In addition to the presence of a UN Representative, other UN officials constantly sent messages to the table of negotiations. Among them, the OHCHR's representative in Colombia played an active role regarding the respect for international standards related to human rights abuses occurred during the conflict but affirming the UN support to the negotiations. At this point, he noted that: "It is quite clear in the international legal framework that an amnesty or a pardon cannot be included but it's not clear how far you must go with criminal law," "U.N. urges Colombia not to concede to FARC," *United Press International* (13 September 2012), available at: https://www.upi.com/Top_News/Special/2012/09/13/UN-urges-Colombia-not-to-concede-to-FARC/UPI-47681347565546/ (accessed on 2 August 2018).
151 UN Security Council, Resolution 2261 (2016); UN Security Council, Resolution 2307 (2016); UN Security Council, Resolution 2366 (2017).
152 Corte Constitucional de Colombia, Sentencia C-574 de 1992.

its constitutionality regarding reparation and justice. In an extensive reference to international law, the Court invoked the ICCPR, the American Convention on Human Rights, the International Convention on Enforced Disappearance, the Geneva Conventions and their Protocol Additional II, the Genocide Convention, the ICC Statute,[153] and several sentences of the Inter-American Court of Human Rights.[154] The Court used all these references to frame the State's international legal obligation to ensure victims' rights to truth, justice, and reparation, especially regarding the prohibition on amnesties for grave violations of IHRL and IHL. Based on this legal framework, the Court modified some aspects of the Law, increasing the perpetrators' measures of accountability and responsibility with respect to reparations for victims.[155]

Another instance is the constitutional exam of the 2012 Legal Framework for Peace.[156] This instrument was adopted, before the peace negotiations with the FARC began, with the purpose of providing a legal basis for the future transitional mechanisms that could be required. In its judgement, the Court extensively examined relevant international treaties, international human rights jurisprudence, and international practice on transitional justice. Using those references, the Court defined the international standards that the Legal Framework for Peace should have observed in terms of reparation to victims[157] and justice for international crimes.[158]

In the third instance, the Court has been a fundamental actor for the normative development of the 2016 Peace Agreement, and its previous decisions had clear influence during the negotiations. In the same way that the threat of a possible intervention by the ICC influenced matters of criminal justice, the parties' knowledge that any norm developing the Agreement would be submitted to the Court's control caused them to carefully follow its previous jurisprudence on transitional justice. In this sense, the Court indirectly influenced the normative internationalization of the Peace Agreement because of the international legal background of its previous jurisprudence on this matter. This was especially the case for the incorporation of international standards on the right to reparation and the prohibition of amnesties for international crimes.

---

153   Corte Constitucional de Colombia, Sentencia C-370/06 paragraph 4.3.
154   Corte Constitucional de Colombia, paragraph 4.4.
155   For the Court, the broad purpose of that law "was valid, but added that the Law had to be more stringent in order to comply with constitutional and international legal standards." Kalmanovitz, 'Introduction: Law and Politics in the Colombian Negotiations with Paramilitary Groups,' 7.
156   Corte Constitucional de Colombia, Sentencia C-579/13.
157   Corte Constitucional de Colombia, paragraph 7.2.
158   Corte Constitucional de Colombia, paragraph 8.1.3.

4.4 The Prosecutor of the International Criminal Court

Under current international law, the ICC should be considered a part of any transitional justice process, and the parties in conflicts should take seriously the possibility of an ICC intervention in cases where negotiation terms do not meet the Rome Statute's standards.[159] This question has been present in Colombia since the very beginning of the ICC's mandate. Indeed, when Colombia deposited its instrument of ratification to the Rome Statute in 2002, a declaration was made in the sense of deferring the competence of the ICC for war crimes for seven years.[160] The declaration was made with the purpose of facilitating peace negotiations with armed groups in the country during the meantime.

In 2003, Colombia initiated a negotiation for the demobilization of paramilitary groups. A year later the ICC Prosecutor put the country under preliminary examination,[161] which she has kept open until now. During these years, the Rome Statute and the examination by the ICC Prosecutor have been invoked by different actors as a reminder of the international legal obligation to ensure justice for crimes under the Court's jurisdiction. The consideration of the ICC was reflected in the discussion of the Justice and Peace Law for that demobilization. When the Constitutional Court examined the constitutionality of this law, most interventions invoked the ICC Statute to claim greater accountability, and the Court used such an instrument as a parameter to support its decision to modify some aspects of the Law.[162]

In 2012, Colombia adopted a constitutional reform developing a Legal Framework for Peace that included the possibility of granting alternative penalties or the suspension of sentences for members of armed groups.[163] This norm was examined by the Constitutional Court in 2013, and the ICC Prosecutor intervened in the process through two letters expressing her concern regarding these benefits. In the first letter she argued that since the suspension of a prison sentence means that the accused does not spend time imprisoned, it would be manifestly inadequate in the case of those most responsible for committing international crimes.[164] In a second letter, sent a few weeks later, the

---

159 Ambos, 'The Legal Framework of Transitional Justice,' 67–68.
160 The Office of the Prosecutor, 'Report on Preliminary Examination Activities 2016,' para. 233.
161 The Office of the Prosecutor, para. 231.
162 Corte Constitucional de Colombia, Sentencia C-370/06 paragraph 4.3.8.
163 Congreso de la República de Colombia, Acto Legislativo 01 de 2012.
164 Letter of 26 July 2013, sent by the Prosecutor of the ICC to the Colombian Constitutional Court. Corte Constitucional de Colombia, Sentencia C-579/13 paragraph 3.16.1.

Prosecutor emphasized that the ICC maintains its competence over individuals who committed crimes enshrined by the Rome Statute, even if they have received judicial benefits under domestic law.[165]

In 2015, in a conference on transitional justice and the ICC in Colombia, the ICC Deputy Prosecutor explained the Prosecutor's position in a more moderate way. In his opinion, criminal sentences can adopt different forms in transitional contexts: absolute suspension of sentences is not possible, but prison time is not an indispensable punishment.[166] This statement supported the idea that in contexts of transition, alternative measures offering effective restrictions of liberty were enough to meet the ICC's standards on punishment.

All of these elements have played a significant role in the transition in Colombia. The mechanism of criminal responsibility and prison sentences applied to paramilitary groups under the 2005 Justice and Peace Law were possible owing to the potential threat of an ICC intervention.[167] This was also the case in the 2016 Peace Agreement with the FARC. Indeed, even though the guerrilla did not accept the same prison sentences as those applied to paramilitaries, the negotiators understood that the ICC Prosecutor would not accept simple restorative sanctions for individuals responsible of the most serious crimes. In this sense, the Final Agreement incorporated the Deputy Prosecutor's perspective, introducing effective restrictions of liberty as a part of the restorative sanctions agreed by the parties.

As such, the ICC Prosecutor welcomed the terms of the Peace Agreement.[168] In a subsequent visit to the country, the Prosecutor declared herself "impressed by the commitment, invaluable experience and high standards of Colombian courts," and reaffirmed the disposition of her office to keep "as a good faith partner of the Colombian government and the Colombian people in this journey towards sustainable peace."[169]

---

165 Letter of 7 August 2013, sent by the Prosecutor of the ICC to the Colombian Constitutional Court. Corte Constitucional de Colombia, paragraph 3.16.2.
166 James Stewart, Deputy ICC Prosecutor, 'Transitional Justice in Colombia and the Role of the International Criminal Court.'
167 Kastner, *Legal Normativity in the Resolution of Internal Armed Conflict*, 168. In the same line, see Jose Arvelo, 'International Law and Conflict Resolution in Colombia: Balancing Peace and Justice in the Paramilitary Demobilization Process,' *Georgetown Journal of International Law* 37, no. 2 (2006): 447.
168 Office of the ICC Prosecutor, 'Statement of ICC Prosecutor, Fatou Bensouda, on the Conclusion of the Peace Negotiations between the Government of Colombia and the Revolutionary Armed Forces of Colombia.'
169 Statement of the Prosecutor of the International Criminal Court, Fatou Bensouda, on the conclusion of her visit to Colombia (10–13 September 2017), https://www.icc-cpi.int//Pages/item.aspx?name=170913-otp-stat-colombia (accessed on 17 April 2018).

These statements reflect the Prosecutor's satisfaction with the way in which the parties in negotiation accepted and applied her recommendations, showing the influence of the ICC in the Colombian transitional justice mechanisms since 2005. This Prosecutor's support plays a very positive role in giving legitimacy and legal certainty to the Agreement. On this point, one can conclude that if criminal accountability is effectively ensured in the agreed terms, a future ICC intervention would be unlikely in this case.[170]

4.5   The Inter-American System of Human Rights

Both the Inter-American Commission and the Inter-American Court of Human Rights have made significant contributions to the development of IHRL regarding truth, justice, and reparation, and they have influenced its incorporation into domestic law and practice.[171] As discussed in the previous chapter regarding the prohibition on amnesties for serious violations of human rights, the Commission and the Court developed a consistent jurisprudence on the State's obligation to investigate and prosecute those crimes, as well as to provide reparation for victims of dictatorial regimes and armed conflicts in the continent. The Court has even rejected the validity of domestic laws involving impunity in those cases.[172]

The Inter-American System of Human Rights' jurisprudence has been invoked by several organizations and by the Constitutional Court during the constitutional control for the norms on transitional justice in Colombia. NGOs and academia's interventions before the Constitutional Court during the exam of the Justice and Peace Law and the Legal Framework for Peace invoked the Inter-American jurisprudence on human rights as a reference for the State's international obligations. And, indeed, the Constitutional Court extensively referred to several Inter-American Court sentences as parameters of constitutional control.[173] Such decisions were mainly related to positive obligations to prevent, investigate, and sanction human rights violations;[174] the

---

170   Sanchez, 'Could the Colombian Peace Accord Trigger an ICC Investigation on Colombia?,' 176.
171   Juan Méndez and Catherine Cone, 'Human Rights Make a Difference: Lessons from Latin America,' in *The Oxford Handbook of International Human Rights Law*, ed. Dinah Shelton (Oxford: Oxford University Press, 2013), 979.
172   Inter-American Court of Human Rights, Case of the Massacres of El Mozote and nearby places v. El Salvador, Judgement of 25 October 2012.
173   Corte Constitucional de Colombia, Sentencia C-370/06; Corte Constitucional de Colombia, Sentencia C-579/13.
174   Caso Godínez Cruz vs. Honduras; Caso Hermanos Gómez Paquiyauri vs. Perú.

inadmissibility of amnesties for those violations[175] and the invalidity of laws granting such amnesties;[176] the victim's right to an effective remedy, including reparation;[177] and the right to truth.[178]

Considering these elements, the Constitutional Court made significant adjustments to the 2005 Justice and Peace Law, which were expressly welcomed by the Inter-American Commission. The Commission issued an official statement analyzing the Law and the Constitutional Court's judgment under the Inter-American standards on human rights. For the Commission, the Court's decision substantially improved the Law's balance between the need to grant judicial benefits in exchange for contributions to peace with the international standards on truth, justice, and reparation. On this matter, the Commission affirmed that the Court's decision constituted an essential tool to interpret and apply the Colombian transitional legal framework according to the State's international human rights obligations.[179] Therefore, the precedents of the Inter-American System became crucial considerations for the parties during the 2012–2016 peace negotiations.

4.6   Victims and Civil Society Organizations

NGOs working on human rights and other related sectors are fundamental actors in the process of transition to peace. As noted by Davis, "their experience in litigation and political incidence have contributed for example to the development of a strong jurisprudence on victims' rights in Latin America."[180] At the same time, IHRL has played a fundamental role in legitimizing different civil society's claims and discourses. NGOs have used international law "in advocacy, campaigning, fact-finding reports, complaints to international bodies, briefs to courts, and to develop the scope and efficacy of the international human rights institutional framework."[181]

---

175   Inter-American Court of Human Rights, Case of the Massacres of El Mozote and nearby places v. El Salvador, Judgement of 25 October 2012. Inter-American Court of Human Rights, Case of 'Mapiripán Massacre' v. Colombia, Judgment of 15 September 2005.
176   Inter-American Court of Human Rights, Case of the Massacres of El Mozote and nearby places v. El Salvador, Judgement of 25 October 2012.
177   Caso Myrna Mack Chang vs Guatemala; Caso comunidad Moiwana vs. Suriname.
178   Caso Bámaca Velásquez vs Guatemala.
179   Inter-American Commission on Human Rights, Pronunciamiento de la Comisión Interamericana de Derechos Humanos sobre la aplicación y el alcance de la Ley de justicia y paz en la República de Colombia, 2006, http://www.cidh.org/countryrep/Colombia2006sp/pronunciamiento.8.1.06esp.htm (accessed on 15 April 2018).
180   Jeffrey Davis, *Seeking Human Rights Justice in Latin America: Truth, Extra-Territorial Courts, and the Process of Justice* (Cambridge: Cambridge University Press, 2014), 224.
181   Andrew Clapham, 'The Use of International Human Rights Law by Civil Society Organisations,' in *Routledge Handbook of International Human Rights Law*, ed. Sheeran Rodley, Sir Nigel Scott (London: Routledge, 2013), 153.

As such, civil society organizations have also contributed to the international legal background of the transition to peace in Colombia. Besides their general advocacy in media and political scenarios, they have held a concrete role in the discussion of transitional justice norms before the Constitutional Court. During the examination of the 2005 Justice and Peace Law and the 2012 Legal Framework for Peace, the Court considered the interventions and briefs submitted by several local NGOs and think tanks, as well as international ones like the International Commission of Jurists,[182] the International Center for Transitional Justice, Human Rights Watch, and Amnesty International.[183] In all of their interventions, these organizations invoked international law asking the Court to ensure international standards on justice and reparations to victims.

Those legal discourses in media and before the Court have impacted the way in which the legal mechanisms were designed and adapted. On the Justice and Peace Law, Evans highlights that "the consistent pressure by international and regional human rights mechanisms, as well as by national civil society organisations, has played a major role in highlighting concerns relating to reparations."[184] Similarly, one could consider the influence of human rights advocacy on matters such as victims' participation during the peace negotiations and the broad gender dimension of the 2016 Peace Agreement. These issues were not present in the initial agenda of negotiations, but they were introduced and accepted by the parties during the process owing to the pressure by victims, NGOs, and other related actors.

On this line, the role of victims during the peace negotiations in Colombia expressed their potential to bring legal standards and discourses to the discussion on matters involving their rights. Victims played a fundamental role both through their public advocacy and through their direct participation in the table of negotiations for having a Peace Agreement observing international legal standards on victim's rights.

4.7 Insights on the Type and Role of Actors of Jus Post Bellum

From the variety of actors and functions played by them in the Colombian transition, one can find relevant insights for understanding the type and role of actors of *jus post bellum* in general. As suggested in this section, an actor of *jus post bellum* is everyone playing a role in defining, bringing, interpreting,

---

182 Corte Constitucional de Colombia, Sentencia C-370/06 paragraph 3.
183 Corte Constitucional de Colombia, Sentencia C-579/13 paragraphs 3, 4.
184 Evans, *The Right to Reparation in International Law for Victims of Armed Conflict*, 221.

and applying relevant international law as a frame for transitioning from armed conflict to sustainable peace.

If *jus post bellum* is a normative framework that guides the contextualized interpretation and application of international law for the transition to peace, the way in which this framework operates and the principles that define its substance, as seen in this chapter, mean that the range of actors that can play a role in this process is wide and open. This section offered a varied list of domestic and international actors in Colombia, without being exhaustive. The common element among them was their contribution to define a normative framework in which the formulas for transition were built on different matters, having as a goal addressing the root causes of armed conflict and observing international standards on human rights, democracy, and the rule of law. Thus, according to the conceptual and empirical analysis presented here, playing a role on such a task can be considered as the distinctive element to identify the actors of *jus post bellum* in any given context.

As such, the Colombian experience shows at least four kind of relevant actors that could be generally seen as the basic categories to classify actors of *jus post bellum* in other contexts.

First, direct parts in negotiation are the main actors of *jus post bellum*. Regardless of the efforts made by other institutions or actors, the parties directly involved in finding a solution to their armed conflict are at the center of decisions, and their understanding and commitment to the normative legal framework guiding transition is a condition to make possible a successful transit from armed conflict to peace under the parameters of *jus post bellum*.

Second, external actors such as mediators, guarantors, the UN, and other relevant international institutions are essential to facilitate the incorporation of international legal norms, discourses, and practices into the specific transitional process. As seen in Colombia, the guarantor countries, the UN representative, the ICC Prosecutor, and even the Inter-American human rights institutions played a role at bringing to the table and to the institutional and public discussions international standards as derived from the State's international obligations and from the comparative practice on the matter. This external contribution was essential to make the parties aware on the legal limits and possibilities shaping their negotiation. The specific actors relevant for other contexts will depend on different conditions but that support by international actors is essential to facilitate transition from a NIAC to peace under the vision of *jus post bellum*.

Third, domestic institutions are also key actors for a successful observance of *jus post bellum* in transitions from NIACs. This section only referred to the Constitutional Court in Colombia, but other actors such as the parliament and other courts, for example, have played a role in the normative internationalization of the Colombian transition. In other contexts, those actors will depend on the institutional design or the institutional situation of the country, but experience from this case study shows how relevant is to have domestic institutions ensuring compliance with international legal standards both for the design and for the implementation of transitional mechanisms.

Fourth, experience in the case study shows how the active involvement of victims and other civil society actors is a fundamental component of *jus post bellum*. As discussed on the principle of inclusiveness, the normative dimension of inclusion is getting increased attention in international law and it plays a vital role for making peace legitimate and sustainable. Then, the participation of victims and other civil society actors not only ensures their involvement in the peacebuilding process but those actors can also bring to the discussion international standards to be observed in the protection of their rights and those of society.

5 The Functions Played by International Law in the Colombian Transition: Possible Functions of *Jus Post Bellum*?

Considering the significant role played by international law in the Colombian transition, this case offers important insights on the possible functions of *jus post bellum* as a framework involving the application of international law to transitions from armed conflict to peace. Based on that view, this section presents some functions played by international law in the transition to peace in Colombia, and how they could be more generally understood as functions of *jus post bellum*.

5.1 *Increasing International Legitimacy of Transitional Mechanisms*

In a global world, the international acceptance of peace agreements and other transitional mechanisms can be a condition for their successful and sustainable implementation. Such acceptance is largely dependent on the conformity of those mechanisms with international law.

In the Colombian case, the adherence of the peace negotiations and the Peace Agreement to international law is at the basis of their broad international support. It is evident, for instance, in the extensive involvement of the UNSC in monitoring implementation, and in the welcoming messages by the ICC Prosecutor regarding transitional justice mechanisms. It creates a favorable environment for donors and external agencies supporting the implementation of the agreement and can also have effects on the domestic level, increasing the credibility of the process and encouraging all actors around its compliance.

5.2 *Offering Legal Certainty to the Peace Agreement*

One of the main reasons why the parties based the Colombian Peace Agreement on international law was to lend it legal certainty beyond domestic law. This can be identified in at least two instances. One is the legal shielding of the Agreement as an international legal accord, which was a purpose shared not only by both parties but also by other actors of civil society and external guarantors facing the threat of future modifications to the Agreement by its opponents. This function is very relevant in the case of NIACs, as usually there are sectors opposing the peace agreement that could have the power to modify what was agreed. Here, the shielding function attributed by the negotiators to international law in the Peace Agreement expresses a creative use of international legal norms and mechanisms, and it constitutes a significant contribution to the debate on the functions that *jus post bellum* as normative framework can play.

Second, the international acceptance of the Peace Agreement, specially by the Office of the ICC Prosecutor and the UNSC, creates an expectation that the deal will be respected by international legal institutions. For instance, in the field of criminal responsibility for international crimes, one could reasonably expect that individuals responsible for such crimes who are duly submitted to the transitional justice system created by the Agreement would not later be prosecuted by those facts in Colombia or abroad. It is an important expression of legal certainty, in view of the risk of any re-opening of criminal processes if the ICL's exigences are not met, and the fact that the ICC keeps competence regardless of the domestic benefits granted by the State. Here, the guidance of international law for the definition of the system of criminal justice was essential to reaching a formula designed to satisfy the ICC's complementarity test. Similarly, it would be expected that the adherence to international standards on truth, justice, and reparation could shield the Agreement from situations like the annulation of domestic laws because of their incompatibility with IHRL standards, as it has occurred in Latin America in some cases following recommendations of the Inter-American System of Human Rights.[185]

---

185   Some examples include Argentina (La Nacion, Diputados derogó la obediencia debida, 25 March 1998, https://www.lanacion.com.ar/politica/diputados-derogo-la-obediencia-debida-nid91500, accessed on 10 March 2017); Chile (Publico, Chile deroga el decreto ley de amnistía aprobado por la dictadura, 12 September 2014, https://www.publico.es/internacional/chile-deroga-decreto-ley-amnistia.html, accessed on 10 March 2017); El Salvador (El Nuevo Herald, Supremo salvadoreño deroga Ley de Amnistía, 10 July 2016,

5.3 Delimitating a Bargaining Zone for Negotiations

In peace negotiations, international law helps to delimit the parties' expectations within a framework external to them. It is particularly important considering that in NIACs non-state armed groups generally reject the state's institutions and norms. Thus, framing the negotiations under international law places state and non-state actors in a certain position of parity regarding their obligations and expectations. In such cases, it would be easier for non-state actors to accept conditions that the state cannot ease on in negotiation because it is constrained by its international obligations.[186]

In the Colombian case, this is especially visible in the field of justice. On the one hand, if the parties wanted the Agreement to be protected and governed by international law, they had to accept that the Additional Protocol II's provision on amnesties needed to be balanced with the State's duty to prosecute international crimes. On the other hand, the fact that the State's margin of decision is limited by its international obligations implies that even if the government wanted to accept lower standards, it cannot ensure that they would be respected domestically and internationally. The ICC's competence, the preceding reopening of domestic judicial processes against beneficiaries of amnesties in Latin America, and the possibility of prosecutions by foreign courts under the principle of universal jurisdiction caused the guerrilla to accept that criminal responsibility was a necessary condition under international law rather than a mere exigence of the government.

5.4 Creating Confidence among the Parties

In a NIAC, at least a non-state actor is fighting the institutional system, including its legal order. Such an actor is likely to distrust a negotiation conducted exclusively under the domestic normative framework it is fighting against. In the Colombian case, framing the negotiation under an international legal angle increased trust among the parties, as they felt backed by norms, actors, and institutions beyond mere domestic law.

---

https://www.elnuevoherald.com/noticias/mundo/america-latina/article89949847.html (accessed on 10 March 2017).

186 On this point, Saffon and Uprimny point out that "legal standards on victims' rights would work not as obstacles to peace, but rather as virtuous restrictions that channel peace negotiations, by restricting the available political options for framing them, and by bringing conflicting interests and expectations of different actors closer–even to the point of generating consensual spaces among them." Saffon and Uprimny, 'Uses and Abuses of Transitional Justice in Colombia,' 388.

On this matter, Kastner argues that "international law may offer a 'shade' under which peace negotiations can take place in a more legitimate, and as a result more effective way, by pulling the actors involved towards this shade and spurring compliance."[187] This confidence can be enhanced by the fact that an international framework offers a certain impartial language in which parties can find common and reconcilable points, at the time that international law recognizes in neutral terms the status of the non-state actors in negotiation.[188]

5.5   Empowering Traditional Marginalized Actors

International law empowered different groups in Colombia in their demands for participation and inclusion in the design of transitional mechanisms and in the peace process. This function of international law is described by Kastner as a legal empowerment allowing vulnerable groups not only to be aware of their rights and the use of law to protect them but also, in the context of transitional processes, "to contribute to forming the legal-normative framework of peace negotiations."[189]

International law gave force to victims' discourses and demands during the peace process and in the Agreement in Colombia. Since 2005, international law has backed victims' claims to increase the exigences of truth, justice, and reparation in the initial *Alternative Penalties Law*, which caused the government and the Congress to move towards a more comprehensive Justice and Peace Law.[190] Victims' demands had true impact because they were grounded on international law. In this way, their discourse transcended a political dimension and attained a normative power.[191] On this point, the 2016 Peace Agreement declares that it seeks to respond to the expectations of the victims and society in general, as well as to the State's national and international obligations.[192]

When people can invoke international legal obligations to support their demands in a context of transition, they receive greater visibility and international support, a result that consequentially improves their chances of being heard and included. This occurs because of international pressure to negotiate

---

187   Kastner, *Legal Normativity in the Resolution of Internal Armed Conflict*, 16–17.
188   Jorge Esquirol, 'Can International Law Help? An Analysis of the Colombian Peace Process,' *Connecticut Journal of International Law* 16, no. 1 (2000): 39.
189   Kastner, *Legal Normativity in the Resolution of Internal Armed Conflict*, 146.
190   Saffon and Uprimny, 'Uses and Abuses of Transitional Justice in Colombia,' 392–93.
191   Saffon and Uprimny, 373.
192   Government of Colombia and FARC, 'Final Agreement to End the Armed Conflict and Build a Stable and Lasting Peace,' 129.

according to international law and the negotiators' growing interest to have an agreement internationally accepted. This is particularly visible with respect to the increased attention paid to women in peace negotiations around the world after UNSC Resolution 1325.[193]

Additionally, the Colombian experience shows that the international legal development on women's participation and inclusion in peace processes can serve as an example for approaching other identity groups, which are equally essential to achieving peace.[194] This is especially the case for LGBTI people, whose rights are receiving increasing legal attention at the international level.[195] Similarly, for ethnic communities, their international legal protection through ILO Convention 169 and UN declarations can be enhanced with the communities' specific participation and inclusion in peace processes, following the example of the framework created for women by UNSC Resolution 1325.

5.6   Promoting Comprehensiveness in the Guarantee of Rights

Following international standards, the Colombian Agreement integrates justice, truth, and reparation as an indivisible whole. The Agreement states that these three components are all aimed at ensuring victims' rights with no one component prevailing over the others.[196] This system looks at accomplishing the State's positive obligations under IHRL, a regime under which states have the responsibility not only to investigate and punish violations of human rights but also to prevent them, search for the truth, repair the victims, guarantee the non-repetition of violence, and maintain public order.[197] This combined

---

193   Helen Durham, 'From Paper to Practice: The Role of Treaty Ratification Post-Conflict,' in *The Role of International Law in Rebuilding Societes After Conflict*, ed. Brett Bowden, Hilary Charlesworth, and Jeremy Farrall (Cambridge: Cambridge University Press, 2009), 194.

194   On this point, Anderlini notes that "where political or identity issues are at the root of conflict, women can use their gendered identities and social experiences to bridge these chasms and set an example for other in their own identity groups." Anderlini, *Women Building Peace: What They Do, What It Matters*, 126.

195   The visibility of LGBT rights at international law level started in 2011 with UN Human Rights Council Resolution 17/19 (2011). In 2016, the Council created a mandate for an Independent Expert on protection against violence and discrimination based on sexual orientation and gender identity, through Resolution 32/2 (2016), UN. Doc. A/HRC/RES/32/2.

196   Government of Colombia and FARC, 'Final Agreement to End the Armed Conflict and Build a Stable and Lasting Peace,' 130.

197   Inter-American Court of Human Rights, Case of the Massacres of El Mozote and nearby places v. El Salvador, Judgement of 25 October 2012 Concurrent Opinion Judge Diego García-Sayán et. al., para. 23. See also Acosta-Lopez, 'The Inter-American Human Rights System and the Colombian Peace: Redefining the Fight Against Impunity,' 179.

approach is the best way to comprehensively satisfy victims' rights in contexts of transition, which is unlikely to be achieved through only criminal retribution for past violations.[198] On this point, it is important to remember that such a comprehensive approach was not envisaged in the agenda of negotiations, in which the guerilla was reluctant to accept any form of justice but agreed to include a component on victims' rights. It was here that, owing to the comprehensive approach to victims' rights in international law, all components on truth, justice, and reparation were finally developed during the peace process.

5.7 Encouraging the Transformative Role of Transition

As discussed above, *jus post bellum* looks for a positive transformation of the *status quo ante* rather than simply its restoration, especially in contexts of transition from NIACs to peace. In the Colombian case, the ways in which international law has shaped transition strengthened the transformative role of transitional mechanisms to build peace. This effect can be seen in at least three components.

First, the establishment of a reparation system, even during the ongoing armed conflict, shows that reparation can also play a transformative role capable of creating conditions for peace. In addition to the five measures of reparation defined by international law, the 2011 Law on Victims established a system of institutions and mechanisms to empower victims and ensure their participation at different levels. It paved the way for the significant victims' support to the 2012–2016 peace negotiations with the guerrilla. Reparation thus assumed a dual role, both correcting violations of human rights and fostering transformation and reconciliation in a broad sense,[199] which definitively helped to create conditions for peace.

Second, by empowering groups to participate and be included in peace talks and agreements, international law can contribute to the openness of societies in transition. If the participation and inclusion of different groups is seen as a legal standard rather than a mere political choice, transitions will be better used as an opportunity to address structural discriminatory dynamics in society.[200] On this point, Kastner claims that "an agreement may not only

---

198 Chetail, 'Introduction,' 23.
199 On this idea, see: Marco Sassòli, 'Reparation,' in *Post-Conflict Peacebuilding: A Lexicon*, ed. Vincent Chetail (Oxford: Oxford University Press, 2009), 283. Ruth Rubio-Marín, 'Gender and Collective Reparations in the Aftermath of Conflict and Political Repression,' in *The Gender of Reparations*, ed. Ruth Rubio-Marín (Cambridge: Cambridge University Press, 2009), 383.
200 According to Maguire, transitional contexts are scenarios in which new frameworks can be established to promote the transformation of social unfair realities, and law plays a

symbolize a concerted attempt to end an armed conflict but may also aspire to solve structural problems and generate fundamental changes in a post-conflict society."[201] In the Colombian case, no previous attempt to negotiate peace has had a similar approach. And though the effects of this inclusiveness are to be seen in the coming years, the fact that different groups were heard during the negotiations and their demands included in the Agreement represents a promising opportunity for shaping a more inclusive country.[202]

Finally, the Colombian peace negotiations gave a central role to the discussion on the root causes of armed conflict. The objective of establishing a sustainable peace requires not only ending armed confrontation but also addressing its causes. On this point, the Peace Agreement looks at improving rural development and political participation in Colombia, ensuring all civil, political, economic, social, and cultural rights. A successful implementation of those measures would bring positive transformations in the quality of life of millions of people in the regions most affected by armed conflict.

5.8 *Insights for the General Functions of* Jus Post Bellum

This section explored the functions played by international law in the Colombian case suggesting how they could reflect possible functions of *jus post bellum*. The seven functions discussed here show the contributions of international law in the Colombian transition, from facilitating negotiations and increasing confidence among the parties to promoting comprehensive transformations and the participation of traditionally marginalized groups. All those functions certainly express the purposes of *jus post bellum*.

---

vital role accomplishing such a task. Therefore, participation of women and other relevant groups must be ensured when creating those frameworks. Amy Maguire, ' "Security Starts with the Law": The Role of International Law in the Protection of Women's Security Post-Conflict,' in *The Role of International Law in Rebuilding Societes After Conflict*, ed. Brett Bowden, Hilary Charlesworth, and Jeremy Farrall (Cambridge: Cambridge University Press, 2009), 223, 242–43.

201   Ibid., 68.
202   Regarding this idea, Bell and O'Rourke note that the very fact of mentioning an issue in the agreement gives a base for interested groups to defend it during the implementation. For them, "[w]hile the terms of a peace agreement do not secure the implementation of its provision, and the omission of an issue does not mean that it cannot be addressed in practice, issues that are not specifically mentioned in the agreement can be difficult to prioritize post-agreement, and importantly, international implementation mechanisms and donor funding flow from the agreement's priorities": Bell and O'Rourke, 'Peace Agreements or Pieces of Paper? The Impact of UNSC Resolution 1325 on Peace Processes and Their Agreements,' 947.

In that way, even if the above-mentioned functions are presented as serving specific features of the Colombian context, most of them are also relevant to other cases. However, to summarize their content towards suggesting more general functions of *jus post bellum* in transition from NIACs to peace, they could be gathered into three possible global functions.

First, helping to delimitate the matters to be addressed in peace negotiations or any other transitional mechanism, by looking to comprehensively address the causes and the consequences of armed conflict under international legal standards. Even though each context has its own conditions, a process conducted under the framework of *jus post bellum* must include matters as reconstruction and transformation, reparations for victims, and criminal accountability for crimes committed during the conflict, among others. Here, as seen in the section on principles, a framework of *jus post bellum* brings to the discussion the international legal norms, discourses, and practices guiding the treatment of the specific matter, delimiting the negotiation and the conclusion of the corresponding mechanisms.

Second, a framework of *jus post bellum* shows the actors that must be involved in transitional processes, giving legal grounds for traditionally marginalized groups to be included in order to make transition to peace legitimate, sustainable, and socially supported. This is an essential component on current peacemaking and peacebuilding, where the more people can participate and their concerns be considered the more accepted and effective can be the construction of sustainable peace.

Third, the framework of *jus post bellum* conveys international legal mechanisms and institutions to facilitate negotiations, the conclusion of peace agreements, and their successful implementation. A normative framework external to the parties in a NIAC helps to create confidence, and the participation of international actors as mediators or guarantors in the negotiation or in the implementation facilitates the discussion on complex matters and secures the effective monitoring and verification in the implementation phase.

6 Conclusions

This chapter developed a comprehensive analysis of *jus post bellum* through the lens of the Colombian case, offering empirical insights for understanding the definition, formation, principles, actors, and functions of this normative framework. The conclusions can be summarized into five components.

First, from the proliferation of theoretical definitions presented in Chapter 1, this chapter suggested a definition based on the evidence provided by the

Colombian case. To this effect, the chapter delineated four basic features of *jus post bellum*: (*i*) its content is given by principles; (*ii*) its object is to help establishing a sustainable peace; (*iii*) it holds a functional rather than a temporal approach; and, (*iv*) its legal nature is a matter of international law. Thus, by referring to empirical elements from the case study, this chapter defined *jus post bellum* as a normative framework of principles offering a space of contextualized interpretation and application of relevant international law in the transition from armed conflict to a sustainable peace. Such a framework contains normative standards and possibilities, which, rather than being restrictive, are aimed at guiding choices in transition.

Second, *jus post bellum* is a dynamic normative framework permanently constructed through the practice of parties involved in transition. Such parties must apply international legal norms that were not meant to regulate transitional processes, and in doing so they interpret and adapt those norms to their specific context. It implies a dual process of application and creation of law, regarding which the chapter provided concrete examples from Colombia.

Third, principles are the constituent substance of *jus post bellum*. They create the normative framework allowing parties to move within a set of relevant norms, discourses, and practices to balance international legal obligations with the political conditions raised by their transitional process. This chapter explored some principles present in the Colombian case, assessing their legal value and their configuration in the transition to peace in the country. Even though such a list is not exhaustive, the principles discussed offered a concrete illustration on the content of *jus post bellum* in practice.

Fourth, the chapter explored how different external and domestic actors played a role in bringing international legal considerations to the Colombian transition. The chapter sustained that the potential actors of *jus post bellum* go beyond the parties directly involved in peace negotiations, and that they concern all the potential actors that have an interest in or a responsibility for ensuring compliance with international law with a view to make transition to peace sustainable. From there, the chapter suggested some basic categories that could identify actors in other contexts.

Fifth, analyzing the functions played by international law in the Colombian transition, the chapter outlined the potential functions of *jus post bellum*. Here, it examined how the normative framework provided by *jus post bellum* can help transition in different ways, as delimiting the bargaining zone of possible agreement in peace negotiations, offering legal certainty to peace deals, increasing confidence among the parties, empowering traditionally marginalized groups, and encouraging the transformative role of transition. Here, the chapter also classified some general functions that could guide *jus post bellum* in other contexts.

General Conclusions

1   A Summary of the Study

This book explored the role of international law in the transition from armed conflict to peace under the analytical framework of *jus post bellum*, using the Colombian transition as a case study. Analyzing this question through three chapters, the study assessed how the theory of *jus post bellum* works in practice, providing new empirical insights for understanding the content and scope of the concept.

Chapter 1 analyzed *jus post bellum* as the concept framing the role of international law in the transition from armed conflict to peace. Different approaches to a definition of the concept showed the complexity of the debate. However, some common points emerged. First, *jus post bellum* is a solid concept whose potential as a framework on the role of law in transitions to peace is evident in the significant literature in this field. Second, although *jus post bellum* has been approached differently as a new legal regime, as an ordering system of norms, and as an interpretative framework, no consensual definition exits for the concept. Nonetheless, each approach unveils features of the concept and can help to build an integrative definition, such as understanding *jus post bellum* as a normative framework of principles guiding the coordination and interpretation of international legal norms applicable to the transition from armed conflict to peace. Third, although the usefulness of *jus post bellum* has been contested, it is a more comprehensive framework for the variety of legal matters involved in transition compared to related concepts: transitional justice, being focused on dealing with past human rights abuses, is narrower than *jus post bellum*, which covers the broad spectrum of aspects involved in peacebuilding; and *lex pacificatoria* is essentially a different name for the same object of *jus post bellum* but has little reception in the scholarship in the field. Fourth, *jus post bellum* is built around its functional approach to guiding transitions toward sustainable peace, which entails both addressing the root causes of the conflict and observing international legal standards on human rights and the rule of law.

Chapter 2 offered an extensive test case on the role played by international law in the transition in Colombia. The parties openly recognized the existence of an international legal framework for their negotiations and applied it in a creative way. First, they subscribed the peace agreement as constituting an international legal accord, seeking to shield it from eventual domestic modifications. Second, socioeconomic and political reforms were adopted to address the root causes of the conflict, following a human rights-based approach through the relevant IHRL instruments on civil, political, economic, social, and cultural rights. Third, a sophisticated system of criminal justice was established by using international law as its main framework. It excluded amnesties for international crimes, establishing that people responsible for those crimes will be judged under a formal system of justice granting restorative sanctions and restrictions on liberty in exchange for contributions to peace. Fourth, a comprehensive system of administrative reparations was adopted according to relevant international standards. Fifth, a broad approach to inclusiveness in the peace negotiations and in the agreement was applied following international guidelines on participation for women and ethnic communities, which was extended to other social groups.

Finally, Chapter 3 assessed the elements from theory presented in Chapter 1 against the elements from practice explored in Chapter 2, offering new insights on the content and scope of *jus post bellum*. This chapter suggested a definition of *jus post bellum* as a normative framework of principles guiding the legal and political choices in transition under the parameters of international law. These principles consist of legal norms, discourses, and practices, offering a bargaining zone with normative constraints and possibilities within which parties in transition can define their own transitional formulas. Through concrete examples from Colombia, the chapter analyzed how *jus post bellum* is a process in permanent development, whose content and scope are continually formed through the practice of actors involved in the transition, in the way they interpret, adapt, and apply relevant international legal norms in relation to their concrete context. Lastly, the chapter explored the multiplicity of potential actors of *jus post bellum* by referring to those involved in the Colombian case and how they brought international normative elements to shape the transition to peace, providing an analysis of the functions that such an international legal influence played in the process. As a result, the chapter found that *jus post bellum* effectively works in practice, and that the Colombian case offers invaluable insights for understanding the concrete content, formation, actors, and functions that *jus post bellum* can play as the normative framework for transition.

2 The Main Contributions of the Colombian Transition to International Law and to *Jus Post Bellum*

From an international legal perspective, the main lesson of the Colombian case is that international law is not a restrictive but a facilitative framework for

GENERAL CONCLUSIONS

the transition from armed conflict to peace. Since 2005, the country has been developing transitional instruments according to international standards, and in the 2012–2016 peace negotiations the parties intentionally appealed to international law as a parameter for their talks and the agreement.[1] Because of this, as analyzed in Chapters 2 and 3, the Colombian transition offers a fairly full picture of how international law can facilitate, protect, and legitimize internal peace processes and agreements.

The parties' decision to reinforce the legal certainty of the peace agreement through its enactment as an international legal accord shows their faith in international law. It reveals how international law can enhance confidence among parties in a NIAC, offering an external framework in which both state and non-state actors can trust. This fact also shows that parties in negotiation can make creative use of international norms according to the specific needs and conditions of their context. This point offers important lessons on the flexibility that international norms must have in order to be applied to internal contexts, especially in transitional periods, as well as on the role of domestic actors applying and creating international law through their practice in transition.

Regarding criminal justice, the Colombian process showed, as no other transition had before, that judicial criminal accountability is not an obstacle to agreements for peace. Unlike preceding negotiated transitions, in which truth and justice were sought through non-judicial mechanisms, the Colombian peace agreement introduced a domestic judicial system framed under ICL, in which people responsible for the most serious crimes will be tried before judges with formal judicial processes and sentences, with the opportunity to receive restorative sanctions if they cooperate to truth and reparations. This approach provides new insights on the uneven practice relating to justice and accountability in peace agreements,[2] offering an innovative way to combine the retributive elements required by ICL for international crimes with the restorative approach necessary to achieving peace and reconciliation, all toward ensuring victim's rights.[3]

---

1 Government of Colombia and FARC, 'Final Agreement to End the Armed Conflict and Build a Stable and Lasting Peace,' 2, 154.
2 Considering the variety of approaches to justice and criminal accountability in peace processes practice, see: UN Secretary-General, 'The Rule of Law and Transitional Justice in Conflict and Post-Conflict Societies,' para. 12.2.
3 On this point, Chetail points out that in contexts of transition, victim's rights and reconciliation could hardly be ensured only through criminal retribution for past violations. Chetail, 'Introduction,' 23.

On reparations to victims of armed conflict, Colombia adopted in 2011 an innovative system of comprehensive reparations based on the UN Basic Principles and Guidelines on Reparations. As noted by Evans, despite the inherent difficulties associated with the shortage of resources and the high number of victims, the transitional debate in Colombia has "set focus on international legal obligations in an unprecedented manner and resulted in recognition of the right of victims to receive reparation."[4] This case shows that it is possible to develop a comprehensive system of reparation following international legal standards, even in the context of extensive violations of human rights and IHL within an armed conflict. Additionally, this case also offers new insights on the obligations and role of non-state armed actors contributing to victims' reparation both as part of the restorative sanctions and as measures of social reintegration and reconciliation.

Similarly, the search for an inclusive transition in Colombia has been marked by a consistent reference to international law. From the Constitutional Court to the negotiators in the peace process, including victims, civil society organizations, and international community, the discourse for inclusiveness was grounded in international law. In this way, the Colombian experience offers important lessons on how inclusive transitions are embedded in international law, and how inclusiveness contributes to a more legitimate, effective, and sustainable peace. International law empowers traditionally marginalized groups in society, allowing their participation and inclusion in peace processes to function as an opportunity to address structural discriminatory factors. On this point, the Colombian process demonstrated that the international legal developments regarding women's participation and inclusion in peace processes can also serve as an approach in relation to other identity groups whose participation is equally essential to achieving peace. It is especially the case for LGBTI people, whose rights are attaining increasing legal attention at the international level, and ethnic communities, whose international legal protection can be enhanced through their specific participation and inclusion in peace processes, following the example of the framework created for women by UNSC Resolution 1325.

All these contributions of the Colombian transition to international law offer new insights on the concept of *jus post bellum* as the normative framework for transition from armed conflict to peace. However, in addition to the elements referred in these general conclusions, four specific contributions to the development of *jus post bellum* are worth mentioning in this section.

---

4 Evans, *The Right to Reparation in International Law for Victims of Armed Conflict*, 222.

First, analyzing the concept of *jus post bellum* in the context of NIACs, the Colombian case showed that the normative framework guiding transition to peace is about international law. Even though most elements of the Agreement are based on and developed through domestic law, the analysis conducted in this book demonstrated how international law defined the common frame of reference in which both the State and the rebel group found a space of mutual understanding.

Second, practice in Colombia showed that despite the parties' common acceptance of international standards, such an international legal framework needed to be adapted to the conditions of the context. Toward this, the negotiators considered legal discourses, interpretations, and practices (e.g. the ICC Prosecutor's statements, NGOs' and victims' advocacy, and the previous transitional instruments in Colombia) to apply international norms in a way compatible with their pursuit of peace. As such, the Colombian case indicates that *jus post bellum* can offer the framework to integrate all relevant legal elements applicable to transition into flexible principles that will guide parties in their transitional choices. In turn, this approach recognizes the norm-creating powers of parties involved in transition, as one could conclude that the formulas designed in Colombia to adapt international standards into its context will likely serve as a reference for future transitions in the world.

Third, the Colombian case unveils the broad set of actors and functions involved in *jus post bellum*. In addition to the direct parties, guarantors, and international delegates for the negotiations, several other actors can play a role in referring to and creating the normative framework for transition. In Colombia those actors included international and domestic institutions, NGOs, victims, and diverse social groups. As analyzed in Chapter 3, all of these actors invoked international law to support their suggestions and demands related to the peace negotiations and the design of transitional instruments in Colombia. From there, one can suggest at least four kind of actors of *jus post bellum* in NIACs: the direct parties in negotiation, domestic institutions, external mediators and guarantors, and victims and other identity and social sectors. Similarly, the normative framework used and developed for transition in Colombia served multiple functions, including facilitating negotiations, increasing legitimacy and legal certainty, and improving the overall quality of mechanisms aimed at building sustainable peace.

Fourth, the Colombian case illustrates the functional rather than temporal approach of *jus post bellum* proposed by most scholars. As argued in this book, *jus post bellum* serves as a normative framework guiding the negotiation and design of mechanisms aimed at transitioning to peace, regardless of the very existence of a peace process or the effective end of armed conflict. As such, transitional efforts undertaken in Colombia since the 2005 Peace and Justice Law, the 2011 Law on Victims, and the 2012 Legal Framework for Peace were all conceived and designed in the perspective of *jus post bellum*, even though they were not developed within a peace negotiation. Additionally, despite the 2012–2016 peace process and the 2016 peace agreement, armed conflict is still ongoing in the country with other armed groups. Thus, no temporal approach could frame the application of *jus post bellum* in Colombia but its function to help to establish sustainable peace.

3   *Jus Post Bellum* from Theory to Practice: Challenges and Opportunities

As noted since the Introduction, despite the significant literature on *jus post bellum* in recent years, at the time of writing only four studies devoted to analyzing the concept in practice were identified. This can be explained by several factors: the concept is still recent in legal scholarship, its usefulness has been contested, and its very definition and content have not reached academic consensus. However, the mentioned studies have been conducted in 2005 and 2012 regarding Iraq,[5] in 2009 on the Afghan case,[6] and in 2011 on Uganda.[7] Almost a decade has passed, and new and important developments have been achieved by the legal scholarship on *jus post bellum*. As such, the Colombian case is a remarkable example with which to conduct a new empirical analysis, testing theory in practice in order to offer new insights to continue the conceptual development of *jus post bellum*.

Previous case studies on *jus post bellum* have only addressed specific matters, such as military occupation (Iraq) and the role of ICL in the context of a peace process (Uganda), or they were conceived from the perspective of the just war theory (Afghanistan). Here, the book offered a comprehensive legal analysis of *jus post bellum* from the perspective of the Colombian transition. As a result, the study was able to exemplify and propose new elements regarding

---

5   Daniel Thürer and Malcom MacLaren, '"Ius Post Bellum" in Iraq: A Challenge to the Applicability and Relevance of International Humanitarian Law?,' in *Weltinnenrecht: Liber Amicorum Jost Delbrück*, ed. Klaus Dicke, and et al. (Berlin: Duncker & Humblot, 2005), 753–82; Christina Benson, '*Jus Post Bellum* in Iraq: The Development of Emerging Norms for Economic Reform in Post Conflict Countries,' *Richmond Journal of Global Law & Business* 11, no. 4 (2012): 315–55.
6   Labonte, '*Jus Post Bellum*, Peacebuilding and Non-State Actors: Lessons from Afghanistan.'
7   Ryngaert and Gould, 'International Criminal Justice and *Jus Post Bellum*: The Challenge of ICC Complementarity: A Case-Study of the Situation in Uganda.'

the definition, principles, object, functions, and actors of *jus post bellum* based on practice.

In this way, some remarks can be made on the challenges and opportunities of carrying the concept from theory to practice. First, *jus post bellum* is still perceived as too closely associated with its moral and philosophical foundations within the just war theory, which has been considered by some authors as an obstacle for its development as a legal concept.[8] In 2012 May proposed the most accepted series of principles of *jus post bellum*, though he sustained that those principles are normative because "they are moral norms" but "not legal principles themselves."[9] In 2015 Kastner developed a comprehensive analysis on the legal normativity for the resolution of internal armed conflicts that advanced many elements of *jus post bellum*, but he decided not to use the concept, arguing that it is more linked to IACs, and it "heavily relies on just war tradition."[10] Then, in 2016, the ILC's Special Rapporteur Marie Jacobsson did not address the concept of *jus post bellum* in her Report on the Protection of the Environment in Relation to Armed Conflicts, affirming that "the legal-political discussion on this concept is wider than positive law and has a clear connection to just war theories."[11] These examples illustrate the challenges ahead to bringing *jus post bellum* from its original moral conception to the legal realm, and how analyzing the concept in practice, as this study did, can offer new insights on its legal background and function.

Second, offering a legal framework for a fundamentally political matter as peacemaking and peacebuilding is a challenging task in practice. The search of sustainable peace involves many elements traditionally not seen as law, such as addressing root causes of armed conflict, building positive peace, reaching reconciliation, and promoting inclusiveness. However, as analyzed in this study, all these matters can be seen from an international legal perspective if a broad understanding of law is assumed. *Jus post bellum* as a normative framework requires viewing law as a social and dynamic process,[12] involving positive

---

8   De Brabandere, 'The Concept of *Jus Post Bellum* in International Law: A Normative Critique'; Vatanparast, 'Waging Peace: Ambiguities, Contradictions, and Problems of a *Jus Post Bellum* Legal Framework.'
9   May, *After War Ends*, 5.
10 Kastner, *Legal Normativity in the Resolution of Internal Armed Conflict*, 17.
11 Jacobsson, 'Third Report on the Protection of the Environment in Relation to Armed Conflicts,' para. 10.
12 On the idea of law as a social process in the context of *jus post bellum*: Pierre Allan and Alexis Keller, 'The Concept of a Just Peace, or Achieving Peace Through Recognition, Renouncement, and Rule,' in *What Is a Just Peace?*, ed. Pierre Allan and Alexis Keller (Oxford: Oxford University Press, 2006), 204.

and soft law norms as well as legal discourses and practices from actors participating in transition. Thus, practice in transitioning to peace permanently offers new normative elements to build *jus post bellum*, recognizing the role of the relevant actors interpreting, applying, and creating law through their own practice.

Third, the variety of definitions and principles around *jus post bellum* complicates the application of the concept in practice. However, practice is the only way to delimitate the content and scope of the concept. The 2014 publication of the University of Leiden's *Jus Post Bellum* Project concluded that many aspects of *jus post bellum* "need to be specified inductively, i.e. through a systematic look at practice."[13] Here, the Colombian case offered invaluable elements, as analyzed in Chapter 3, testing theory in practice to better understand the content and functioning of *jus post bellum* as the normative framework for transitions. As such, this study reveals why more cases and comparative practices should be analyzed in order to identify "what is systematic about the law that applies to the process of achieving a sustainable peace."[14]

4 The Future of *Jus Post Bellum*

Despite roughly two decades of scholarly development of *jus post bellum*, in 2017 Iverson referred to "the newness of the term,"[15] and Bruch argued that "the effort to articulate and elaborate *jus post bellum* is valuable and necessary" but that it "is still early in the process."[16] These views convey the significant challenges and opportunities entailed in the future of the concept that only can be handled, as noted above, through a systematic look at practice.

This study advanced basic elements showing how *jus post bellum* can find a content and applicability in practice. However, as sustained in Chapter 3, the concept is still limited to academic scholarship, and Special Rapporteur Jacobsson's argument for not addressing *jus post bellum* in her Report to the ILC in 2016 is an example of the challenges ahead to bringing the concept into

---

13   Iverson, Easterday, and Stahn, 'Epilogue: *Jus Post Bellum*—Strategic Analysis and Future Directions,' 545.
14   Iverson, 'Contrasting the Normative and Historical Foundations of Transitional Justice and *Jus Post Bellum*: Outlining the Matrix of Definitions in Comparative Perspective,' 101.
15   Iverson, 'The Function of *Jus Post Bellum* in International Law,' 12.
16   Carl Bruch, 'Considerations in Framing the Environmental Dimensions of *Jus Post Bellum*,' in *Environmental Protection and Transitions from Conflict to Peace: Clarifying Norms, Principles, and Practices*, ed. Carsten Stahn, Jens Iverson, and Jennifer Easterday (Oxford: Oxford University Press, 2017), 35.

official use. Unlike transitional justice, for example, which has expanded its academic foundation to achieve broad usage in legal and political practice, *jus post bellum* still requires significant development before reaching a similar status. The good news, as showed by this study, is that the concept has the capacity to embody international legal values for building peace under the rule of law, human rights, and positive peace, constituting an effective normative framework for transitions from armed conflict to peace. Additionally, as noted in the 2017 publication of the *Jus Post Bellum* Project in reference to the Draft Principles on Environmental Protection in Relation to Armed Conflicts proposed to the ILC in 2016, many of those principles "may not be formally labeled as *post bellum* principles, but reflect arguments that have been made in *jus post bellum* scholarship."[17]

The main challenge for the development of the concept is posed by its context-specificity. Although some authors have considered that a universal instrument of *jus post bellum* would be possible through a convention regulating transitions from armed conflict to peace,[18] this study analyzed how the inner flexibility and context-specificity of *jus post bellum* make such a task neither possible nor desirable. On this matter, Chetail argues that *jus post bellum* must facilitate the "contextualized interpretation" and the "contextualized application"[19] of norms relevant to transition, which, according to Easterday, means offering "a space for devising a context-specific, comprehensive, and coordinated approach to post-conflict peacebuilding."[20] Similarly, De Brabandere highlights that transitional instruments "vary widely from case to case according to the expectations in the territories,"[21] which Stahn supports with his remark that "each post-conflict engagement requires a situation-specific response."[22] Likewise, defining *jus post bellum* as an interpretative framework, Gallen concludes that "each transitional society will interpret its own practices, its own *jus post bellum*."[23]

The future of *jus post bellum* will therefore be determined by a systematic analysis of practice to find what is common in different contexts, assuming

---

17 Stahn, Iverson, and Easterday, 'Introduction: Protection of the Environment and *Jus Post Bellum*: Some Preliminary Reflections,' 24.
18 Orend, '*Jus Post Bellum*: The Perspective of a Just-War Theorist'; Österdahl and van Zadel, 'What Will *Jus Post Bellum* Mean? Of New Wine and Old Bottles.'
19 Chetail, 'Introduction,' 18.
20 Easterday, 'Peace Agreements as a Framework for *Jus Post Bellum*,' 385.
21 De Brabandere, 'The Responsibility for Post-Conflict Reforms: A Critical Assessment of *Jus Post Bellum* as a Legal Concept,' 145.
22 Stahn, 'R2P and *Jus Post Bellum*. Towards a Polycentric Approach,' 105.
23 Gallen, '*Jus Post Bellum*: An Interpretive Framework,' 69.

that this is a framework in permanent construction. Even though the formulas developed in Colombia offered significant lessons on how law can guide choices for transition to peace, they are not automatically replicable in other contexts. As examined in Chapters 2 and 3, there are many context-specific factors explaining why the country had such receptiveness to international law and to integrating several principles of *jus post bellum*. Then, a systematic analysis on practice from other contexts could led to general guidelines or policy documents on *jus post bellum* to guide relevant actors on the matter while it helps advancing the concept in theory and practice.

In short, this book departed from the theoretical background on *jus post bellum* and analyzed the concept in practice, within the context of NIACs and by using the Colombian transition as a case study. This work offered new insights, which in turn point to the need to delve into the empirical analysis of the concept if we want *jus post bellum* to fully develop its potential.

Bibliography

Acosta-Lopez, Juana. "The Inter-American Human Rights System and the Colombian Peace: Redefining the Fight Against Impunity." *American Journal of International Law* 110 AJIL Unbound Symposium on the Colombian Peace Talks and International Law (2016): 178–82.

Allan, Pierre, and Alexis Keller. "The Concept of a Just Peace, or Achieving Peace Through Recognition, Renouncement, and Rule." In *What Is a Just Peace?*, edited by Pierre Allan and Alexis Keller, 195–215. Oxford: Oxford University Press, 2006.

Ambos, Kai. "The Legal Framework of Transitional Justice." In *Building a Future on Peace and Justice: Studies on Transitional Justice, Conflict Resolution and Development: The Nuremberg Declaration on Peace and Justice*, edited by Kai Ambos, Judith Large, and Marieke Wierda, 19–103. Berlin: Springer, 2009.

Anderlini, Sanam. *Women Building Peace: What They Do, What It Matters*. Boulder: Lynne Rienner, 2007.

Arnson, Cynthia, ed. *In the Wake of War: Democratization and Internal Armed Conflict in Latin America*. Stanford: Stanford University Press, 2012.

Arvelo, Jose. "International Law and Conflict Resolution in Colombia: Balancing Peace and Justice in the Paramilitary Demobilization Process." *Georgetown Journal of International Law* 37, no. 2 (2006): 411–76.

Bartels, Rogier. "From Jus in Bello to *Jus Post Bellum*: When Do Non-International Armed Conflicts End?" In *Jus Post Bellum: Mapping the Normative Foundations*, edited by Carsten Stahn, Jennifer Easterday, and Jens Iverson, 297–314. Oxford: Oxford University Press, 2014.

Bass, Gary. "*Jus Post Bellum*." *Philosophy & Public Affairs*, 2004.

Bell, Christine. "Lex Pacificatoria Colombiana: Colombia's Peace Accord in Comparative Perspective." *American Journal of International Law* 110 AJIL Unbound Symposium on the Colombian Peace Talks and International Law (2016): 165–71.

Bell, Christine. "Of *Jus Post Bellum* and Lex Pacificatoria: What's in a Name?" In *Jus Post Bellum: Mapping the Normative Foundations*, edited by Carsten Stahn, Jennifer Easterday, and Jens Iverson, 181–206. Oxford: Oxford University Press, 2014.

Bell, Christine. *On the Law of Peace: Peace Agreements and the Lex Pacificatoria*. Oxford: Oxford University Press, 2008.

Bell, Christine. *Peace Agreements and Human Rights*. Oxford: Oxford University Press, 2003.

Bell, Christine. "Peace Agreements: Their Nature and Legal Status." *American Journal of International Law* 100, no. 2 (2006): 373–412.

Bell, Christine. "Peace Settlements and International Law: From Lex Pacificatoria to Jus Post Bellum." In *Research Handbook on International Conflict and Security Law*.

Jus Ad Bellum, Jus in Bello and Jus Post Bellum, edited by Nigel White and Christian Henderson. 499–546: Edward Elgar Publishing, 2013.

Bell, Christine. "Post-Conflict Accountability and the Reshaping of Human Rights and Humanitarian Law." In *International Humanitarian Law and International Human Rights Law*, edited by Orna Ben-Naftali, 328–70. Oxford: Oxford University Press, 2011.

Bell, Christine, and Catherine O'Rourke. "Does Feminism Need a Theory of Transitional Justice? An Introductory Essay." *International Journal of Transitional Justice* 1, no. 1 (2007): 23–44.

Bell, Christine, and Catherine O'Rourke. "Peace Agreements or Pieces of Paper? The Impact of UNSC Resolution 1325 on Peace Processes and Their Agreements." *International and Comparative Law Quarterly* 59, no. 4 (2010): 941–80.

Bell, Christine, and Catherine O'Rourke. "The People's Peace? Peace Agreements, Civil Society, and Participatory Democracy." *International Political Science Review* 28, no. 3 (2007): 293–324.

Benson, Christina. "*Jus Post Bellum* in Iraq: The Development of Emerging Norms for Economic Reform in Post Conflict Countries." *Richmond Journal of Global Law & Business* 11, no. 4 (2012): 315–55.

Bergsmo, Morten, and Pablo Kalmanovitz, eds. *Law in Peace Negotiations*. Oslo: Torkel Opsahl Academic EPublisher, 2010.

Betancur, Laura. "The Legal Status of the Colombian Peace Agreement." *American Journal of International Law* 110 AJIL Unbound Symposium on the Colombian Peace Talks and International Law (2016): 188–92.

Bois-Pedain, Antje du. *Transitional Amnesty in South Africa*. Cambridge: Cambridge University Press, 2007.

Boon, Kristen. "Legislative Reform in Post-Conflict Zones: *Jus Post Bellum* and the Contemporary Occupant's Law-Making Powers." *McGill Law Journal* 50, no. 2 (2005): 285–326.

Boon, Kristen. "The Application of *Jus Post Bellum* in Non-International Armed Conflicts." In *Jus Post Bellum: Mapping the Normative Foundations*, edited by Carsten Stahn, Jennifer Easterday, and Jens Iverson, 259–68. Oxford: Oxford University Press, 2014.

Botero, Catalina. *La Ley de Alternatividad Penal y Justicia Transicional*. Bogota: DeJusticia, 2004.

Botero, Catalina, and Esteban Restrepo. "Estándares Internacionales y Procesos de Transición En Colombia." In *¿Justicia Transicional Sin Transición? Verdad, Justicia y Reparación Para Colombia*, edited by Rodrigo Uprimny, Maria Saffon, Catalina Botero, and Esteban Restrepo, 45–108. Bogota: DeJusticia, 2006.

Bottigliero, Ilaria. *Redress for Victims of Crimes under International Law*. Leiden: Nijhoff, 2004.

Bowden, Brett, Hilary Charlesworth, and Jeremy Farrall, eds. *The Role of International Law in Rebuilding Societes After Conflict*. Cambridge: Cambridge University Press, 2009.

Braithwaite, John. *Restorative Justice & [and] Responsive Regulation*. Oxford: Oxford University Press, 2002.

Broomhall, Bruce. *International Justice and the International Criminal Court: Between Sovereignty and the Rule of Law*. Oxford: Oxford University Press, 2003.

Bruch, Carl. "Considerations in Framing the Environmental Dimensions of *Jus Post Bellum*." In *Environmental Protection and Transitions from Conflict to Peace: Clarifying Norms, Principles, and Practices*, edited by Carsten Stahn, Jens Iverson, and Jennifer Easterday, 29–39. Oxford: Oxford University Press, 2017.

Burbidge, Peter. "Justice and Peace?—The Role of Law in Resolving Colombia's Civil Conflict." *International Criminal Law Review* 8, no. 3 (2008): 557–87.

Carrillo, Arturo. "Justice in Context: The Relevance of the Inter-American Human Rights Law and Practice to Repairing the Past." In *The Handbook of Reparations*, edited by Pablo de Greiff, 504–38. Oxford: Oxford University Press, 2006.

Céspedes-Báez, Lina. "Gender Panic and the Failure of a Peace Agreement." *American Journal of International Law* 110 AJIL Unbound Symposium on the Colombian Peace Talks and International Law (2016): 183–87.

Chayes, Antonia. "Chapter VII½: Is *Jus Post Bellum* Possible?" *European Journal of International Law* 24, no. 1 (2013): 291–305.

Chernick, Marc. "Negotiating Peace amid Multiple Forms of Violence: The Protracted Search for a Settlement to the Armed Conflicts in Colombia." In *Comparative Peace Processes in Latin America*, edited by Cynthia Arnson, 159–99. Stanford: Stanford University Press, 1999.

Chetail, Vincent. "Introduction: Post-Conflict Peacebuilding: Ambiguity and Identity." In *Post-Conflict Peacebuilding: A Lexicon*, edited by Vincent Chetail, 1–33. Oxford: Oxford University Press, 2009.

Chetail, Vincent, ed. *Post-Conflict Peacebuilding: A Lexicon*. Oxford: Oxford University Press, 2009.

Chetail, Vincent, and Oliver Jütersonke, eds. *Peacebuilding*. Critical Concepts in Political Science. London: Routledge, 2015.

Clamp, Kerry. *Restorative Justice in Transition*. London: Routledge, 2014.

Clapham, Andrew. "Human Rights and International Criminal Law." In *Cambridge Companion to International Criminal Law*, edited by William Schabas, 11–33. Cambridge University Press, 2016.

Clapham, Andrew. *Human Rights Obligations of Non-State Actors*. Oxford: Oxford University Press, 2006.

Clapham, Andrew. "Non-State Actors." In *Post-Conflict Peacebuilding: A Lexicon*, edited by Vincent Chetail, 200–212. Oxford: Oxford University Press, 2009.

Clapham, Andrew. "The Use of International Human Rights Law by Civil Society Organisations." In *Routledge Handbook of International Human Rights Law*, edited by Sheeran Rodley, Sir Nigel Scott, 153–67. London: Routledge, 2013.

Coady, Cecil Anthony. "The *Jus Post Bellum*." In *New Wars and New Soldiers: Military Ethics in the Contemporary World*, edited by Jessica Wolfendale and Paolo Tripodi, 49–66. London: Ashgate Press, 2011.

Cohen, Jean. "The Role of International Law in Post-Conflict Constitution-Making: Toward a *Jus Post Bellum* for 'Interim Occupations.'" *New York Law School Law Review* 51 (2007 2006): 497–532.

Corten, Olivier. "Le *Jus Post Bellum* Remet-Il En Cause Les Règles Traditionnelles Du Jus Contra Bellum?" *Revue Belge de Droit International*, 2011.

Corten, Olivier, and Pierre Klein. "Are Agreements between States and Non-State Entities Rooted in the International Legal Order?" In *The Law of Treaties Beyond the Vienna Convention*, edited by Enzo Cannizzaro, 3–23. Oxford: Oxford University Press, 2011.

Davis, Jeffrey. *Seeking Human Rights Justice in Latin America: Truth, Extra-Territorial Courts, and the Process of Justice*. Cambridge: Cambridge University Press, 2014.

De Brabandere, Eric. "International Territorial Administrations and Post-Conflict: Reflections on the Need of a *Jus Post Bellum* as Legal Framework." *Revue Belgue de Droit International* 44, no. 1–2 (2011): 69–90.

De Brabandere, Eric. "The Concept of *Jus Post Bellum* in International Law: A Normative Critique." In *Jus Post Bellum: Mapping the Normative Foundations*, edited by Carsten Stahn, Jennifer Easterday, and Jens Iverson, 123–41. Oxford: Oxford University Press, 2014.

De Brabandere, Eric. "The Responsibility for Post-Conflict Reforms: A Critical Assessment of *Jus Post Bellum* as a Legal Concept." *Vanderbilt Journal of Transnational Law* 43, no. 1 (2010): 119–49.

De Greiff, Pablo. "Justice and Reparations." In *The Handbook of Reparations*, edited by Pablo De Greiff, 451–77. Oxford: Oxford University Press, 2006.

DiMeglio, Richard. "The Evolution of the Just War Tradition: Defining *Jus Post Bellum*." *Military Law Review* 186 (2006): 116–63.

Durham, Helen. "From Paper to Practice: The Role of Treaty Ratification Post-Conflict." In *The Role of International Law in Rebuilding Societes After Conflict*, edited by Brett Bowden, Hilary Charlesworth, and Jeremy Farrall, 177–97. Cambridge: Cambridge University Press, 2009.

Easterday, Jennifer. "Peace Agreements as a Framework for *Jus Post Bellum*." In *Jus Post Bellum: Mapping the Normative Foundations*, edited by Carsten Stahn, Jennifer Easterday, and Jens Iverson, 379–415. Oxford: Oxford University Press, 2014.

Easterday, Jennifer, and Hana Ivanhoe. "Conflict, Cash, and Controversy: Protecting Environmental Rights in Post-Conflict Settings." In *Environmental Protection and Transitions from Conflict to Peace: Clarifying Norms, Principles, and Practices*, edited by Carsten Stahn, Jens Iverson, and Jennifer Easterday, 274–98. Oxford: Oxford University Press, 2017.

BIBLIOGRAPHY

Easterday, Jennifer, Jens Iverson, and Carsten Stahn. "Exploring the Normative Foundations of *Jus Post Bellum*: An Introduction." In *Jus Post Bellum: Mapping the Normative Foundations*, edited by Carsten Stahn, Jennifer Easterday, and Jens Iverson, 1–11. Oxford: Oxford University Press, 2014.

Ellerby, Kara. "(En)Gendered Security? Gender Mainstreaming and Women's Inclusion in Peace Processes." In *Gender, Peace and Security: Implementing UN Security Council Resolution 1325*, edited by Theodora-Ismene Gizelis and Louise Olsson, 185–209. Abingdon: Routledge, 2015.

Escola de Cultura de Pau. *Peace Talks in Focus 2018. Report on Trends and Scenarios*. Barcelona: Icaria, 2018.

Escola de Cultura de Pau. *Peace Talks in Focus 2019. Report on Trends and Scenarios*. Barcelona: Icaria, 2019.

Escola de Cultura de Pau. *Yearbook of Peace Processes 2016*. Edited by Vicenç Fisas. Barcelona: Icaria, 2016.

Escola de Cultura de Pau. *Yearbook of Peace Processes 2015*. Edited by Vicenç Fisas. Barcelona: Icaria, 2015.

Esquirol, Jorge. "Can International Law Help? An Analysis of the Colombian Peace Process." *Connecticut Journal of International Law* 16, no. 1 (2000): 23–93.

Evans, Christine. *The Right to Reparation in International Law for Victims of Armed Conflict*. Cambridge: Cambridge University Press, 2012.

Evans, Mark. "At War's End: Time to Turn to *Jus Post Bellum*?" In *Jus Post Bellum: Mapping the Normative Foundations*, edited by Carsten Stahn, Jennifer Easterday, and Jens Iverson, 26–42. Oxford: Oxford University Press, 2014.

Fabre, Cecile. "Cosmopolitanism, Just War Theory and Legitimate Authority." *International Affairs* 84, no. 5 (2008): 963–76.

Farrall, Jeremy. "Impossible Expectations? The UN Security Council's Promotion of the Rule of Law After Conflict." In *The Role of International Law in Rebuilding Societes After Conflict*, edited by Brett Bowden, Hilary Charlesworth, and Jeremy Farrall, 134–56. Cambridge: Cambridge University Press, 2009.

Fleck, Dieter. "*Jus Post Bellum* as a Partly Independent Legal Framework." In *Jus Post Bellum: Mapping the Normative Foundations*, edited by Carsten Stahn, Jennife Easterday, and Jens Iverson, 43–57. Oxford: Oxford University Press, 2014.

Fleck, Dieter. "Legal Protection of the Environment. The Double Challenge of Non-International Armed Conflict and Post- Conflict Peacebuilding." In *Environmental Protection and Transitions from Conflict to Peace: Clarifying Norms, Principles, and Practices*, edited by Carsten Stahn, Jens Iverson, and Jennifer Easterday, 203–19. Oxford: Oxford University Press, 2017.

Freeman, Mark, and Drazan Djukic. "*Jus Post Bellum* and Transitional Justice." In *Jus Post Bellum. Towards a Law of Transition from Conflict to Peace*, edited by Carsten Stahn and Jann Kleffner, 213–27. The Hague: T.M.C. Asser Press, 2008.

Gallen, James. "*Jus Post Bellum*: An Interpretive Framework." In *Jus Post Bellum: Mapping the Normative Foundations*, edited by Carsten Stahn, Jennifer Easterday, and Jens Iverson, 58–79. Oxford: Oxford University Press, 2014.

Gallen, James. "Odious Debt and *Jus Post Bellum*." *Journal of World Investment & Trade* 16, no. 4 (2015): 666–94.

Galtung, Johan. "Violence, Peace, and Peace Research." *Journal of Peace Research* 6, no. 3 (1969): 167–91.

Gardam, Judith, and Michelle Jarvis. *Women, Armed Conflict, and International Law*. The Hague: Kluwer Law International, 2001.

Garraway, Charles. "The Relevance of *Jus Post Bellum*: A Practitioner's Perspective." edited by Carsten Stahn and Jann Kleffner, 153–62. The Hague: T.M.C. Asser Press, 2008.

Gibson, James. "The Contributions of Truth to Reconciliation: Lessons from South Africa." *Journal of Conflict Resolution* 50, no. 3 (2006): 409–32.

Gillett, Matthew. "Eco-Struggles: Using International Criminal Law to Protect the Environment During and After Non-International Armed Conflict." In *Environmental Protection and Transitions from Conflict to Peace: Clarifying Norms, Principles, and Practices*, edited by Carsten Stahn, Jens Iverson, and Jennifer Easterday, 220–53. Oxford: Oxford University Press, 2017.

Goldstone, Richard. "Past Human Rights Violations: Truth Commissions and Amnesties or Prosecutions." *Northern Ireland Legal Quarterly* 51, no. 2 (2000): 164–73.

Guerrero, Julian, and Mariana Goetz. "Reparations for Victims in Colombia: Colombia's Law on Justice and Peace." In *Reparations for Victims of Genocide, War Crimes and Crimes against Humanity: Systems in Place and Systems in the Making*, edited by Carla Ferstman, Mariana Goetz, and Alan Stephens, 435–58. Leiden: Martinus Nijhoff, 2009.

Heffes, Ezequiel, and Marcos Kotlik. "Special Agreements as a Means of Enhancing Compliance with IHL in Non-International Armed Conflicts: An Inquiry into the Governing Legal Regime." *International Review of the Red Cross* 96, no. 895/896 (2014): 1195–1224.

Hehn, Arist von. *The Internal Implementation of Peace Agreements after Violent Intrastate Conflict*. Leiden: Martinus Nijhoff, 2011.

Henckaerts, Jean-Marie, and Louise Doswald-Beck. *Customary International Humanitarian Law. Volume I: Rules*. Cambridge: Cambridge University Press, 2005.

Hofmann, Ursign, and Pascal Rapillard. "Post-Conflict Mine Action: Environment and Law." In *Environmental Protection and Transitions from Conflict to Peace: Clarifying Norms, Principles, and Practices*, edited by Carsten Stahn, Jens Iverson, and Jennifer Easterday, 396–419. Oxford: Oxford University Press, 2017.

Huneeus, Alexandra, and Rene Urueña. "Introduction to Symposium on the Colombian Peace Talks and International Law." *American Journal of International Law* 110

AJIL Unbound Symposium on the Colombian Peace Talks and International Law (2016): 161–64.

Iasiello, Louis. "*Jus Post Bellum*: The Moral Responsibilities of Victors in War." *Naval War College Review* 57, no. 3–4 (2004): 33–52.

ICRC. *Commentary of 1987 on Protocol Additional II*. Geneva, 1987.

ICRC. *Commentary on the First Geneva Convention*. 2nd ed. Geneva, 2016.

Iverson, Jens. "Contrasting the Normative and Historical Foundations of Transitional Justice and *Jus Post Bellum*: Outlining the Matrix of Definitions in Comparative Perspective." In *Jus Post Bellum: Mapping the Normative Foundations*, edited by Carsten Stahn, Jennifer Easterday, and Jens Iverson, 80–101. Oxford: Oxford University Press, 2014.

Iverson, Jens. "The Function of *Jus Post Bellum* in International Law." Leiden University, 2017. https://openaccess.leidenuniv.nl/handle/1887/55949.

Iverson, Jens. "Transitional Justice, *Jus Post Bellum* and International Criminal Law: Differentiating the Usages, History and Dynamics." *The International Journal of Transitional Justice* 7 (2013): 413–33.

Iverson, Jens, Jennifer Easterday, and Carsten Stahn. "Epilogue: *Jus Post Bellum*—Strategic Analysis and Future Directions." In *Jus Post Bellum: Mapping the Normative Foundations*, edited by Carsten Stahn, Jennifer Easterday, and Jens Iverson, 542–53. Oxford: Oxford University Press, 2014.

Jeffery, Renée. *Amnesties, Accountability, and Human Rights*. Philadelphia: University of Pennsylvania Press, 2014.

Jessup, Philip. "Should International Law Recognize an Intermediate Status between Peace and War?" *American Journal of International Law* 48, no. 1 (1954): 98–103.

Kalmanovitz, Pablo. "Introduction: Law and Politics in the Colombian Negotiations with Paramilitary Groups." In *Law in Peace Negotiations*, edited by Morten Bergsmo and Pablo Kalmanovitz, 1–25. Oslo: Torkel Opsahl Academic EPublisher, 2010.

Kastner, Philipp. *Legal Normativity in the Resolution of Internal Armed Conflict*. Cambridge: Cambridge University Press, 2015.

Kennedy, David. *Of War and Law*. Princeton: Princeton University Press, 2006.

Kerr, Rachel, and Eirin Mobekk. *Peace and Justice: Seeking Accountability after War*. Cambridge: Polity, 2007.

Kleffner, Jan. "Towards a Functional Conceptualization of Temporal Scope of *Jus Post Bellum*." In *Jus Post Bellum: Mapping the Normative Foundations*, edited by Carsten Stahn, Jennifer Easterday, and Jens Iverson, 287–96. Oxford: Oxford University Press, 2014.

Kleffner, Jann. "Introduction: From Here to There ... And the Law in the Middle." In *Jus Post Bellum: Towards a Law of Transition from Conflict to Peace*, edited by Carsten Stahn and Jann Kleffner, 1–5. The Hague: T.M.C. Asser Press, 2008.

Kooijmans, P.H. "The Security Council and Non-State Entities as Parties to Conflicts." In *International Law: Theory and Practice: Essays in Honour of Eric Suy*, edited by Eric Suy and Karell Wellens, 333–46. The Hague: Martinus Nijhoff Publishers, 1998.

Kreß, Claus. "War Crimes Committed in Non-International Armed Conflict and the Emerging System of International Criminal Justice." *Israel Yearbook on Human Rights* 30 (2001): 103–77.

Kreß, Claus, and Leena Grover. "International Criminal Law Restraints in Peace Talks to End Armed Conflicts of a Non-International Character." In *Law in Peace Negotiations*, edited by Morton Bergsmo and Pablo Kalmanovitz, 41–84. Oslo: Torkel Opsahl Academic EPublisher, 2010.

Kulkarni, Anupma. "Criminal Justice for Conflict-Related Violations. Developments during 2014." In *Peace and Conflict 2016*, edited by David Backer, Ravi Bhavnani, and Paul Huth, 192–209. New York: Routledge, 2016.

Labonte, Melissa. "*Jus Post Bellum*, Peacebuilding and Non-State Actors: Lessons from Afghanistan." In *Ethics, Authority, and War: Non-State Actors and the Just War Tradition*, edited by Eric Heinze and Brent Steele, 205–57. New York: Palgrave Macmillan, 2009.

Lackey, Douglas. "Postwar Environmental Damage: A Study in *Jus Post Bellum*." In *International Criminal Law and Philosophy*, edited by Larry May and Zachary Hoskins, 141–52. Cambridge: Cambridge University Press, 2010.

Laplante, Lisa. "Transitional Justice and Peace Building: Diagnosing and Addressing the Socioeconomic Roots of Violence through a Human Rights Framework." *International Journal of Transitional Justice* 2, no. 3 (2008): 331–355.

Lewkowicz, Grégory. "*Jus Post Bellum*: Vieille Antienne Ou Nouvelle Branche Du Droit? Sur Le Mythe de l'origine Vénérable Du *Jus Post Bellum*." *Revue Belge de Droit International*, 2011.

Lewkowicz, Grégory. "Présentation. Le *Jus Post Bellum* : Nouveau Cheval de Troie Pour Le Droit Des Conflit Armés?" *Revue Belge de Droit International* 44, no. 1–2 (2011): 5–10.

Lucas, George. "Jus Ante and Post Bellum. Completing the Circle, Breaking the Circle." In *Ethics Beyond War's End*, edited by Eric Patterson, 47–64. Washington: Georgetown University Press, 2012.

Maguire, Amy. " 'Security Starts with the Law': The Role of International Law in the Protection of Women's Security Post-Conflict." In *The Role of International Law in Rebuilding Societes After Conflict*, edited by Brett Bowden, Hilary Charlesworth, and Jeremy Farrall, 218–43. Cambridge: Cambridge University Press, 2009.

Mallinder, Louise. "Amnesties in the Pursuit of Reconciliation, Peacebuilding, and Restorative Justice." In *Restorative Justice, Reconciliation and Peacebuilding*, edited by Jennifer Llewellyn and Daniel Philpott, 138–73. Oxford: Oxford University Press, 2014.

Mallinder, Louise. "Can Amnesties and International Justice Be Reconciled?" *International Journal of Transitional Justice* 1 (2007): 208–30.

Mallinder, Louise. "The End of Amnesty or Regional Overreach? Interpreting the Erosion of South America's Amnesty Laws." *International and Comparative Law Quarterly* 65, no. 3 (2016): 645–80.

Marieke, Wierda. "The Positive Role of International Law in Peace Negotiations: Implementing Transitional Justice in Afghanistan and Uganda." In *Law in Peace Negotiations*, edited by Morten Bergsmo and Pablo Kalmanovitz, 281–93. Oslo: Torkel Opsahl Academic EPublisher, 2010.

May, Larry. *After War Ends: A Philosophical Perspective*. Cambridge: Cambridge University Press, 2012.

May, Larry. "*Jus Post Bellum*, Grotius, and Meionexia." In *Jus Post Bellum: Mapping the Normative Foundations*, edited by Carsten Stahn, Jennifer Easterday, and Jens Iverson, 15–25. Oxford: Oxford University Press, 2014.

May, Larry. "*Jus Post Bellum*, Proportionality and the Fog of War." *European Journal of International Law* 24, no. 1 (2013): 315–33.

May, Larry. "Reparation, Restitution, and Transitional Justice." In *Morality, Jus Post Bellum, and International Law*, edited by Larry May and Andrew Forcehimes, 32–48. Cambridge: Cambridge University Press, 2012.

May, Larry, and Andrew Forcehimes, eds. *Morality, Jus Post Bellum, and International Law*. Cambridge: Cambridge University Press, 2012.

McCready, Doug. "Ending the War Right: *Jus Post Bellum* and the Just War Tradition." *Journal of Military Ethics* 8, no. 1 (2009): 66–78.

Mégret, Frédéric. "Should Rebels Be Amnestied?" In *Jus Post Bellum: Mapping the Normative Foundations*, edited by Carsten Stahn, Jennifer Easterday, and Jens Iverson, 519–41. Oxford: Oxford University Press, 2014.

Méndez, Juan, and Catherine Cone. "Human Rights Make a Difference: Lessons from Latin America." In *The Oxford Handbook of International Human Rights Law*, edited by Dinah Shelton, 955–79. Oxford: Oxford University Press, 2013.

Murphy, Colleen, and Linda Radzik. "*Jus Post Bellum* and Political Reconciliation." In *Jus Post Bellum and Transitional Justice*, edited by Larry May and Elizabeth Edenberg, 305–25. New York: Cambridge University Press, 2013.

Naert, Frederik. "International Humanitarian Law and Human Rights Law in Peace Operations as Parts of a Variable Ius Post Bellum." *Revue Belge de Droit International* 44, no. 1–2 (2011): 26–37.

Naqvi, Yasmin. "The Right to the Truth in International Law: Fact or Fiction?" *International Review of the Red Cross* 88, no. 862 (2006): 245–73.

Ní Aoláin, Fionnuala, and Dina Haynes. "The Compatibility of Justice for Women with *Jus Post Bellum* Analysis." In *Jus Post Bellum: Mapping the Normative Foundations*, edited by Carsten Stahn, Jennifer Easterday, and Jens Iverson, 161–77. Oxford: Oxford University Press, 2014.

Olsson, Louise, and Theodora-Ismene Gizelis. "An Introduction to Resolution 1325: Measuring Progress and Impact." In *Gender, Peace and Security: Implementing UN Security Council Resolution 1325*, edited by Theodora-Ismene Gizelis and Louise Olsson, 1–15. Abingdon: Routledge, 2015.

Orend, Brian. "*Jus Post Bellum*." *Journal of Social Philosophy* 31, no. 1 (2000): 117–37.

Orend, Brian. "*Jus Post Bellum*: A Just War Theory Perspective." In *Jus Post Bellum. Towards a Law of Transition from Conflict to Peace*, edited by Carsten Stahn and Jann Kleffner, 31–52. The Hague: T.M.C. Asser Press, 2008.

Orend, Brian. "*Jus Post Bellum*: The Perspective of a Just-War Theorist." *Leiden Journal of International Law* 20, no. 3 (2007): 571–91.

Orend, Brian. "Justice After War. Toward a New Geneva Convention." In *Ethics Beyond War's End*, edited by Eric Patterson, 175–96. Washington: Georgetown University Press, 2012.

Orend, Brian. *War and International Justice: A Kantian Perspective*. Wilfrid Laurier University Press, 2000.

O'Rourke, Catherine. "Transitioning to What? Transitional Justice and Gendered Citizenship in Chile and Colombia." In *Gender in Transitional Justice*, edited by Susane Buckley-Zistel and Ruth Stanley, 136–60. Basingstoke: Palgrave Macmillan, 2012.

Orozco Abad, Iván. *Sobre los límites de la conciencia humanitaria: Dilemas de la paz y la justicia en América Latina*. Bogotá: Temis, 2005.

Österdahl, Inger. "Just War, Just Peace and the '*Jus Post Bellum*.'" *Nordic Journal of International Law* 81, no. 3 (2012): 271–93.

Österdahl, Inger. "The Gentle Modernizer of the Law of Armed Conflict." In *Jus Post Bellum: Mapping the Normative Foundations*, edited by Carsten Stahn, Jennifer Easterday, and Jens Iverson, 207–28. Oxford: Oxford University Press, 2014.

Österdahl, Inger, and Esther van Zadel. "What Will *Jus Post Bellum* Mean? Of New Wine and Old Bottles." *Journal of Conflict and Security Law* 14, no. 2 (2009): 175–207.

Patterson, Eric. "Conclusion. Toward a Twenty-First Century *Jus Post Bellum*." In *Ethics Beyond War's End*, edited by Eric Patterson, 221–29. Washington: Georgetown University Press, 2012.

Patterson, Eric. *Ending Wars Well: Order, Justice, and Conciliation in Contemporary Post-Conflict*. New Haven: Yale University Press, 2012.

Patterson, Eric, ed. *Ethics Beyond War's End*. Washington: Georgetown University Press, 2012.

Payne, Cymie. "Defining the Environment: Environmental Integrity." In *Environmental Protection and Transitions from Conflict to Peace: Clarifying Norms, Principles, and Practices*, edited by Carsten Stahn, Jens Iverson, and Jennifer Easterday, 40–70. Oxford: Oxford University Press, 2017.

Payne, Cymie. "The Norm of Environmental Integrity in Post-Conflict Legal Regimes." In *Jus Post Bellum: Mapping the Normative Foundations*, edited by Carsten Stahn, Jennifer Easterday, and Jens Iverson, 502–18. Oxford: Oxford University Press, 2014.

Peperkamp, Lonneke. "*Jus Post Bellum*: A Case of Minimalism versus Maximalism?" *Ethical Perspectives* 21, no. 2 (2014): 255–88.

Philpott, Daniel, and Jennifer J. Llewellyn. "Restorative Justice and Reconciliation: Twin Frameworks for Peacebuilding." In *Restorative Justice, Reconciliation and Peacebuilding*, edited by Llewellyn Philpott, Daniel Jennifer, 14–36. Oxford: Oxford University Press, 2014.

Porter, Elisabeth. *Connecting Peace, Justice and Reconciliation*. Boulder: Lynne Rienner Publishers, 2015.

Porter, Elisabeth. *Peacebuilding: Women in International Perspective*. London: Routledge, 2007.

Rigby, Andrew. "Forgiveness and Reconciliation in *Jus Post Bellum*." In *Just War Theory: A Reappraisal*, edited by Mark Evans, 177–200. Edinburgh: Edinburgh University Press, 2005.

Roberts, Anthea, and Sandesh Sivakumaran. "Lawmaking by Nonstate Actors: Engaging Armed Groups in the Creation of International Humanitarian Law." *Yale Journal of International Law* 13, no. 1 (2012): 107–52.

Roht-Arriaza, Naomi. "After Amnesties Are Gone: Latin American National Courts and the New Contours of the Fight against Impunity." *Human Rights Quarterly* 37 (2015): 341–82.

Roht-Arriaza, Naomi, and Lauren Gibson. "The Developing Jurisprudence on Amnesty." *Human Rights Quarterly* 20 (1998): 843–85.

Roucounas, Emmanuel. "Peace Agreements as Instruments for the Resolution of Intrastate Conflicts." In *Conflict Resolution: New Approaches and Methods*, by UNESCO, 113–40. Paris: UNESCO, 2000.

Rubio-Marín, Ruth. "Gender and Collective Reparations in the Aftermath of Conflict and Political Repression." In *The Gender of Reparations*, edited by Ruth Rubio-Marín, 381–402. Cambridge: Cambridge University Press, 2009.

Ryngaert, Cédric, and Lauren Gould. "International Criminal Justice and *Jus Post Bellum*: The Challenge of ICC Complementarity: A Case-Study of the Situation in Uganda." *Revue Belge de Droit International* 44, no. 1–2 (2011): 91–124.

Saffon, Maria, and Rodrigo Uprimny. "Uses and Abuses of Transitional Justice in Colombia." In *Law in Peace Negotiations*, edited by Morgen Bergsmo and Pablo Kalmanovitz, 354–99. Oslo: Torkel Opsahl Academic EPublisher, 2010.

Sanchez, Nelson Camilo. "Could the Colombian Peace Accord Trigger an ICC Investigation on Colombia?" *American Journal of International Law* 110 AJIL Unbound Symposium on the Colombian Peace Talks and International Law (2016): 172–77.

Sari, Aurel. "The Status of Foreign Armed Forces Deployed in Post-Conflict Environments: A Search for Basic Principles." In *Jus Post Bellum: Mapping the Normative Foundations*, edited by Carsten Stahn, Jennifer Easterday, and Jens Iverson, 467–501. Oxford: Oxford University Press, 2014.

Saul, Matthew. "Creating Popular Governments in Post-Conflicts Situations: The Role of International Law." In *Jus Post Bellum: Mapping the Normative Foundations*, edited by Carsten Stahn, Jennifer Easterday, and Jens Iverson, 447–66. Oxford: Oxford University Press, 2014.

Schabas, William. "Amnesty, the Sierra Leone Truth and Reconciliation Commission and the Special Court for Sierra Leone." *University of California Davis Journal of International Law and Policy* 11 (2004): 145–169.

Schaller, Christian. "Towards an International Legal Framework for Post-Conflict Peacebuilding." *Research Paper, German Institute for International and Security Affairs* 3 (2009): 3–21.

Sivakumaran, Sandesh. "The Addressees of Common Article 3." In *The 1949 Geneva Conventions. A Commentary*, edited by Andrew Clapham, Paola Gaeta, and Marco Sassòli, 415–31. Oxford: Oxford University Press, 2015.

Stahn, Carsten. " 'Jus Ad Bellum', 'jus in Bello' ... 'Jus Post Bellum'?—Rethinking the Conception of the Law of Armed Force." *European Journal of International Law* 17, no. 5 (2006): 921–43.

Stahn, Carsten. "*Jus Post Bellum*: Mapping the Discipline(s)." *American University International Law Review* 23, no. 2 (2007): 311–47.

Stahn, Carsten. "*Jus Post Bellum*: Mapping the Discipline(s)." In *Jus Post Bellum. Towards a Law of Transition from Conflict to Peace*, edited by Carsten Stahn and Jann Kleffner, 93–112. The Hague: T.M.C. Asser Press, 2008.

Stahn, Carsten. "R2P and *Jus Post Bellum*. Towards a Polycentric Approach." In *Jus Post Bellum: Mapping the Normative Foundations*, edited by Carsten Stahn, Jennifer Easterday, and Jens Iverson, 102–22. Oxford: Oxford University Press, 2014.

Stahn, Carsten. "The Future of *Jus Post Bellum*." In *Jus Post Bellum. Towards a Law of Transition from Conflict to Peace*, edited by Carsten Stahn and Jann Kleffner, 231–37. The Hague: T.M.C. Asser Press, 2008.

Stahn, Carsten, Easterday, Jennifer, and Iverson, Jens, eds. *Jus Post Bellum: Mapping the Normative Foundations*. Oxford: Oxford University Press, 2014.

Stahn, Carsten, Jens Iverson, and Jennifer Easterday, eds. *Environmental Protection and Transitions from Conflict to Peace: Clarifying Norms, Principles, and Practices*. Oxford: Oxford University Press, 2014.

Stahn, Carsten, Jens Iverson, and Jennifer Easterday, eds. *Environmental Protection and Transitions from Conflict to Peace: Clarifying Norms, Principles, and Practices*. Oxford: Oxford University Press, 2017.

Stahn, Carsten, Jens Iverson, and Jennifer Easterday. "Introduction: Protection of the Environment and *Jus Post Bellum*: Some Preliminary Reflections." In *Environmental Protection and Transitions from Conflict to Peace: Clarifying Norms, Principles, and Practices*, edited by Carsten Stahn, Jens Iverson, and Jennifer Easterday, 1–25. Oxford: Oxford University Press, 2017.

Stahn, Carsten, and Jan Kleffner, eds. *Jus Post Bellum: Towards a Law of Transition from Conflict to Peace*. The Hague: T.M.C. Asser Press, 2008.

Teitel, Ruti. "Rethinking *Jus Post Bellum* in an Age of Global Transitional Justice: Engaging with Michael Walzer and Larry May." *European Journal of International Law* 24, no. 1 (2013): 335–42.

Teitel, Ruti. *Transitional Justice*. Oxford: Oxford University Press, 2000.

Teitel, Ruti. "Transitional Justice Genealogy." *Harvard Human Rights Journal* 16 (2003): 69–94.

Teitel, Ruti G. *Globalizing Transitional Justice: Contemporary Essays*. Oxford: Oxford University Press, 2014.

Thürer, Daniel, and Malcom MacLaren. "'Ius Post Bellum' in Iraq: A Challenge to the Applicability and Relevance of International Humanitarian Law?" In *Weltinnenrecht: Liber Amicorum Jost Delbrück*, edited by Klaus Dicke, and et al., 753–82. Berlin: Duncker & Humblot, 2005.

Transitional Justice Institute. *The Belfast Guidelines on Amnesty and Accountability*. Belfast: University of Ulster, 2013.

Turgis, Noémi. "What Is Transitional Justice?" *International Journal of Rule of Law, Transitional Justice and Human Rights* 1 (2010): 9–14.

Catherine Turner, "Mapping a Norm of Inclusion in the *Jus Post Bellum*", in *Just Peace After Conflict. Jus Post Bellum and the Justice of Peace*, ed. Carsten Stahn and Jens Iverson (Oxford: Oxford University Press, 2020), 130–146.

Uprimny, Rodrigo. "Las Enseñanzas del Análisis Comparado: Procesos Transicionales, Formas de Justicia Transicional y el Caso Colombiano." In *¿Justicia Transicional Sin Transición? Verdad, Justicia y Reparación para Colombia*, edited by Rodrigo Uprimny, Maria Saffon, Catalina Botero, and Esteban Restrepo, 17–44. Bogota: DeJusticia, 2006.

Uprimny, Rodrigo, and Maria Saffon. "Derecho a La Verdad: Alcances y Límites de La Verdad Judicial." In *¿Justicia Transicional Sin Transición? Verdad, Justicia y Reparación Para Colombia*, edited by Rodrigo Uprimny, Maria Saffon, Catalina Botero, and Esteban Restrepo, 139–72. Bogota: DeJusticia, 2006.

Uprimny, Rodrigo, Maria Saffon, Catalina Botero, and Esteban Restrepo, eds. *¿Justicia Transicional Sin Transición? Verdad, Justicia y Reparación Para Colombia*. Bogota: DeJusticia, 2006.

Vatanparast, Roxana. "Waging Peace: Ambiguities, Contradictions, and Problems of a *Jus Post Bellum* Legal Framework." In *Jus Post Bellum: Mapping the Normative*

Foundations, edited by Carsten Stahn, Jennifer Easterday, and Jens Iverson, 142–60. Oxford: Oxford University Press, 2014.

Venturini, Gabriella. "The Temporal Scope of Application of the Conventions." In *The 1949 Geneva Conventions*, edited by Andrew Clapham, Paola Gaeta, and Marco Sassoli, 51–68. Oxford: Oxford University Press, 2015.

Verdirame, Guglielmo. "What to Make of *Jus Post Bellum*: A Response to Antonia Chayes." *European Journal of International Law* 24, no. 1 (2013): 307–13.

Vianès, Emmanuel. "Le *Jus Post Bellum*: Rupture Ou Continuité?" *Études Internationales*, 2013.

Vierucci, Luisa. "Applicability of the Conventions by Means of Ad Hoc Agreements." In *The 1949 Geneva Conventions. A Commentary*, edited by Andrew Clapham, Paola Gaeta, and Marco Sassòli, 509–21. Oxford: Oxford University Press, 2015.

Wählisch, Martin. "Conflict Termination from a Human Rights Perspective: State Transitions, Power-Sharing, and the Definition of the 'Post.'" In *Jus Post Bellum: Mapping the Normative Foundations*, edited by Carsten Stahn, Jennifer Easterday, and Jens Iverson, 315–33. Oxford: Oxford University Press, 2014.

Walzer, Michael. *Arguing About War*. New Haven: Yale University Press, 2004.

Walzer, Michael. *Just and Unjust Wars. A Moral Argument with Historical Illustrations*. New York: Basic Books, 2006.

Walzer, Michael. "The Aftermath of War. Reflections on *Jus Post Bellum*." In *Ethics Beyond War's End*, edited by Eric Patterson, 35–46. Washington: Georgetown University Press, 2012.

Wanis-St. John, Anthony, and Darren Kew. "Civil Society and Peace Negotiations: Confronting Exclusion." *International Negotiation* 13 (2008): 11–36.

Williams, Robert, and Dan Caldwell. "*Jus Post Bellum*: Just War Theory and the Principles of Just Peace." *International Studies Perspectives* 7, no. 4 (2006): 309–20.

Zegveld, Liesbeth. *Accountability of Armed Opposition Groups in International Law*. Cambridge: Cambridge University Press, 2002.

Index

American Convention on Human Rights 76n93, 103, 103n243, 106, 116, 153
amnesty 67, 83–84, 85n147, 85–86, 86n149, 86n150, 87n153, 87n156, 88n161, 88n164, 90n173, 88–92, 92n184, 92n185, 92n186, 94, 94n196, 95n200, 97, 100, 122, 138, 152n150, 185–187, 190–191

Basic Principles and Guidelines on the Right to a Remedy and Reparation for Victims 6n20, 10n44, 28n33, 103n246, 103n247, 103–105, 106n261, 108, 116, 116n316, 129n19, 139, 139n80, 172, 191

civil society 13, 15, 112, 114, 114n301, 116–117, 119, 121, 123, 130, 145–146, 157–158, 160–161, 172
Constitutional Court 14n77, 14–15, 15n84, 21, 56, 58, 59n22, 63, 65, 94, 94n198, 97–98, 100n228, 107, 111, 117–118, 130, 152, 154, 154n164, 155n165, 155–159, 172
criminal accountability 18, 91, 96, 98, 100, 136, 138, 156, 167, 171, 171n2
criminal justice 22, 96, 107, 136–137, 161, 171

differential approach 111–112, 118–120
domestic law 15–16, 27, 58–59, 63, 83, 121, 128, 135, 139, 150, 152, 155–156, 161–162, 173

environmental protection 11, 75, 77, 80, 122, 147n122, 147–148

gender 18, 112n291, 112–113, 115, 117–120, 146, 158, 164n195
Geneva Conventions 36n81, 58, 63n40, 61–65, 65n48, 65n49, 67, 73, 84, 87, 92n183, 153, 191, 193
  Common Article 3 58, 65n48, 61–67, 191
  special agreements 13, 58, 66n51, 61–67, 71, 73, 122, 130
guarantor countries 2, 14n73, 73, 123, 151, 159, 161, 167, 173

inclusiveness 2, 6, 21, 31, 53, 110–112, 117, 121, 123, 126, 131, 144–145, 160, 166, 170, 172, 175
indigenous 80, 111, 115, 118, 121, 121n349, 144–146
Inter-American Commission on Human Rights x, 88, 88n162, 88n163, 88n164, 88n165, 89n166, 157n179
Inter-American Court of Human Rights x, 73, 74n86, 89, 89n167, 89n168, 89n169, 90n171, 103n245, 106, 106n262, 141n94, 143, 143n103, 153, 156, 156n172, 157n175, 157n176, 164n197
International Armed Conflicts 7, 18, 32, 49–52, 128, 175
International Covenant on Civil and Political Rights 75, 79, 90, 90n173, 102, 116, 122, 153
International Covenant on Economic, Social and Cultural Rights 76, 79, 102, 118, 121–122
International Criminal Court 2, 5, 13–14, 14n74, 14n74, 14n77, 17, 73, 83, 84n137, 86, 88, 94n198, 95n199, 94–96, 98–100, 104, 116, 122–123, 126, 130, 138, 144, 151, 154n164, 155n165, 155n166, 155n168, 155n169, 153–156, 156n170, 159–162, 173
International Criminal Law 1, 4, 13, 17, 50, 52, 83–84, 95–96, 100, 105, 122, 126, 130, 132, 139, 143–144, 148, 161, 171, 174
International Human Rights Law x–1, 4–5, 6n20, 13, 15, 47n140, 50, 53, 63–64, 71, 74, 76–79, 79n118, 82–84, 88, 100n224, 100–102, 103n246, 103–104, 106n261, 108, 110, 116n316, 118n326, 122, 132, 139, 139n80, 148, 152–153, 156n171, 156–157, 157n181, 161, 164, 170, 180, 182, 188
International Humanitarian Law x–1, 3n8, 3–4, 10, 13, 15, 17, 36, 50, 52–53, 62–67, 71–73, 77–78, 83–84, 87–88, 88n164, 91, 100n224, 100–101, 104–106, 108, 118n326, 122–123, 126, 130, 132, 137–139, 148–149, 152–153, 172

International Law Commission 71, 73, 125, 148n128, 148–149, 149n138, 175–177

jus ad bellum 7–8, 25–26, 34n66, 36, 39–40, 51, 85, 149
jus in bello 7–8, 25–26, 34n66, 36, 39–40, 49, 149
jus post bellum ix, 3, 3n8, 11n54, 11n59, 6–12, 16n87, 20n101, 23n3, 29n43, 31n54, 32n60, 34n63, 34n65, 34n66, 34n67, 35n69, 35n73, 35n74, 39n95, 15–42, 43n117, 46n133, 46n134, 47n137, 49n147, 49n148, 43–53, 74, 77, 82, 100, 110–111, 121, 127n11, 128n15, 128n16, 134n48, 123–137, 141n86, 141–147, 149–150, 158–161, 165–170, 175n12, 172–178
  actors of *jus post bellum* 2, 13–14, 14n73, 16, 16n87, 18–19, 22, 29, 29n43, 32, 47, 48, 52, 54–55, 57, 59–60, 62–63, 92, 93n190, 99n218, 97–100, 105, 110–111, 113, 116–117, 122–124, 126, 128–131, 135, 138, 140, 142, 145–146, 149–151, 154, 162n186, 157–163, 167–168, 170–173, 175–176, 178
  functions of *jus post bellum* 124, 160
  principles of 10, 17, 21, 31–35, 35n73, 39, 50, 52, 124, 136–137, 150, 175, 178
just war theory 9, 17, 20, 20n101, 23, 31, 33, 34n65, 39–40, 125, 174–175
Justice and Peace Law 56, 96–97, 99, 107, 126, 137, 152, 154–158, 163

law of armed force 25–26, 51
Law on Victims and Land Restitution 101, 108–109, 111, 118, 165, 174
lex pacificatoria 11, 11n59, 21, 30, 43, 47n137, 47–48, 52, 169
LGBTI 118, 120, 126, 131, 146, 164, 172

minorities 13, 114–115, 118–119, 121, 144, 146

non-international armed conflict 1, 3, 6–7, 12, 16–19, 24, 26–27, 32, 34, 36, 36n80, 49n147, 49n148, 50n151, 49–52, 58–59, 61–62, 64–65, 74–75, 78, 84–85, 87, 87n153, 89, 91–92, 105, 110, 115, 128, 133–134, 138, 145, 150, 159, 161–162, 165, 167, 171, 173, 178
non-state actors 17, 27, 58–59, 65, 66n51, 72n82, 110, 128, 139–140, 150, 162–163, 171

Nuremberg Declaration on Peace and Justice 42n112, 45n127, 48n141, 91, 91n182, 115, 115n306, 117, 117n318, 179–180

participation 13, 47, 57, 75, 77, 80, 95, 107, 112n288, 114n301, 111–117, 119–120, 122–123, 126, 130, 135, 144–145, 152, 158, 160, 166n200, 163–167, 170, 172
peace agreement 1, 1n2, 1n4, 5–6, 12n64, 12n65, 14, 14n74, 18, 21–22, 34n67, 39n95, 39–40, 42n116, 45, 53, 57–63, 68n61, 65–70, 72n79, 72n82, 72–73, 83–84, 86, 90–91, 94, 107, 110, 114n301, 113–115, 117, 119, 127, 130, 134, 145–146, 148, 151–152, 160–161, 166n202, 166–167, 169, 171, 174
peace process 1, 14n73, 13–15, 18, 21–22, 39, 42, 53, 55, 57, 69, 83, 92, 99n218, 101, 111–112, 120, 125, 127, 130, 138, 140, 142, 145, 148, 150, 163, 165, 172–174
peacebuilding 1, 1n3, 4–7, 16–17, 19–20, 26, 35n69, 43n117, 43–45, 51, 74–78, 80, 82, 111, 128n16, 128–129, 134, 140, 160, 167, 169, 175, 177
peacekeeping 4, 45
peacemaking 1, 5–7, 10, 16–17, 19–20, 26, 43, 47–48, 51, 76, 83, 85, 111, 126, 129, 140, 144, 167, 175
positive peace 37, 42, 75, 134, 175, 177
proportionality 10, 17, 32, 132, 142–143

reconciliation 9–10, 17–18, 31–32, 42–43, 77–78, 80, 82–83, 85, 86n149, 93n186, 91–95, 97, 107, 127, 132, 137, 140–142, 147, 165, 171n3, 171–172, 175
reconstruction 9, 29, 32, 50, 52, 78, 82, 133–135, 147, 167
reintegration 57, 69, 74–75, 77–78, 80, 135, 142n98, 172
reparations 2, 6, 9–10, 13–15, 18, 21–22, 31–32, 37, 39, 42, 44, 53, 56–57, 81, 83, 89, 92, 93n186, 95–97, 99, 104n247, 101–110, 114, 116, 118, 120, 123, 127, 132, 138n74, 139n81, 139n82, 141n86, 138–142, 142n97, 144, 147, 153, 156–158, 161, 163–165, 167, 170–172
restorative sanctions 81, 100, 122, 138, 142, 155, 170–172
root causes of armed conflict 13n65, 75, 80, 127, 135, 159, 166, 175

INDEX

Special Jurisdiction for Peace   81, 83, 98–100, 100n224, 109, 121, 138, 140
sustainable peace   3, 5, 7, 16, 21, 24, 29n43, 29–30, 37–39, 41–43, 45, 47, 52, 74–75, 77, 79, 82, 122, 125, 127–128, 132, 135, 141n86, 141–142, 144–146, 149, 155, 159, 166–169, 172–176

transitional justice   15, 21, 44n123, 43–46, 46n133, 57, 83, 94, 100, 126, 137, 153, 155
truth   2, 13–14, 42, 44, 57, 81n131, 83, 89, 92–93, 93n186, 95–96, 99–100, 104, 109, 119–120, 138, 140–142, 153, 156–157, 161, 163–164, 171

unilateral declaration   13, 58, 62, 67, 71n74, 70–72, 122

United Nations Security Council   6n20, 6n21, 6n22, 13n72, 13–14, 58, 62, 68n58, 68n59, 68n60, 68n61, 68n62, 68n63, 67–69, 69n70, 70n73, 70–72, 87, 113, 117, 126, 130, 145, 152, 160–161, 164, 172
  Resolution 1325   6n20, 13, 77n104, 113n299, 113–114, 114n300, 114n303, 117, 126, 130, 145, 152, 164, 166n202, 172, 180, 183, 189

victims   13, 15, 18, 37, 44, 56–57, 65–66, 80, 83, 89, 93n190, 97–99, 101, 104–109, 109n275, 112, 114, 116–119, 123, 137, 139n82, 139–142, 144–146, 152–153, 156–158, 160, 162n186, 162–165, 167, 172–173

women   13, 77, 112n288, 114n301, 110–115, 117–120, 126, 130, 144–145, 152, 164, 164n194, 166n200, 170, 172

Printed in the United States
by Baker & Taylor Publisher Services